Delight Thyself also in the Lord

A SIMPLE DAILY DEVOTIONAL

VOLUME 2

Delight Thyself
DESIGN MINISTRIES

delightthyself.com

*"Delight thyself also in the LORD;
and he shall give thee the desires of thine heart."*
Psalm 37:4

*"But the meek shall inherit the earth;
and shall delight themselves in the abundance of peace."*
Psalm 37:11

Copyright © 2021 by Delight Thyself Design Ministries, Inc.

All Scripture quotations are taken from the King James Bible.

Published by Delight In Him Publications,
a division of Delight Thyself Design Ministries in Hurricane, WV.

Delight Thyself Design Ministries, Inc. is a non-profit organization whose mission is to design and distribute Gospel tracts for the furtherance of the Gospel of Jesus Christ. Our ministry is 100% faith supported by Independent Baptist Churches and individuals. All Scriptures are from the King James Bible.

All rights reserved. No part of this book may be reproduced or transmitted in any form or by any means - electronic, mechanical, photocopy, recording, or otherwise without written permission of the publisher, except for brief quotations in online or printed reviews.

Delight Thyself Design Ministries, Inc.
PO Box 725
Hurricane, WV 25526
delightthyself.com

Special thanks to my Momma who took the time to proofread these pages.

The contents of this book are the result of years of spiritual growth in life and ministry. Every effort has been made to give proper credit and attribution to quotes and information that is not original. It is not our intent to claim originality with any quote or thought that could not be tied to an original source.

Printed in the United States of America.

ISBN-13: 978-0-9995175-9-8

Table of Contents

Prologue 6

Dedications 7

January 8

February 39

March 68

April 99

May 129

June 160

July 190

August 221

September 252

October 282

November 313

December 343

Title Index 374

Holidays 383

About Us 385

What Can One Tract Do? 387

The Bible Way To Heaven 388

Prologue

Just like the first book, **this devotional is simply meant to point you to Jesus Christ through His Word.** If we delight ourselves in Him, He has promised to give us desires according to His will for our lives.

It is hard to put into words what the Lord has done through the first volume. We have heard countless stories of how the Lord has touched the hearts of readers all across the globe. Many have trusted Christ, read through the entire Bible for the first time, and found the help they needed as a result of reading those pages. We know that is only because of the power of the printed Word woven throughout each page. To God be the glory for every thing we have heard, and for any fruit that we will find on streets of gold.

My prayer for Volume 2 is simply that the Lord will use each of these new pages to only bring Him more glory.

Holidays

There are themes throughout the year that center around specific holidays. **Each theme is meant to direct our focus toward how we can best delight in the Lord throughout each holiday season.** Since some holidays do not fall on the same date each year, listed below are the dates where these can be found.

Resurrection Sunday - April 12-17, 19-22

These 10 days are themed around the season that we celebrate the death, burial and resurrection of our Lord and Saviour, Jesus Christ.

Thanksgiving - November

The entire month of November has a theme of thankfulness woven throughout each page. My hope is that we can focus our hearts and minds toward a revival of thanksgiving that is shown in our day-to-day lives all throughout the year.

Christmas - December

The first 25 days of December are centered around the miraculous birth of Jesus Christ and the reason He came.

Dedications

The past four years since the first devotional book was printed, to say the least, have not been easy. I was even convinced that Volume 2 would never be printed. But the Lord has taught me through His Word that even in our affliction, it is possible to find an abundance of peace if we delight ourselves in Him.

Through the study of the Scriptures, and trusting Him to direct the writing of each day, the Lord has healed my heart. I am eternally thankful for His goodness in making this new book possible.

As before, certain days throughout the year are dedicated to some of the people behind the scenes of this ministry who are the Aarons & Hurs that hold up my hands through their love, friendship and support. These people will recognize the theme or verse significance on their birthdays, days that have special meaning, etc. This is just a small way to say thank you to those who the Lord has used to make a difference in my life. You know who you are, and I love each one of you.

I am fervently praying that the Lord will speak to you through each day of this devotional book, pointing you not to the words that I have written, but only to Him through His Word.

Psalm 28:7
*"The LORD is my strength and my shield;
my heart trusted in him, and I am helped:
therefore my heart greatly rejoiceth;
and with my song will I praise him."*

Allison McKay
Delight Thyself Design Ministries

01.01 | January 1

Where God Guides, He Provides.

Isaiah 58:11
"And the LORD shall guide thee continually, and satisfy thy soul in drought, and make fat thy bones: and thou shalt be like a watered garden, and like a spring of water, whose waters fail not."

With every new year, come new expectations, frustrations and opportunities. More often than not, even with the best intentions, our resolutions fizzle out before winter gives way to spring.

Even though our motives may be sincere, our flesh usually gets in the way much sooner than we had hoped.

Instead of relying upon ourselves to accomplish a resolution, may we choose to cling to this promise that we shall be guided by the Lord not just occasionally…but continually.

He can and will continually guide us, if only we allow Him to do so.

Psalm 32:8
"I will instruct thee and teach thee in the way which thou shalt go: I will guide thee with mine eye."

Even in the midst of drought, we shall be satisfied.

No matter the desert, famine or wilderness we find ourselves in…
He is enough.

Sometimes He guides us out of a situation just so He can direct and protect us, all the while providing for our every need.

Proverbs 3:5-6
"Trust in the LORD with all thine heart; and lean not unto thine own understanding. In all thy ways acknowledge him, and he shall direct thy paths."

Where God guides… He provides.
Trust Him today, and every day.

Bible Reading
Genesis 1-2 | John 1

January 2 | 01.02

Acts 10:20
"Arise therefore, and get thee down, and go with them, doubting nothing: for I have sent them."

Have you ever felt the Holy Spirit nudge you to do something or speak to someone; yet you end up having an internal tug-of-war in an effort to convince yourself that you do not need to follow through? Peter was there.

The Holy Spirit told Peter to go.

But He did not stop there,
He continued with another admonishment…*"doubting nothing"*.

**The Lord knows that our flesh wants us
to doubt everything that He tells us to do.**

When Peter was told to go and not doubt, he was also given a specific reason why there was no sense in worrying or doubting the direction.

"…for I have sent them."

What better reason could he have heard for the fact that there was no reason to doubt? None. The Lord had sent them, and that was all Peter needed to know.

The Word of God is full of promises and encouragement of how we too have no reason to doubt when He directs our path.

Isaiah 41:10
"Fear thou not; for I am with thee: be not dismayed; for I am thy God: I will strengthen thee; yea, I will help thee; yea, I will uphold thee with the right hand of my righteousness."

There is no reason to doubt when He directs you.

Bible Reading
Genesis 3-4 | John 2

01.03 | January 3

Most Unlikely.

1 Corinthians 1:26-27
"For ye see your calling, brethren, how that not many wise men after the flesh, not many mighty, not many noble, are called: But God hath chosen the foolish things of the world to confound the wise; and God hath chosen the weak things of the world to confound the things which are mighty;"

Have you ever noticed that God seems to call the most unlikely people to do His work? This is no accident, for there are no accidents or coincidences with God. He chooses the most improbable people and situations to manifest His power, grace and love through.

1 Corinthians 2:5
"That your faith should not stand in the wisdom of men, but in the power of God."

If He only used those who we in our human flesh deem worthy to be called we would put our faith in the ability of a person instead of God's power to use them. God gets the most glory when a situation seems most unlikely.

Luke 1:37
"For with God nothing shall be impossible."

Moses had a stammering tongue and considered himself to be a worthless speaker. But God called him, and used him beyond both Moses' ability and the opinions of others. He allowed Moses to lead the children of Israel through the wilderness and used him to display God's power in many miracles along the way. When they reached the Red Sea they had nowhere to turn…except to God. That impossible moment allowed God to manifest His power in an incredible way that no one even thought possible at the time.

You may feel like there is nothing you can offer the Lord in service to Him. That is how He wants us to feel, for it is then that He can work through us. He is not looking for the wisest person to do His work; He simply wants the willing. Disregard your ability or inability to accomplish something for Him. Ask Him to use you in spite of you. When we get ourselves out of the way, it is then that He can use us. **What situation seems most unlikely to happen in your life?** You may feel as if you are standing at the edge of the Red Sea with nowhere to turn. This is where God wants to use the weak things of this world to confound the mighty. **He knows right where you stand and just what you need.**

Bible Reading
Genesis 5-6 | John 3

January 4 | 01.04

Speechless.

Acts 4:14
"And beholding the man which was healed standing with them, they could say nothing against it."

The rulers, elders, scribes, the High Priest, and many others gathered together in Jerusalem to question Peter and John. (Acts 4:7)

The Sanhedrin had seen the evidence of the power of the Name of Jesus when the impotent man was healed. He now stood before them whole. Peter was filled with the Holy Ghost when he answered their question. He went on to declare that no other name can bring salvation.

Acts 4:10,12
"Be it known unto you all, and to all the people of Israel, that by the name of Jesus Christ of Nazareth, whom ye crucified, whom God raised from the dead, even by him doth this man stand here before you whole...Neither is there salvation in any other: for there is none other name under heaven given among men, whereby we must be saved."

The boldness of Peter and John had an effect on those around them.

Acts 4:13
"Now when they saw the boldness of Peter and John, and perceived that they were unlearned and ignorant men, they marvelled; and they took knowledge of them, that they had been with Jesus."

Does anyone marvel at your boldness? We can be bold in many things, but these men set an example for us to strive for because they were known to have been with Jesus. **Could someone say that about you?**

Proverbs 28:1
"The wicked flee when no man pursueth: but the righteous are bold as a lion."

Their boldness reminded the people that God had miraculously healed the impotent man as he stood in their midst. Those who were once questioning with an agenda became silent because it was evident that God alone had done the work.

When God does something, no critic can overthrow it.

May we be bold enough to proclaim the Truth, and silent enough to allow the works of the Lord to speak for themselves.

Bible Reading
Genesis 7-8 | John 4

01.05 | January 5

Counted Worthy.

Acts 5:41
"And they departed from the presence of the council, rejoicing that they were counted worthy to suffer shame for his name."

They were beaten.
They were commanded not to speak in the Name of Jesus.

Acts 5:40
"And to him they agreed: and when they had called the apostles, and beaten them, they commanded that they should not speak in the name of Jesus, and let them go."

They were released.
Instead of choosing to run away and hide,
they did what would have likely been the furthest from our minds…

They rejoiced.
While wounded from the beating they had endured at the hands of their persecutors, they chose to rejoice.

**How could they find a reason to rejoice
in the midst of their pain and suffering?**

They were counted worthy to suffer shame for the Name of Jesus.

We may not find ourselves with physical wounds of persecution, but we often bear scars from what we endure in our service to Him.

He suffered for us as He took our place.

**May we choose to rejoice
because we have been counted worthy to suffer for Him.**

Acts 5:42
"And daily in the temple, and in every house, they ceased not to teach and preach Jesus Christ."

Proclaim His Name today, and every day.

Bible Reading
Genesis 9-10 | John 5

January 6 | 01.06

Acts 5:11
*"And great fear came upon all the church,
and upon as many as heard these things."*

Barnabas, among others, sold his land then brought the money and laid it at the apostles feet for it to be used for the ministry. Ananias and Sapphira saw how Barnabas was received of the disciples, and must have wanted the same reception, so they too sold a possession.

Acts 5:1-2
"But a certain man named Ananias, with Sapphira his wife, sold a possession, And kept back part of the price, his wife also being privy to it, and brought a certain part, and laid it at the apostles' feet."

However, they chose to keep back part of the price.

They brought a certain part of the money and laid it at the feet of the apostles expecting to receive the same reward. Peter discerned right away that there was a different motive behind the couple's gift.

Acts 5:3-4
"But Peter said, Ananias, why hath Satan filled thine heart to lie to the Holy Ghost, and to keep back part of the price of the land? Whiles it remained, was it not thine own? and after it was sold, was it not in thine own power? why hast thou conceived this thing in thine heart? thou hast not lied unto men, but unto God."

Our motives will always come through eventually.

Ananias fell down and died immediately after Peter rebuked him. This caused great fear to come upon all that heard of what had occurred. Sapphira was then given an opportunity to confess what they had done, and she chose to lie again. She too fell down and died immediately after she made her choice.

What has to happen to cause us to fear the Lord?

God may use us as an example to cause great fear to come upon those around us if we continue to choose our own motives over Him.

Our actions have consequences.
Choose to obey Him today.

Bible Reading
Genesis 11-12 | John 6

01.07 | January 7

Speak His Name.

Acts 4:20
"For we cannot but speak the things which we have seen and heard."

Peter and John admitted they could not obey the command of the Sanhedrin.

Acts 4:18
"And they called them, and commanded them not to speak at all nor teach in the name of Jesus."

They were told point blank not to speak the name of Jesus.
How would you respond to such an order?

Unfortunately, the day is likely soon coming that each of us will be faced with the same situation as the disciples.

How will you respond when you are told that you cannot speak the Name of Jesus anymore?

Peter and John simply stated they had no choice. There was no deliberation or weighing the pros and cons. They knew immediately that they would continue to speak the Name of Jesus regardless of the consequences.

They knew it was better to obey God rather than men.
When persecution comes, remember how Peter and John responded.

Acts 4:21
"So when they had further threatened them, they let them go, finding nothing how they might punish them, because of the people: for all men glorified God for that which was done."

The Lord was glorified in their boldness to proclaim His Name no matter the cost.

In times of distress, we must choose Him.
Trials will come, but His grace is sufficient.

Any circumstance we face is another opportunity for God to get the glory.

Speak His Name today.

Bible Reading
Genesis 13-14 | John 7

Declare His Name.

Romans 9:17
"For the scripture saith unto Pharaoh, Even for this same purpose have I raised thee up, that I might shew my power in thee, and that my name might be declared throughout all the earth."

In Exodus 9, the Lord had Moses go unto Pharoah and speak for Him.

Exodus 9:1
"Then the LORD said unto Moses, Go in unto Pharaoh, and tell him, Thus saith the LORD God of the Hebrews, Let my people go, that they may serve me."

Moses obeyed. He went to Pharoah multiple times and told him what the Lord had said. He did not proclaim his own opinion, but he spoke *"Thus saith the Lord"*.

In Romans, Paul writes *"For the scripture saith unto Pharoah..."*

This further illustrates that when Moses spoke for the Lord, it was not to be taken as Moses' words or even as what he would have done. No, it was the LORD, the Almighty God speaking.

Paul reminds the church at Rome of this Truth as he explains the great heaviness and continual sorrow he had for his people.

Romans 10:1
"Brethren, my heart's desire and prayer to God for Israel is, that they might be saved."

When we listen to the preaching of the Word of God, we must remind ourselves that it is not the preacher delivering the message who speaks the Truth, but the very Words of God which he proclaims. Today it seems, more than ever, that we substitute the truth of the man of God for the Truth of the Word of God.

May we listen with open hearts to what the Lord has to say, while also being willing to declare His Name to all around us as we have opportunity. Although not everyone is called to be a pastor, we are all responsible to carry out the Great Commission of the Gospel of Jesus Christ.

Declare His Name today.

Bible Reading
Genesis 15-16 | John 8

01.09 | January 9

Acts 8:36
"And as they went on their way, they came unto a certain water: and the eunuch said, See, here is water; what doth hinder me to be baptized?"

Chapter 8 of the Book of The Acts gives us a clear picture as to the process of a baptism. We are introduced to the eunuch of Ethiopia in verses 27 and 28 as he is riding in his chariot reading out of Isaiah 53.

Philip obeyed the Holy Spirit as He nudged him to go to the eunuch.

Acts 8:30
"And Philip ran thither to him, and heard him read the prophet Esaias, and said, Understandest thou what thou readest?"

How many times has the Holy Spirit told us to talk with or visit someone, and we refused?
The eunuch's response is convicting. (Acts 8:31)

The eunuch began asking questions, and Philip showed him Who Jesus was.

Someone is waiting for us to show them the Truth of the Word of God.

Then as they continued to travel, the eunuch saw a certain water, and asked what he had to do to be baptized.
Philip gave him a simple answer.

Acts 8:37
*"And Philip said, **If thou believest with all thine heart, thou mayest.** And he answered and said, I believe that Jesus Christ is the Son of God."*

Many modern day translations of the Bible omit this verse. Doing so, changes the whole context of this portion of Scripture. To read verse 36, then immediately continue to verse 38, we miss the answer to the eunuch's question. Without the answer to his question, it implies that someone can be baptized any time they want without anything taking place beforehand. And more importantly, it implies that baptism leads to salvation, which is simply not true. One must believe the Gospel of Jesus Christ before they are baptized. Many people are being taught the false doctrine of baptismal regeneration because the translation they use simply does not teach them they must be saved before they are baptized.

Baptism is an outward expression of an inward transformation that has already taken place within the life of a believer.

Bible Reading
Genesis 17-18 | John 9

January 10 | 01.10

Justified.

Romans 3:24
*"Being justified freely by his grace
through the redemption that is in Christ Jesus:"*

What does it mean to be justified?
Someone years ago came up with the phrase…"Just-If-I'd Never Sinned."
That is how God sees those who have trusted Christ as their Saviour.
He sees the righteousness of Jesus Christ and not our own.
That is justification, or the means of being justified.

We have no righteousness in and of ourselves.
Romans 3:10-12
*"As it is written, There is none righteous, no, not one:
There is none that understandeth, there is none that seeketh after God.
They are all gone out of the way, they are together become unprofitable;
there is none that doeth good, no, not one."*

We are nothing without Him.
John 15:5
*"I am the vine, ye are the branches: He that abideth in me, and I in him,
the same bringeth forth much fruit: for without me ye can do nothing."*

But through Him…
We are redeemed.
"…through the redemption that is in Christ Jesus:"
Redemption is only found in Jesus Christ.

We are justified.
Justification is only found in Jesus Christ.
"…justified freely…"
Salvation is a gift… and gifts are free.

"…by his grace…"
Grace is being given something we do not deserve…and it is only
by the grace of God that we have the opportunity
to place our faith in Jesus Christ.

Ephesians 2:8-9
*"For by grace are ye saved through faith; and that not of yourselves:
it is the gift of God: Not of works, lest any man should boast."*

Bible Reading
Genesis 19-20 | John 10

01.11 | January 11

The Lord Hath Heard.

Psalm 6:9
"The LORD hath heard my supplication; the LORD will receive my prayer."

In times of need, often our first reaction is to seek someone to listen.

Someone who cares.
Someone who understands.

How often do we seek help from anyone or anything
other than the Lord?

The first instinct of our flesh is to find comfort anywhere else but Him.
He created us,
but sin often gets in the way of our good intentions.
Psalm 6:8
*"Depart from me, all ye workers of iniquity;
for the LORD hath heard the voice of my weeping."*

He cares.
1 Peter 5:7
"Casting all your care upon him; for he careth for you."

He understands.
Hebrews 4:15
*"For we have not an high priest which cannot be touched
with the feeling of our infirmities; but was in all points tempted
like as we are, yet without sin."*

When we go to Him, He not only hears and rescues us,
but He also secures and directs us.

Psalm 40:1-2
*"I waited patiently for the LORD; and he inclined unto me, and heard my
cry. He brought me up also out of an horrible pit, out of the miry clay, and
set my feet upon a rock, and established my goings."*

Bible Reading
Genesis 21-22 | John 11

January 12 | 01.12

The Promise Of Salvation.

Romans 10:13
"For whosoever shall call upon the name of the Lord shall be saved."

In this verse we find the simple way of salvation.

"For whosoever…"
This tells us who is eligible.

Whosoever simply means anyone.
No one is disqualified no matter their circumstance.
While anyone is able, there is something
that everyone must adhere to in order to receive salvation.

The Condition
"…shall call upon the name of the Lord…"
We must call upon the Name of the Lord Jesus Christ,
for it is only through Him that salvation is found.

The Blessing
"…shall be saved."
Salvation is the free gift that we receive when we call upon Him.

Romans 6:23
*"For the wages of sin is death; but the gift of God
is eternal life through Jesus Christ our Lord."*

Romans 10:13 is a summary of three previous verses in Chapter 10 which explain what it means to *"call upon the name of the Lord."*
Romans 10:8-10
*"But what saith it? The word is nigh thee, even in thy mouth, and in thy heart: that is, the word of faith, which we preach;
That if thou shalt confess with thy mouth the Lord Jesus, and shalt believe in thine heart that God hath raised him from the dead, thou shalt be saved. For with the heart man believeth unto righteousness; and with the mouth confession is made unto salvation."*

When we call upon His Name, we do so by confessing and believing in Him by faith. It is not a prayer that saves us,
but our faith in Jesus Christ and what He has done for us.

Ephesians 2:8-9
"For by grace are ye saved through faith; and that not of yourselves: it is the gift of God: Not of works, lest any man should boast."

Bible Reading
Genesis 23-24 | John 12

01.13 | January 13

Willing To Lose.

Philippians 3:7
"But what things were gain to me, those I counted loss for Christ."

In this life we are given many things and people.

Many times, we fail to remember where,
or rather Who, these gifts come from.
James 1:17
*"Every good gift and every perfect gift is from above,
and cometh down from the Father of lights,
with whom is no variableness, neither shadow of turning."*

God in His infinite wisdom gives us everything and everyone we have.
The very breath of life inside of us came from Him.
The lungs we breathe with, He created.

He freely gives us everything.

With His gifts, comes purpose.
Purpose for us,
and a purpose for which He wants us to use the gifts He has given.

Many times, He gives so that we may be willing to lose for Him.
Mark 8:35
"For whosoever will save his life shall lose it; but whosoever shall lose his life for my sake and the gospel's, the same shall save it."

Paul was willing to lose everything he had for the sake of knowing Christ. He was willing to have nothing if it meant he could know Jesus Christ more.

Could that be said of us today?
God simply wants us to be willing to lose even the dearest thing to us in order for us know Him more.

The truth of the matter is, when we think we have lost something or someone for the sake of Christ, we end up receiving so much more that we had before.

Bible Reading
Genesis 25-26 | John 13

January 14 | 01.14

The Reason To Lose.

Philippians 3:8-11

"Yea doubtless, and I count all things but loss for the excellency of the knowledge of Christ Jesus my Lord: for whom I have suffered the loss of all things, and do count them but dung, that I may win Christ, And be found in him, not having mine own righteousness, which is of the law, but that which is through the faith of Christ, the righteousness which is of God by faith: That I may know him, and the power of his resurrection, and the fellowship of his sufferings, being made conformable unto his death; If by any means I might attain unto the resurrection of the dead."

None of us like to lose. None. Of. Us. Whether it is family game night, our favorite team is playing, or a race to the best parking spot in front of [enter your choice of store here], we do not like finishing second, much less last. But that is not the type of losing Paul writes about in Philippians 3. The loss that he refers to are those times in life when we no longer have something or someone we once did. Sometimes God removes situations, places or people from our lives so that our focus is no longer on our surroundings, but on our Saviour.

The Realization of Christ
Philippians 3:8
"…for the excellency of the knowledge of Christ Jesus my Lord…"
Knowing more about Christ is worth any loss we experience.

The Reward of Christ
Philippians 3:8
"…that I may win Christ …"
Though we may suffer while we lose, there is no better reward than Him.

The Reception of Christ
Philippians 3:9
"And be found in him …"
Because of our faith in Christ, God sees His righteousness instead of our unrighteousness. We were once lost, but through Him we are found.

The Reality of Christ
Philippians 3:10
"That I may know him…"
The more we lose, the more we can know Him. It is in those times when we feel like we have lost it all, that we must pick up the Word of God and look within those precious pages in order to find ourselves once again…in Him.

Bible Reading
Genesis 27-28 | John 14

01.15 | January 15

The Cost Of Being Fruitful.

John 15:1-2
"I am the true vine, and my Father is the husbandman. Every branch in me that beareth not fruit he taketh away: and every branch that beareth fruit, he purgeth it, that it may bring forth more fruit."

In John 15, we have a beautiful picture of our relationship with Jesus Christ and God the Father. Imagine a man walking the fields of a vineyard, observing the fruit of his labourers. He walks up and down each row, inspecting the condition of the branches of the vines. Some have no grapes, so he uproots the plant and removes it from the field. Some have a few grapes, so he prunes the shoots in order to produce more growth, and therefore more fruit. The pruning hurts the branch some, but the man knows that this is what is best in the long run. Not too long later, he will return to find this pruned branch bearing more fruit and therefore fulfilling its true purpose.

This analogy is very similar to how we are able to produce more fruit as children of God. We are connected to the True Vine, the Lord Jesus Christ, the moment we trust in Him by faith for salvation.

John 15:5
"I am the vine, ye are the branches: He that abideth in me, and I in him, the same bringeth forth much fruit: for without me ye can do nothing."

Each of us are branches being inspected by our Father, and our fruitfulness depends upon our connection to His Son, Jesus Christ. When we produce some fruit, God sees the areas of our lives that prevent us from bearing much fruit, and often chooses to purge or prune those areas in order to enable us to produce more fruit for His glory. See John 15:8

The purging is hurtful at the time, but like a good parent chastens their children in order to teach them to do right, so does our Heavenly Father as He sees what we don't. Trust Him in the midst of your purging season, and look forward to the promise that this situation will allow you to become more fruitful for His glory.

John 15:11
"These things have I spoken unto you, that my joy might remain in you, and that your joy might be full."

We can have joy in the midst of the purging seasons as we abide in Him.

Bible Reading
Genesis 29-30 | John 15

January 16 | 01.16

His Ways.

Isaiah 55:8-9
"For my thoughts are not your thoughts, neither are your ways my ways, saith the LORD. For as the heavens are higher than the earth, so are my ways higher than your ways, and my thoughts than your thoughts."

Losing leads to gaining.
Humility leads to exaltation.
Dying leads to living.

Although these statements may sound contradictory to how our minds think, they are truthful examples of how God's thoughts and ways are so much higher than ours.

How can losing become gaining?
Matthew 16:25
"For whosoever will save his life shall lose it: and whosoever will lose his life for my sake shall find it."

How can humility lead to exaltation?
James 4:10
"Humble yourselves in the sight of the Lord, and he shall lift you up."

How can death bring forth life?
Galatians 2:20
"I am crucified with Christ: nevertheless I live; yet not I, but Christ liveth in me: and the life which I now live in the flesh I live by the faith of the Son of God, who loved me, and gave himself for me."

In those times when we do not understand what is happening or why circumstances occur in our lives, may we remember that His ways are higher and so much better than ours.

His ways bring salvation.
His ways bring eternal life.
His ways bring joy.
His ways bring peace.

"God always gives His best to those who leave the choice with Him."
Jim Elliot

Bible Reading
Genesis 31-32 | John 16

01.17 | January 17

Romans 1:15
"So, as much as in me is, I am ready to preach the gospel to you that are at Rome also."

Paul was ready to preach.

Not everyone is called or able to be what we know of as a preacher today, but all of us are called to be ready to do something for the glory of God.

Being ready does not necessarily mean you are fully prepared at the time, but that you are preparing by seeking what the Lord has for you.

Prepare by searching the Scriptures.
John 5:39
"Search the scriptures; for in them ye think ye have eternal life: and they are they which testify of me."

Prepare by sanctifying your heart.
1 Peter 3:15
"But sanctify the Lord God in your hearts: and be ready always to give an answer to every man that asketh you a reason of the hope that is in you with meekness and fear:"

Prepare by submitting to the power of God.
Romans 1:16
"For I am not ashamed of the gospel of Christ: for it is the power of God unto salvation to every one that believeth; to the Jew first, and also to the Greek."

Are you diligently seeking what the Lord has for you to do?

Prepare to be ready to do something for His glory today, and every day.

Bible Reading
Genesis 33-34 | John 17

January 18 | 01.18

But Thou, O LORD.

These four words are found together seven times within the Scriptures. Within the context of each of the passages where these verses are found lie seven Truths for us to remember Who the LORD is to us each and every single day of our lives.

Jehovah, the Self-existing One, He is the LORD.

Whatever our situation, He is the LORD.
Whatever our surroundings, He is the LORD.
Whatever storm we find ourselves in, He is the LORD.

He Protects Us. - Psalm 3:3
"But thou, O LORD, art a shield for me; my glory,
and the lifter up of mine head."

He Chastens Us. - Psalm 6:3
"My soul is also sore vexed: but thou, O LORD, how long?"

He Sustains Us. - Psalm 41:10
"But thou, O LORD, be merciful unto me, and raise me up,
that I may requite them."

He Fights For Us. - Psalm 59:8
"But thou, O LORD, shalt laugh at them;
thou shalt have all the heathen in derision."

He Cares About Us. - Psalm 86:15
"But thou, O Lord, art a God full of compassion, and gracious,
longsuffering, and plenteous in mercy and truth."

He Is Always There For Us. - Psalm 102:12
"But thou, O LORD, shalt endure for ever;
and thy remembrance unto all generations."

He Knows Us. - Jeremiah 12:3
"But thou, O LORD, knowest me…"

He knows our every need, and is willing and able to help us in every aspect of our lives. What comfort there is knowing Him.

In times of doubt or fear remember…
"But thou, O LORD…"

Bible Reading
Genesis 35-36 | John 18

01.19 | January 19

Romans 1:20
"For the invisible things of him from the creation of the world are clearly seen, being understood by the things that are made, even his eternal power and Godhead; so that they are without excuse:"

A beautiful sunset.
A peaceful waterfall.
A mountain range surrounded by fog.
A wave crashing onto the shore.

These and countless other breathtaking experiences remind us each and every day of the God Who created them.

Psalm 19:1
"The heavens declare the glory of God; and the firmament sheweth his handywork."

This world does not exist by accident.
No Big Bang occurred to begin the process of all that we see around us.

There is only One explanation.

Genesis 1:1
"In the beginning God created the heaven and the earth."

One Creator, Who spoke it all into existence.

Genesis 1:3-4
"And God said, Let there be light: and there was light. And God saw the light, that it was good: and God divided the light from the darkness."

Every human being He created is without excuse of knowing Him because He is clearly seen all around us.

Those of us who know Him are without excuse of telling others about Him.

The world He created speaks more boldly than we often do.

Bible Reading
Genesis 37-38 | John 19

January 20 | 01.20

From Burdens To Blessings.

Psalm 55:22
"Cast thy burden upon the LORD, and he shall sustain thee: he shall never suffer the righteous to be moved."

There are at least two types of burdens in the Bible.

Burden: a heaviness, weight, trouble

These are the burdens that are trials. The weight of them hurts and we often desire for them to be lifted off of us, but they are ultimately for our good and His glory. **We are told to bear these types of burdens FOR someone else.**

Galatians 6:2
"Bear ye one another's burdens, and so fulfil the law of Christ."

But there's another type of burden…

This type of burden is also heavy and weighs upon our hearts. It can also cause pain, but it's a different type of pain. Instead of carrying the burden FOR someone else, **we are to carry this type of burden TO someone else.** This is when we are so burdened for someone else to receive something that we are willing to bring it to them. The Apostle Paul had this burden for the people of Israel.

Romans 9:2
"That I have great heaviness and continual sorrow in my heart."

Romans 10:1
"Brethren, my heart's desire and prayer to God for Israel is…"

What is our heart's desire and prayer to God today?

Paul's was very specific.

Romans 10:1
"Brethren, my heart's desire and prayer to God for Israel is that they might be saved."

This is the type of burden that we should desire to have!

Can we say, like Paul, that our hearts' desire and prayer to God is to see people saved? If that is true, what are we doing about it?

The greatest burden someone can have is being without Christ, while the greatest blessing we can receive is bringing someone to Christ. If we will allow ourselves to have a burden for lost souls, we will see an abundance of blessings from the Lord.

Proverbs 11:30
"The fruit of the righteous is a tree of life; and he that winneth souls is wise."

Bible Reading
Genesis 39-40 | John 20

01.21 | January 21

The Hedge.

Job 1:10
"Hast not thou made an hedge about him, and about his house, and about all that he hath on every side? thou hast blessed the work of his hands, and his substance is increased in the land."

Most know the testimony of Job quite well. He lived in the land of Uz, and was known as a perfect and upright man, who feared God and eschewed evil. People who knew Job knew his priorities. He had a reputation of living for God and for being a man of faith in Him. Satan even knew Job. When he came into His presence, the Lord Himself spoke of Job to Satan, and in verses 9-11 we find his response to the Lord's suggestion.

Job 1:9-11
"Then Satan answered the LORD, and said, Doth Job fear God for nought? Hast not thou made an hedge about him, and about his house, and about all that he hath on every side? thou hast blessed the work of his hands, and his substance is increased in the land. But put forth thine hand now, and touch all that he hath, and he will curse thee to thy face."

Satan also knew that Job was living inside the hedge that the Lord had placed around him. He knew that if he was to do anything to him, the Lord Himself would have to remove the hedge from Job in order for Satan to be able to touch him. The Lord had put him inside a hedge of divine protection. That's what the Lord does for His children. He did it for Noah and his family just before the earth was destroyed by the flood.

Genesis 7:15-16
"And they went in unto Noah into the ark, two and two of all flesh, wherein is the breath of life. And they that went in, went in male and female of all flesh, as God had commanded him: and the LORD shut him in."

Have you ever been aware of the hedge of protection God has around you? Maybe you've experienced trials where you knew that God had allowed Satan to inflict your life. When trials come, remember that God had to have allowed it. He works all things together for our good and His glory.

Romans 8:28
"And we know that all things work together for good to them that love God, to them who are the called according to his purpose."

Thank God for the hedge today.

Bible Reading
Genesis 41-42 | John 21

January 22 | 01.22

We Know.

Romans 8:28
"And we know that all things work together for good to them that love God, to them who are the called according to his purpose."

When it comes to this verse, most of the time we jump straight to focusing on *"that all things work together for good"*, often jumping right over the first three words. *"And we know…"*

What do we know?
"…that all things work together for good…"

If we truly know that, how come we so often need the reminder of the Truth of Romans 8:28? **We know… but sometimes we forget.**

We forget that the condition to the blessing in this verse is that we must first love God. Without a love for Him, we have no promise of all things working together for good. With a love for Him, we are never alone; no matter what may come our way.

Romans 8:35-39
"Who shall separate us from the love of Christ? shall tribulation, or distress, or persecution, or famine, or nakedness, or peril, or sword? As it is written, For thy sake we are killed all the day long; we are accounted as sheep for the slaughter. Nay, in all these things we are more than conquerors through him that loved us. For I am persuaded, that neither death, nor life, nor angels, nor principalities, nor powers, nor things present, nor things to come, Nor height, nor depth, nor any other creature, shall be able to separate us from the love of God, which is in Christ Jesus our Lord."

We forget that God is always working out the details of our lives for our good, and ultimately for His glory. Sometimes that means things do not happen like we want, and rarely as quickly as we desire. **It is His purpose that truly matters, not ours.** That Truth hurts sometimes to be reminded of, but His purpose is so far greater than ours, and anything we could imagine.

We forget He is Able to do exceeding abundantly above all that we ask or even think.

Ephesians 3:20
"Now unto him that is able to do exceeding abundantly above all that we ask or think, according to the power that worketh in us,"

Instead of forgetting…
May we remind ourselves today what we know to be True.
Bible Reading
Genesis 43-44 | Matthew 1

01.23 | January 23

Fully Persuaded.

Romans 4:21
"And being fully persuaded that, what he had promised, he was able also to perform."

When the situations around us cause doubt and discouragement to creep into our hearts and minds, our level of persuasion, or belief, that God is Able to meet our every need begins to decrease.

It is in these times that we must be conscious of our condition, and remind ourselves of the ability of our Saviour.

2 Timothy 1:12
"For the which cause I also suffer these things: nevertheless I am not ashamed: for I know whom I have believed, and am persuaded that he is able to keep that which I have committed unto him against that day."

We must be fully persuaded that He is Able.

When He begins something,
we can be certain that He will finish what He started.

Philippians 1:6
*"Being confident of this very thing,
that he which hath begun a good work in you
will perform it until the day of Jesus Christ:"*

How persuaded are you today?

**May we be able to say
that we are fully persuaded that He is Able.**

Bible Reading
Genesis 45-46 | Matthew 2

January 24 | 01.24

Seeking To Devour.

1 Peter 5:8-9
"Be sober, be vigilant; because your adversary the devil, as a roaring lion, walketh about, seeking whom he may devour: Whom resist stedfast in the faith, knowing that the same afflictions are accomplished in your brethren that are in the world."

The moment we are fully persuaded that the Lord is Able to meet our need, the devil takes notice of our faith. Like a bullseye on our backs, he is after us with the intent to devour us any way he can.

We must be sober and vigilant.
1 Peter 1:13
"Wherefore gird up the loins of your mind, be sober, and hope to the end for the grace that is to be brought unto you at the revelation of Jesus Christ;"

If we are not calm and collected in our spirit, we will not be aware of when the fiery darts of the wicked are being thrown at us.

We must resist him with purpose.
Ephesians 6:11-12
"Put on the whole armour of God, that ye may be able to stand against the wiles of the devil. For we wrestle not against flesh and blood, but against principalities, against powers, against the rulers of the darkness of this world, against spiritual wickedness in high places."

There is no excuse for attempting to stand defenseless against him when we have been given specific instructions and equipment at our disposal. Failing to place the armour of God upon our lives will only lead to heartache and defeat.

Ephesians 6:13
"Wherefore take unto you the whole armour of God, that ye may be able to withstand in the evil day, and having done all, to stand."

It is not our responsibility to defend ourselves.
Exodus 14:14
"The LORD shall fight for you, and ye shall hold your peace."

When we try to fight for ourselves,
we surrender the perfect peace that only He supplies.
Isaiah 26:3
"Thou wilt keep him in perfect peace, whose mind is stayed on thee: because he trusteth in thee."

Bible Reading
Genesis 47-48 | Matthew 3

01.25 | January 25

Wonderfully Made.

Psalm 139:14
"I will praise thee; for I am fearfully and wonderfully made: marvellous are thy works; and that my soul knoweth right well."

Life is such a precious possession, yet in the day we live in we must fight for the sanctity of human life. Never before has the satanic attack on the life of a baby in the womb been as prevalent as it is today.

The breath of life is a gift from God.

Genesis 2:7
"And the LORD God formed man of the dust of the ground, and breathed into his nostrils the breath of life; and man became a living soul."

James 1:17
"Every good gift and every perfect gift is from above, and cometh down from the Father of lights, with whom is no variableness, neither shadow of turning."

He makes no mistakes.

Psalm 18:30
"As for God, his way is perfect: the word of the LORD is tried: he is a buckler to all those that trust in him."

Regardless of the circumstance, when life begins, God has a purpose. May we pray today for every mother who is contemplating the future of her child.

We are made in the image of God.
We are His creation.

Genesis 1:27
"So God created man in his own image, in the image of God created he him; male and female created he them."

May we choose to fight to protect the right to life of every child that He has created, for each of them are fearfully and wonderfully made.

Bible Reading
Genesis 49-50 | Matthew 4

January 26 | 01.26

Divine Appointments.

Psalm 37:23
*"The steps of a good man are ordered by the LORD:
and he delighteth in his way."*

Have you ever had a divine appointment where you knew without a shadow of a doubt that God had orchestrated every detail? His power is evident when things happen and there is no other explanation, but Him alone.

Sometimes it is a specific amount of money just before an unexpected bill is due. Sometimes it's crossing paths with someone you haven't seen in years hundreds of miles from home. Sometimes it's speaking with a waitress about the Lord as her eyes fill with tears. Sometimes it's a phone call or text of encouragement just when you need it. Sometimes it's just riding in a car with your best friend thanking the Lord for some quality time together.

The Lord has no limits.
There is nothing that He cannot do or accomplish if He desires.

He is willing and able to create divine appointments for us every day if only we will yield ourselves to Him, allowing Him to order our steps.

Psalm 119:133
*"Order my steps in thy word:
and let not any iniquity have dominion over me."*

Being "in the right place at just the right time" does not happen by accident. There are no coincidences with God. Yet, He has given us the freewill to choose whether we will allow Him to guide and direct us.

Proverbs 4:26
"Ponder the path of thy feet, and let all thy ways be established."

Who is ordering your steps today?

Bible Reading
Exodus 1-2 | Matthew 5

01.27 | January 27

Divine Protection.

Psalm 91:1-2
"He that dwelleth in the secret place of the most High shall abide under the shadow of the Almighty. I will say of the LORD, He is my refuge and my fortress: my God; in him will I trust."

Just as there are divine appointments,
there is also without a doubt divine protection.

Think of the many people on 9/11 that had situations arise that prevented them from getting to work at the World Trade Center towers that fateful day. What they thought was an inconvenience absolutely saved their lives.

The LORD orchestrates peculiar events in order to protect His children.
Psalm 32:7
"Thou art my hiding place; thou shalt preserve me from trouble; thou shalt compass me about with songs of deliverance. Selah."

That extra-long traffic light, flat tire, or simply getting "stuck" by a train could be a delay that prohibits you being involved in an accident down the road.

Thieves breaking into cars is an inconvenience, but a blessing when the alternative is them carrying out a terror attack on a congregation.

Psalm 61:3
"For thou hast been a shelter for me, and a strong tower from the enemy."

Children of the Lord have a hedge of divine protection around them. Anything the devil tries to threaten or discourage them with must first be given permission by our Heavenly Father.

Have you ever been aware of divine protection in your life?
Perhaps there may not be a specific instance that comes to mind, but in reality, there are many times the Lord had protected us from harm and we are simply unaware.

He protects us in love by His mercy and His grace.
Thank Him for divine protection today, and every day.

Bible Reading
Exodus 3-4 | Matthew 6

Praying For Others.

Colossians 1:3
"We give thanks to God and the Father of our Lord Jesus Christ, praying always for you,"

Intercessory prayer cannot be overvalued.

Paul knew how important it is that we make praying for others a priority in our lives.

He prayed purposefully.
Colossians 1:9
"For this cause…"

He prayed immediately.
Colossians 1:9
"…since the day we heard it…"

He prayed consistently.
Colossians 1:9
"…do not cease to pray for you …"

How often do you pray for others?

In the first chapter of the Book of Colossians, the Apostle Paul pinned down a recipe for how we can pray for others. Colossians 1:9-12

Pray for them...
…to seek the Lord and His will. - v.9
…to walk with the Lord. - v. 10
…to be fruitful. - v. 10
…to grow spiritually. - v. 10
…to be strong in the Lord. - v. 11-12

If you have not made praying for others a priority, start today.

It will bless your heart as you see the Lord moving in their lives, just as you prayed He would.

Send a text to someone today
letting them know you are praying for them.

Bible Reading
Exodus 5-6 | Matthew 7

01.29 | January 29

When We Pray.

Acts 4:31-32
"And when they had prayed, the place was shaken
where they were assembled together;
and they were all filled with the Holy Ghost, and they spake the word of
God with boldness. And the multitude of them that believed were of one
heart and of one soul: neither said any of them that ought of the things
which he possessed was his own; but they had all things common."

Have you ever really thought about what happens when we pray?
Think about Who hears our prayers…the Lord Himself, Jehovah hears the cries of His children. The Creator hears His creation.

What could happen as a result of our prayers?
Matthew 21:22
"And all things, whatsoever ye shall ask in prayer,
believing, ye shall receive."

If we will bind together to pray for our churches,
we will see them shaken for the glory of God.

The church in Acts were of one heart and one soul.
They prayed together for one purpose…
that the Lord would get the glory.

1 Peter 4:11
"If any man speak, let him speak as the oracles of God;
if any man minister, let him do it as of the ability which God giveth:
that God in all things may be glorified through Jesus Christ, to whom be
praise and dominion for ever and ever. Amen."

Too often we focus on praying for our own needs.
What could happen if we made praying for others a priority?

Our churches could be shaken, if we will pray.
Our families could be shaken, if we will pray.
Our relationships could be shaken, if we will pray.

What are you praying about today?
Who are you praying for God to bless?

Pour yourself into someone else who you know is struggling this week.
If the Lord brings a name or face to your mind, reach out to them.

Bible Reading
Exodus 7-8 | Matthew 8

January 30 | 01.30

Drinking From The Saucer.

Psalm 23:5
"Thou preparest a table before me in the presence of mine enemies: thou anointest my head with oil; my cup runneth over."

In spite of the desire of our enemies for us to suffer destruction, the Lord prepares a table from which we can feast. What a picture of the abundant blessings we receive from the Lord!

Psalm 16:5
"The LORD is the portion of mine inheritance and of my cup: thou maintainest my lot."

When we make praying for others a priority, we will see a difference in our lives as well.

Picture a few glasses side-by-side, each filled with differing levels of water. One glass nearly full, two about half-full, and one with just a small amount of water inside. If the levels of water represented how our week was going and the level of encouragement and blessings we possessed today, which glass would best represent you? Is your glass half-full or half-empty? Are you full almost to the brim, or are you just barely getting by?

Those days when our glass is nearly full are the times when we can pour ourselves into other people so that they too can remember to find comfort in the Lord.

Psalm 23:4
"Yea, though I walk through the valley of the shadow of death, I will fear no evil: for thou art with me; thy rod and thy staff they comfort me."

Sometimes we need a friend to remind us that the Lord is our Shepherd, and He is Able to restore us.

Psalm 23:3
"He restoreth my soul: he leadeth me in the paths of righteousness for his name's sake."

The abundance of the Lord's blessings will make our cup overflow.
When our cup runs over, drinking from the saucer should make us want more of Him.

Psalm 23:6
"Surely goodness and mercy shall follow me all the days of my life: and I will dwell in the house of the LORD for ever."

Bible Reading
Exodus 9-10 | Matthew 9

01.31 | January 31

What Do You Battle?

Ephesians 6:12
"For we wrestle not against flesh and blood, but against principalities, against powers, against the rulers of the darkness of this world, against spiritual wickedness in high places."

Everyone fights some type of battle. Too often we blame our circumstances on someone or something, when the Truth of the matter is that every battle comes from the same source. Spiritual wickedness is real, and the devil is our real enemy. He is the root cause of whatever struggle we face today.

Distractions - 1 Corinthians 10:13
Possibly the easiest weapon in his toolbox is causing us to move our focus onto anything but what truly matters.

Discouragement - Isaiah 41:10
It is so easy to look around us and hang our heads. This wicked world has nothing to offer us but defeat. Look to Jesus today.

Depression - 2 Corinthians 10:5
Though few admit to this ailment, many feel the weight of depression upon them every day. You are not alone in the battle.

Distress - Psalm 18:6
Stress is more than just a buzzword. Our flesh craves anything that deters us from calling out to the Lord for help in our situation. Help is available if only we will call out to Him.

Disobedience - Psalm 51:1-2
Sometimes our situation is because of our own choosing. When we give in to temptation, our actions have consequences. We must confess and repent of our iniquities.

Disease - James 5:15-16
When health decreases, we can turn to the Great Physician. He desires to hear the prayers of His children for those who are sick.

Delay - Psalm 27:14
No one likes to wait, but the reality is that our timetable rarely, if ever, lines up with His. Choose to trust His timing, for He knows what is best. He is working all things for our good and His glory.

**Whatever battle you are facing today,
the Lord has the solution. He is the Answer to every problem.**

Bible Reading
Exodus 11-12 | Matthew 10

February 1 | 02.01

The Battle Is The LORD'S.

1 Samuel 17:47
"And all this assembly shall know that the LORD saveth not with sword and spear: for the battle is the LORD'S, and he will give you into our hands."

Goliath was a champion. He was known for winning any battle in which he participated. He had quite a collection of armour and weapons. His pride caused him to seek out an opponent to fight.

1 Samuel 17:8-9
"…choose you a man for you, and let him come down to me. If he be able to fight with me, and to kill me, then will we be your servants: but if I prevail against him, and kill him, then shall ye be our servants, and serve us."

What a picture of our greatest enemy.
The devil seeks to call us into battle seeking us to fear our defeat.

1 Samuel 17:24
"And all the men of Israel, when they saw the man, fled from him, and were sore afraid."

Only David had the courage to fight the champion.
Despite the fearful warnings of others, he chose to enter the battle in faith that Someone else was on his side.

1 Samuel 17:45
"Then said David to the Philistine, Thou comest to me with a sword, and with a spear, and with a shield: but I come to thee in the name of the LORD of hosts, the God of the armies of Israel, whom thou hast defied."

David chose to participate in the battle for one purpose.
1 Samuel 17:46
"…that all the earth may know that there is a God in Israel."

He knew that the battle was the LORD'S.

What if we approached our battles the way that David did?
Face to face with the enemy trusting that the Lord would give the victory.

No matter what the devil has thrown at you this week,
it is not your battle to fight.

The Lord has purpose for the trial you are facing today.
Remember Who's battle your situation truly is,
and yield the fight to Him.

Bible Reading
Exodus 13-14 | Matthew 11

02.02 | February 2

He Fights For Us.

Exodus 14:14
"The LORD shall fight for you, and ye shall hold your peace."

The children of Israel had no where to turn. Their enemies were close behind them, the Red Sea in front of them. They were sore afraid. Moses admonished them to stand still, and see the salvation of the Lord.

The Lord commanded that they go forward.
Exodus 14:16
"But lift thou up thy rod, and stretch out thine hand over the sea, and divide it: and the children of Israel shall go on dry ground through the midst of the sea."

Moses obeyed, and we know the rest of the story…they all walked across on dry ground. A miracle. A wall of water was beside each of their hands. Their feet were not even wet. Dry ground…on the sea floor.

The Lord fought for them just as He had promised.
How many times have we been at our own Red Sea?
Unsure of where to turn, unsure of what lied ahead.

Maybe our enemies were not physically chasing us to our death, but they were definitely in pursuit. It is in those times, when just as Moses commanded God's chosen people, we must choose to stop, and stand still. The salvation of the Lord is just ahead, only dependent upon our allowing the Lord to fight for us. In the Book of Deuteronomy, we find this same principle reiterated to the children of Israel at least three times. Seems they needed a reminder just as we often do.

He goes before us. Deuteronomy 1:30
He fights so that we have no need to fear. Deuteronomy 3:22
He goes with us. Deuteronomy 20:4

What comfort we too can find in these verses.

The Lord goes before us to clear the way so that He can direct us according to His will. He reminds us not to be fearful, regardless of what surrounds us. Then He goes with us so that we are not alone.

He speaks victory through His Word.
Allow the Lord to fight for you today.

Bible Reading
Exodus 15-16 | Matthew 12

February 3 | 02.03

Who Can Be Against Us?

Romans 8:31
*"What shall we then say to these things?
If God be for us, who can be against us?"*

Can you imagine going into a battle knowing you cannot lose?
That is exactly what happens when we allow the Lord to fight for us!
With Him on our side, we need not even say a word.
His Words are the only ones that truly matter.

Psalm 27:1
*"The LORD is my light and my salvation; whom shall I fear?
the LORD is the strength of my life; of whom shall I be afraid?"*

**He is our Refuge.
He is our Strength.
He is our Help.**

Psalm 46:1-3
"God is our refuge and strength, a very present help in trouble. Therefore will not we fear, though the earth be removed, and though the mountains be carried into the midst of the sea; Though the waters thereof roar and be troubled, though the mountains shake with the swelling thereof. Selah."

When you feel that the earth is being removed from beneath your feet…
He is there.
When your mountain is moved into the midst of a stormy sea…
He is there.
When the waters roar, and the waves crash around you…
He is there.

**He is a very present help in trouble.
He is a very present help in time of need.**

Hebrews 4:16
*"Let us therefore come boldly unto the throne of grace,
that we may obtain mercy, and find grace to help in time of need."*

Trust Him today.
Call out to Him in prayer, and talk to Him
like you do your very best friend…because He is.

Bible Reading
Exodus 17-18 | Matthew 13

02.04 | February 4

Communication.

Jeremiah 33:3
*"Call unto me, and I will answer thee,
and shew thee great and mighty things, which thou knowest not."*

We carry one around with us every day. Constantly checking the time. Hoping for another message. Looking for the latest news, or even what is about to happen. It is our communication line to others. It's a sad reminder that we are more faithful to our phones than we are to the Word of God. We are more concerned about communicating with someone through our phone than we are through our Bible. Not fun to think about, but it is so true for each and every one of us, if we are honest.

Communication is a such a needful thing.
A call from our best friend can brighten our day.
A text of encouragement from anyone can change our perspective.

Communication is a two-way street.
When we talk to someone, we expect an answer;
because that is how communication works.

As children of God, we can open our Bibles for the Lord to speak to us.
In return, we have the privilege of talking to Him through prayer.

In troubled times, we must return to prioritizing the basics.
Prayer and Bible Study.

Jeremiah 33:3
"Call unto me, and I will answer thee…"

Call to Him in prayer today.
He is waiting to hear from us, and the line is never busy.

Psalm 119:105
"Thy word is a lamp unto my feet, and a light unto my path."

Open the pages of His Word today.
He always says just what we need to hear.

Bible Reading
Exodus 19-20 | Matthew 14

February 5 | 02.05

Waiting To Be Led.

Psalm 25:4-5
"Shew me thy ways, O LORD; teach me thy paths. Lead me in thy truth, and teach me: for thou art the God of my salvation; on thee do I wait all the day."

There is no shame in waiting.
Psalm 25:3
"Yea, let none that wait on thee be ashamed: let them be ashamed which transgress without cause."

We live in a world that does not want to wait on anything.

Yet, in the context of his enemies battling against him, David is still lifting up his soul unto the Lord because he truly trusts Him.
Psalm 25:1-2
"Unto thee, O LORD, do I lift up my soul. O my God, I trust in thee: let me not be ashamed, let not mine enemies triumph over me."

David then shifts his prayer from exalting the LORD and pleading for divine protection to asking for direction. He was willing to wait on the LORD. We see that all throughout the Book of Psalms. David was constantly waiting for the LORD to work on his behalf.

David understood the value of waiting on the LORD.
When we wait on Him, we cannot lose.
David desired to learn the Ways and Paths of the LORD, and be lead by Him in every thing that he did.

Do we desire the same?
The Truth of Who is behind something, always comes out.
Acts 5:38-39
"And now I say unto you, Refrain from these men, and let them alone: for if this counsel or this work be of men, it will come to nought: But if it be of God, ye cannot overthrow it…"

When we wait until we know it is the Lord that is leading us to do something, we can rest assured that it will not fail.

Ecclesiastes 3:14
"I know that, whatsoever God doeth, it shall be for ever: nothing can be put to it, nor any thing taken from it: and God doeth it, that men should fear before him."

Wait to be led by Him.

Bible Reading
Exodus 21-22 | Matthew 15

02.06 | February 6

He Is Our Help.

Psalm 28:7
*"The LORD is my strength and my shield; my heart trusted in him,
and I am helped: therefore my heart greatly rejoiceth;
and with my song will I praise him."*

Sometimes the Lord allows circumstances to come into our lives simply for the purpose of refocusing our fleshly tendencies.

Remember when Peter stepped out of the boat and walked on the water until he saw the wind instead of Jesus? A miracle was performed because of his faith, but his fear quickly got in the way.

Our weaknesses remind us of our need for Him.
2 Corinthians 12:10
"Therefore I take pleasure in infirmities, in reproaches, in necessities, in persecutions, in distresses for Christ's sake: for when I am weak, then am I strong."

Our vulnerabilities allow us to see that only He can truly protect us.
Psalm 91:4
"He shall cover thee with his feathers, and under his wings shalt thou trust: his truth shall be thy shield and buckler."

**Because He is our strength and shield, we can trust Him.
When we trust Him, we find help.**
Psalm 121:1-2
"I will lift up mine eyes unto the hills, from whence cometh my help. My help cometh from the LORD, which made heaven and earth."

Look unto the hills of the Word of God today.
The help we receive leads us to rejoice and praise Him.

Psalm 63:7
*"Because thou hast been my help,
therefore in the shadow of thy wings will I rejoice."*

How has the Lord helped you recently?
If it's been awhile since you can say the Lord truly helped you through His Word, perhaps it is because you have not fully trusted in Him.

Trust Him today, and rest in the comfort of knowing He is your help.

Bible Reading
Exodus 23-24 | Matthew 16

February 7 | 02.07

Overwhelmed.

Psalm 61:2
*"From the end of the earth will I cry unto thee,
when my heart is overwhelmed: lead me to the rock that is higher than I."*

Although this verse is typically referred to as a desperate and prayerful plea in the time of distress, is it possible for the Lord to show us something else out of this passage? It is easy to have glass half empty kind of day and run to the Truth of this verse that when we are overwhelmed in sadness or languishing in pain, the Lord is our Rock that we can run to for comfort and safety. But is it possible that this verse can still apply to us if we choose to look at this Truth from a glass half full perspective? If we are able to read this chapter with the blessings of the Lord in mind, we soon find that our glass is not just half full, but running over.

Have you ever been overwhelmed by the Goodness of the Lord?
Psalm 31:19
"Oh how great is thy goodness, which thou hast laid up for them that fear thee; which thou hast wrought for them that trust in thee before the sons of men!"

**Have you ever been overwhelmed by the blessings
He has bestowed upon you?**
1 Samuel 12:24
"Only fear the LORD, and serve him in truth with all your heart: for consider how great things he hath done for you."

Have you ever just been overwhelmed by the thought of Him?
Psalm 33:8
*"Let all the earth fear the LORD:
let all the inhabitants of the world stand in awe of him."*

The Scriptures are full of Truth to cause us to stand in awe of Him.
Psalm 119:161
*"Princes have persecuted me without a cause:
but my heart standeth in awe of thy word."*

Maybe it was an unexpected blessing or an unspoken need that was met… a solution to an infirmity or a surprise gesture from someone you love…or that thing that may seem so small to everyone else, but God knows means the world to you. Whatever it is, if you have ever had a clear glimpse of Him and His glory, you have been overwhelmed. **Ask Him to do it again.**

Bible Reading
Exodus 25-26 | Matthew 17

02.08 | February 8

My Heart's Desire.

Romans 10:1
"Brethren, my heart's desire and prayer to God for Israel is, that they might be saved."

The middle part of Romans 10 is frequently referred to in regards to salvation, and leading someone to the Lord.

Romans 10:9,13
"That if thou shalt confess with thy mouth the Lord Jesus, and shalt believe in thine heart that God hath raised him from the dead, thou shalt be saved...For whosoever shall call upon the name of the Lord shall be saved."

But what about the rest of the chapter?
The first verse shows Paul's heart and burden for Israel.
Most of his people had a zeal for God, yet they did not know Him.

What is our heart's desire?
If we agree with Paul that our heart's desire is for people to be saved, then what are we doing about it?

Romans 10:11
"For the scripture saith, Whosoever believeth on him shall not be ashamed."

If we truly believe on Him, then why are we sometimes ashamed enough that we do not make sharing the Gospel with others a priority?

Romans 10:14
"How then shall they call on him in whom they have not believed? and how shall they believe in him of whom they have not heard? and how shall they hear without a preacher?"

Sharing the Gospel is not reserved for those who have the position of a preacher as we know it in this modern day. Paul was referring to someone who publishes or proclaims the Word of God openly.

Romans 10:17
"So then faith cometh by hearing, and hearing by the word of God."
There can be no salvation without belief and repentance.
No belief without faith.
No faith without hearing.
No hearing without the Word of God.
We must share the Word with others.

Bible Reading
Exodus 27-28 | Matthew 18

February 9 | 02.09

The Worth Of A Soul.

Psalm 126:5-6
"They that sow in tears shall reap in joy. He that goeth forth and weepeth, bearing precious seed, shall doubtless come again with rejoicing, bringing his sheaves with him."

A woman named Lisa is lost without Christ.
She is someone's mom.
She is someone's grandmother.
She is someone's friend.
She is someone's co-worker.
She is someone's wife.

What if she was your mom?
What if she was your friend?
Would you not want someone to share the Gospel with her?

Pray that someone will help her see the Truth of the Gospel and how much God truly loves her.

Just as someone told you.
Imagine if that person had neglected to share the Gospel with you?

Too often, we have lost our tears for the lost.
If we do not sow in tears, there will be no reaping in joy.

Bear the Precious Seed of the Word of God on your shoulders today and tell someone what He has done for you.

Maybe a friend.
Maybe a family member.
Maybe a waitress.
Maybe a cashier.
Whoever it is…tell someone.

Matthew 16:26
"For what is a man profited, if he shall gain the whole world, and lose his own soul? or what shall a man give in exchange for his soul?"

How much is a soul worth to you?

Bible Reading
Exodus 29-30 | Matthew 19

02.10 | February 10

Only Believe.

Mark 5:36
*"As soon as Jesus heard the word that was spoken,
he saith unto the ruler of the synagogue, Be not afraid, only believe."*

Those last five words may have been said to Jarius, the ruler of the synagogue, but they were pinned within the pages of the Holy Scriptures for us to read today. Five words. The power is not so much in the Words themselves, but in the One Who said them.

"Be not afraid, only believe."
**Five words literally full of the grace of God,
spoken by the Word Himself.**

Regardless of our situation today,
they hold the Answer for any problem that we face.

"Be not afraid, only believe."

Jesus did not add any other words after the phrase *"only believe"*.
Perhaps because the Word Himself had spoken.

There is no room to fear when we truly believe in Him.
No room for doubt. No room for indecision.
No room for anxiety. No room for confusion.
No room for panic. No room for distress.
No room for anything, other than believing.

"Be not afraid, only believe."

Time after time within the pages of Scripture
we see how belief made the difference.

Where there was unbelief,
there were not many mighty works.

Where there was doubt, the people missed out.

"Be not afraid, only believe."
Choose today to only believe in Him.

Bible Reading
Exodus 31-32 | Matthew 20

February 11 | 02.11

God Given Power.

Matthew 28:18-20

"And Jesus came and spake unto them, saying, All power is given unto me in heaven and in earth. Go ye therefore, and teach all nations, baptizing them in the name of the Father, and of the Son, and of the Holy Ghost: Teaching them to observe all things whatsoever I have commanded you: and, lo, I am with you alway, even unto the end of the world. Amen."

The Great Commission applies to each and every one of God's children. If it does not, why would God not call us to Heaven the moment after we are saved? **We have work to do.** At the very end of the Book of Matthew, we find these three verses which give us three parts to what we commonly refer to as the Great Commission.

Go
"And Jesus came and spake unto them, saying, All power is given unto me in heaven and in earth. Go ye therefore…"
All of us are commanded to go. Whether it is across the world, across the country, across town, or across the street.

Teach
"…and teach all nations… Teaching them to observe all things whatsoever I have commanded you…"
All of us are commanded to teach. But what do we teach? There are no degrees required to teach this Subject. We must simply teach the Gospel that we have been taught.

Baptize
"…baptizing them in the name of the Father, and of the Son, and of the Holy Ghost…"
Some are commanded to baptize. This is reserved for the pastors of a local church; however, those they baptize must first hear and place faith in the Gospel of Jesus Christ, which any one of us can share.

We are all called to do something.
But how can we do what God has called us to do?
Only through God given power!
Matthew 28:18-19
"And Jesus came and spake unto them, saying, All power is given unto me in heaven and in earth. Go ye therefore…"

Therefore we must go and teach the Gospel of Jesus Christ!
Someone's eternity is depending upon our obedience to His command.

Bible Reading
Exodus 33-34 | Matthew 21

02.12 | February 12

Witnessing The Gospel.

1 Corinthians 15:3-4
"For I delivered unto you first of all that which I also received, how that Christ died for our sins according to the scriptures; And that he was buried, and that he rose again the third day according to the scriptures:"

What is the Gospel?
The Death, Burial and Resurrection of Jesus Christ.

Did you know that one woman witnessed them all?
Mary Magdalene.

She saw Christ's Death. - Matthew 27:54-56
She saw Christ's Burial. - Matthew 27:59-61
She saw Christ's Resurrection. - Mark 16:9

She was there for ALL three.
She literally witnessed the Gospel as it became the Good News.

She was the FIRST to…
See Him alive. - Mark 16:9
Hear His Voice. - John 20:15-16
Be Commissioned. - John 20:17
Share The Gospel. - John 20:18

She obeyed the Lord and shared the Good News.

What an example this woman,
who is often known for her sinful past, has left for us today.

**She witnessed the Gospel,
and was the first to share the Gospel with others.**
It was her that informed the disciples that Jesus was risen.

The Lord gave her the honor of being the first to do many things.

**May we seek to apply her testimony to our own lives
and be a witness for Him!**

[Excerpt from She: Delighting In The Examples Of The Women Of The Bible - Volume 2]

Bible Reading
Exodus 35-36 | Matthew 22

Wait.

Psalm 39:7
"And now, Lord, what wait I for? my hope is in thee."

There are differences in how and why we wait, especially when it comes to the Lord. Within the pages of the Word of God, there are at least three different phrases about waiting and the Lord.

Wait For The Lord
Psalm 130:5
"I wait for the LORD, my soul doth wait, and in his word do I hope."

The word *"for"* denotes waiting with the Object or the purpose of the Object. It means intending to belong to, or be used in connection with something or Someone.

Have you ever felt like you were waiting for the Lord to show you exactly what He intends for you to do? That is when we must wait while hoping in His Word, for He is sure to speak direction as we look to Him in faith.

Wait On The Lord
Psalms 27:14
*"Wait on the LORD: be of good courage,
and he shall strengthen thine heart: wait, I say, on the LORD."*

The word *"on"* signifies being attached to or unified with. When we faithfully wait on the Lord, we are showing those around us that we are attached to or unified with Him.

Wait Upon The Lord
Isaiah 40:31
"But they that wait upon the LORD shall renew their strength; they shall mount up with wings as eagles; they shall run, and not be weary; and they shall walk, and not faint."

The word *"upon"* implies being in complete or approximate contact with. Waiting upon the Lord renews our strength because in order to do so, we must be in contact with Him. We have the opportunity to call upon Him in prayer as we wait for Him to move in our situation or storm.

Wait for, on, and upon Him today, and every day.

Bible Reading
Exodus 37-38 | Matthew 23

02.14 | February 14

The More Excellent Way.

1 Corinthians 12:31
*"But covet earnestly the best gifts:
and yet shew I unto you a more excellent way."*

What is this *"more excellent way"*? Paul writes to the church at Corinth, and through this entire chapter refers to the ministry of the gifts of a child of God, and our place in the body of Christ, the church. The last verse of the chapter is used as a springboard into Chapter 13, where *"a more excellent way"* is unveiled and described.

1 Corinthians 13:1
"Though I speak with the tongues of men and of angels, and have not charity, I am become as sounding brass, or a tinkling cymbal."
Regardless of what we say or do, if we do not have charity, we are nothing. We cannot accomplish anything without the love of Christ being at the root of it all. Charity is that agapē love…the highest form of love…the love of God for man and of man for God.

The love of Christ in us is significant evidence of our possession of Him.

Commonly referred to as "the love chapter", 1 Corinthians 13 describes what charity is, and how we are to utilize it.

1 Corinthians 13:4-7
"Charity suffereth long, and is kind; charity envieth not; charity vaunteth not itself, is not puffed up, Doth not behave itself unseemly, seeketh not her own, is not easily provoked, thinketh no evil; Rejoiceth not in iniquity, but rejoiceth in the truth; Beareth all things, believeth all things, hopeth all things, endureth all things."

The word *"charity"* is found nine times within this chapter.
What are there nine parts of within the pages of Scripture?
Galatians 5:22-23

1 John 4:7-8
"Beloved, let us love one another: for love is of God; and every one that loveth is born of God, and knoweth God. He that loveth not knoweth not God; for God is love."

God is love; and without Him, we can do nothing.
Choose love, and choose Him today.
He is the *"more excellent way"*.

Bible Reading
Exodus 39 | Matthew 24

February 15 | 02.15

Daniel 3:18
"But if not, be it known unto thee, O king, that we will not serve thy gods, nor worship the golden image which thou hast set up."

These three Hebrew boys understood the ultimatum they were given. They were told to bow and worship the golden image setup by Nebuchadnezzar or be thrown into the burning fiery furnace.

Would they obey the king and live, or stand for the Lord and suffer the consequences? When faced with a choice, their faith was bold.

Proverbs 28:1
*"The wicked flee when no man pursueth:
but the righteous are bold as a lion."*

They knew God was able to deliver them.
It was only a matter of if He would.

Our God is truly able to deliver us from any circumstance we face!
But what if He doesn't?

What if He doesn't intervene exactly like we think He should?
What if we are faced with the same decision of who we will obey?

Sooner or later, we too will face an ultimatum like the three Hebrew boys did. Our consequence may not be a burning fiery furnace, but when faced with the same choice to stand or bow to whatever situation is thrown at us, how will we react?

Will we still choose to serve Him?
Will we stand fast despite the pressure?

Daniel 3:16-18
"Shadrach, Meshach, and Abednego, answered and said to the king, O Nebuchadnezzar, we are not careful to answer thee in this matter. If it be so, our God whom we serve is able to deliver us from the burning fiery furnace, and he will deliver us out of thine hand, O king. But if not, be it known unto thee, O king, that we will not serve thy gods, nor worship the golden image which thou hast set up."

When you are faced with a *"But if not..."*
will you stand and proclaim that He is still good?

Bible Reading
Exodus 40 | Matthew 25

02.16 | February 16

Changed At His Feet.

Luke 7:38
"And stood at his feet behind him weeping, and began to wash his feet with tears, and did wipe them with the hairs of her head, and kissed his feet, and anointed them with the ointment."

Many times throughout the pages of Scripture we find people at the feet of Jesus. This is not an accident nor a coincidence; for there are none of those within the inspired and preserved Word of God. It is also noteworthy that many, if not most, of these people were women. From this, we can glean many Truths of what may be found… at His feet.

One of those women was an unnamed woman who is only referred to as a sinner.
Luke 7:37
"And, behold, a woman in the city, which was a sinner, when she knew that Jesus sat at meat in the Pharisee's house, brought an alabaster box of ointment,"

She was a woman, and she was a sinner.
That means we ALL qualify!

Perhaps her name is not recorded so that we can better see that we all can relate to her. She knew Jesus was in the Pharisee's house and she brought with her an alabaster box of ointment.

She was at the feet of Jesus for a purpose.

She sincerely washed His feet with her tears, wiped them with the hairs of her head, and then anointed His feet with the ointment.

She did all of this to express her faith in Him.

Luke 7:47-50
"Wherefore I say unto thee, Her sins, which are many, are forgiven; for she loved much: but to whom little is forgiven, the same loveth little. And he said unto her, Thy sins are forgiven. And they that sat at meat with him began to say within themselves, Who is this that forgiveth sins also? And he said to the woman, Thy faith hath saved thee; go in peace."

Her faith in Him made the difference. She was changed at His feet.
She bowed down a sinner,
and came up a sinner saved by grace through faith!

We can find salvation at His feet.
If you have questions about salvation, please contact us.

Bible Reading
Leviticus 1-2 | Matthew 26

February 17 | 02.17

The Choice At His Feet

Luke 10:39
*"And she had a sister called Mary,
which also sat at Jesus' feet, and heard his word."*

Being at the feet of Jesus is not limited to our physical position. If our hearts are not first laid at His feet, it does not matter what bodily position we are in. Another woman in the New Testament is known for being at His feet, Mary of Bethany. She was the sister of Martha and Lazarus. She and Martha hosted Jesus in their home many times. He was their friend, and they were His…what a thought to be considered a friend of Jesus! In the last five verses of Luke 10, there is much Truth for us to learn from regarding these sisters. Martha received Jesus into her house, and Mary sat at His feet.

Martha was cumbered about, even by good things. She was busy serving the Saviour. However, it is important to note that Martha was once also at the feet of Jesus. Verse 39 tells us this by the word *"also"*. **Both of the sisters were once at His feet, and Martha got up to attend to His needs.**

Those who have served in the ministry in any capacity can relate to how easy it is to get cumbered about with the cares of life, the people whom we are serving, or just the day-to-day aspects. Martha did not just serve a little; she served much. **If we are not watchful, our serving can turn into cumbering…just like it did for Martha.**

> Cumbering can then lead to complaining and commanding.
> Jesus lovingly rebuked Martha for her outburst,
> while commending Mary for remaining at His feet.
> Mary made a choice to sit at His feet and hear His Word.
> **Now it was time for Martha to choose to sit at His feet again.**

If we do not hear the Word of God, our faith will never come. When we neglect His Word, our faith suffers. Have you ever gone awhile without truly sitting at His feet and hearing the Word? Then when you came back, even the first time, can you not notice the difference? Something was missing.

The Word makes the difference.

Like a dried up plant, the refreshing Water from the Word of God revives us just when we need it the most. Regardless of our physical position, your heart can be at His feet by opening your Bible, and spending time in His presence by reading and studying the Word of God that He has preserved for you. **Choose to sit at His feet today, and every day.**

Bible Reading
Leviticus 3-4 | Matthew 27

02.18 | February 18

A Cure At His Feet.

John 11:32
*"Then when Mary was come where Jesus was,
and saw him, she fell down at his feet, saying unto him,
Lord, if thou hadst been here, my brother had not died."*

Have you ever had a problem that seemed impossible to solve? Or maybe a situation that just seemed hopeless? Is there no solution in sight or no light at the end of your tunnel of confusion? That is exactly where Mary and Martha found themselves in John 11. It's a familiar story. Notice how Mary and Martha reacted in the middle of their darkness. They called for Jesus to intercede. **We too can stop and pray when we feel hopeless.** Jesus gave them Words of comfort…just as He has given us in the Scriptures, if only we will take the time to read.

But Jesus did not come when they thought He should.
He did not show up on their timetable.
As far as they were concerned, He was late…four days late.

His timing is rarely on our schedule, isn't it?
We don't like to wait. We want the answer now…or even yesterday.

These sisters believed that if He came when Lazarus was sick, He could miraculously heal him as He did so many others. But Lazarus died. All hope seemed gone. Can you relate?

When Jesus arrived in Bethany, Martha went and met Him expressing her faith that even though her brother was dead, He could help. Jesus then preached the Gospel to her.

John 11:25-26
"Jesus said unto her, I am the resurrection, and the life: he that believeth in me, though he were dead, yet shall he live: And whosoever liveth and believeth in me shall never die. Believest thou this?"
That question is also asked to every one of us.
Do we believe in Him?
Do we believe He can do the impossible in our lives?

Mary ran to Jesus with her problem, believing He could solve it. Jesus saw her faith and her tears. Just as He sees ours when we choose to believe that He is the Answer to our problem. We know the rest of the story. Jesus raised Lazarus from the dead. Lazarus died, and lived again. **Whatever you need today, you can find it at His feet.**

Bible Reading
Leviticus 5-6 | Matthew 28

February 19 | 02.19

Reminded.

Isaiah 40:28
"Hast thou not known? hast thou not heard, that the everlasting God, the LORD, the Creator of the ends of the earth, fainteth not, neither is weary? there is no searching of his understanding."

We have read from the Scriptures. We have heard the Word preached. We have held the Truth in our hands, and flipped through those holy pages. Yet, sometimes… we need reminded. Our flesh often gets in the way so much that we forget what we know to be True.

We need reminded that He is an everlasting God.
Isaiah 57:15
"For thus saith the high and lofty One that inhabiteth eternity, whose name is Holy; I dwell in the high and holy place, with him also that is of a contrite and humble spirit, to revive the spirit of the humble, and to revive the heart of the contrite ones."

We need reminded that He is the LORD.
Jeremiah 32:27
"Behold, I am the LORD, the God of all flesh: is there any thing too hard for me?"

We need reminded that He is the Creator.
Jeremiah 32:17
"Ah Lord GOD! behold, thou hast made the heaven and the earth by thy great power and stretched out arm, and there is nothing too hard for thee:"

We need reminded that He always knows best.
Psalm 147:5
"Great is our Lord, and of great power: his understanding is infinite."

Whatever has distracted you from the Truth today, set it aside.
The Lord started a work in you, and He will finish it.
Philippians 1:6
"Being confident of this very thing, that he which hath begun a good work in you will perform it until the day of Jesus Christ:"

Sometimes we just need reminded.

Bible Reading
Leviticus 7-8 | Luke 1

02.20 | February 20

Redeem The Time.

Ephesians 5:16
"Redeeming the time, because the days are evil."

The time you spent reading the verse above can never return. Think of the photos we take with our phones… it literally freezes and records a moment in time that we can never get back. It is only a memory.

You can hold on to the picture of that memory as long as you want, but you cannot go back and change it.

Use your time wisey while you have it, for there will be no more present time…all will be future time…all will be eternity.

We are not promised tomorrow.
Proverbs 27:1
*"Boast not thyself of to morrow;
for thou knowest not what a day may bring forth."*

Once time passes, an opportunity is lost and gone forever.
Ecclesiastes 9:10
*"Whatsoever thy hand findeth to do, do it with thy might;
for there is no work, nor device, nor knowledge,
nor wisdom, in the grave, whither thou goest."*

What opportunities have you let pass you by?
Telling a friend how much they mean to you?
Inviting someone to church?

Galatians 6:10
"As we have therefore opportunity, let us do good unto all men, especially unto them who are of the household of faith."

Giving someone a tract?
Witnessing when someone asks a question?
Colossians 4:5
"Walk in wisdom toward them that are without, redeeming the time."

Redeem the time that the Lord has given you while you have it.

Bible Reading
Leviticus 9-10 | Luke 2

February 21 | 02.21

Understanding His Will.

Ephesians 5:17
*"Wherefore be ye not unwise,
but understanding what the will of the Lord is."*

When Solomon could have asked for anything, he asked for wisdom.
1 Kings 3:9-10
"Give therefore thy servant an understanding heart to judge thy people, that I may discern between good and bad: for who is able to judge this thy so great a people? And the speech pleased the Lord, that Solomon had asked this thing."

The Wisdom he received allowed him to discern what the will of the Lord was in the matters of leading the children of Israel. **The same Wisdom is available to us, if only we would ask and seek Him.**

James 1:5
"If any of you lack wisdom, let him ask of God, that giveth to all men liberally, and upbraideth not; and it shall be given him."

Wisdom reveals the will of the Lord.
Be not conformed.
Romans 12:2
"And be not conformed to this world: but be ye transformed by the renewing of your mind, that ye may prove what is that good, and acceptable, and perfect, will of God."

Be pure.
1 Thessalonians 4:3-4
"For this is the will of God, even your sanctification, that ye should abstain from fornication: That every one of you should know how to possess his vessel in sanctification and honour;"

Be thankful.
1 Thessalonians 5:18
"In every thing give thanks: for this is the will of God in Christ Jesus concerning you."

The only way we can discern and understand the will of the Lord is to seek Him through His Word. These areas are a good starting place for finding the will of God for our lives. Seek Him today, and allow Him to guide you.

Bible Reading
Leviticus 11-12 | Luke 3

02.22 | February 22

His Way Is The Way.

Psalm 5:8
"Lead me, O LORD, in thy righteousness because of mine enemies; make thy way straight before my face."

Those last seven words are part of a prayer David prayed in Psalm 5, that can also be our prayer when seeking the will of the Lord in whatever situation lies before us.

He wanted clear direction.
"Lead me, O LORD"

Psalm 143:9-10
"Deliver me, O LORD, from mine enemies: I flee unto thee to hide me. Teach me to do thy will; for thou art my God: thy spirit is good; lead me into the land of uprightness."

Even in the face of his enemies, he desired for the Lord to lead him according to His will. **No matter who opposes us, if we seek the Lord's direction we cannot go wrong.**

Psalm 119:10
"With my whole heart have I sought thee: O let me not wander from thy commandments."

He wanted obvious decisions.
"…make thy way straight before my face."
He wanted nothing more and nothing less than the Lord's will for his life.

Psalm 27:11
"Teach me thy way, O LORD, and lead me in a plain path, because of mine enemies."

When we truly desire for the Lord to lead us, He will make our path plain through His Word.

Psalm 119:105
"Thy word is a lamp unto my feet, and a light unto my path."

His Word will guide our next step like a lantern, and then in His timing will light the Way ahead.

Trust Him today, for His way is the Way.

Bible Reading
Leviticus 13-14 | Luke 4

February 23 | 02.23

I Will.

Psalm 9:1-2
*"I will praise thee, O LORD, with my whole heart;
I will shew forth all thy marvellous works. I will be glad and rejoice in thee:
I will sing praise to thy name, O thou most High."*

Four *"I will"* statements are found in the first two verses of Psalm 9. What purpose they can bring to our walk with the Lord, if only we will determine within our hearts to apply them to our lives. They are what some could call simple principles, yet they are so profound and powerful.

Will you determine today to live a life of *"I will…"*?
Psalm 119:16
"I will delight myself in thy statutes: I will not forget thy word."

"I will praise thee, O LORD…"
David sought to praise His Lord with everything in him.
Psalm 9:1 - *"with my whole heart"*

Are we that dedicated to praising Him?
Many times we are guilty of only partial praise.

"I will shew forth all thy marvellous works."
How can we not but speak of the works of the Lord?
David said they are marvellous.

How can we not agree with David? The Lord has done so many truly marvellous things in our lives; yet so often, we neglect to thank Him privately…much less publicly.

"I will be glad and rejoice in thee"
Even on those days when things do not go the way we had hoped, we can choose to be glad and rejoice simply because we know Him.

"I will sing praise to thy name, O thou most High."
When we praise the Lord with our whole heart, we cannot help but sing praise to His Name. The Name above all names. That Name is Jesus. He is the Reason we have a song to sing.

Determine today to say, *"I will"*.

Bible Reading
Leviticus 15-16 | Luke 5

02.24 | February 24

Now Unto Him.

Ephesians 3:20
*"Now unto him that is able to do exceeding abundantly above
all that we ask or think, according to the power that worketh in us,"*

Every now and then we need reminded that God truly is Able.
Not only is He Able, but He is Willing and Able to do exceeding abundantly above all that we could ever ask or even think.
What a Powerful God we serve!
When the Lord gives us Ephesians 3:20 moments, we must always point back to Him for He is the only One worthy of praise and honour.
Pray for Ephesians 3:20 moments.

He is the Source of our prayer.
"Now unto him"
This shows us the Person of God.
"that is able"
This shows us His power.
"to do"
This shows us the performance He is willing and Able to do
for and through us.

He is the Substance of our prayer.
"exceeding"
He is willing to go beyond any distance for His children.
"abundantly"
His power is shown in the depth of His love.
"above"
Whatever we can comprehend He is Able to do,
and still He goes beyond that direction.

He is the Solution of our prayer.
"all that we ask or think"
We must pursue His power through prayer
in order to see it within our situation.
"according to the power"
We must then yield to His power so that we can witness the impossible.
"that worketh in us"
He desires to work in us and through us when we yield our will to His.
Ephesians 3:20 moments occur in our lives for one purpose...His glory.

Bible Reading
Leviticus 17-18 | Luke 6

February 25 | 02.25

By Strength Of Hand.

Exodus 13:3
"And Moses said unto the people, Remember this day, in which ye came out from Egypt, out of the house of bondage; for by strength of hand the LORD brought you out from this place: there shall no leavened bread be eaten."

Pharoah repeatedly would not let Moses and the children of Israel go out from bondage.

Exodus 6:1
"Then the LORD said unto Moses, Now shalt thou see what I will do to Pharaoh: for with a strong hand shall he let them go, and with a strong hand shall he drive them out of his land."

Has there ever been a time in your life where you felt you were in bondage? Maybe there were not physical shackles on your hands and feet, but you felt as though you could not move. You tried to follow the Lord's leading into a different phase or place in your life, but you were held captive by something or someone.

The strength of the hand of the Lord is Able to deliver you today.

Three times within the Scriptures we find the phrase *"by strength of hand"*. Each time is found in Exodus 13, and each time refers to the strength of the hand of the LORD.

A generic place - Exodus 13:3
"…for by strength of hand the LORD brought you out from this place…"

Whatever your situation, no matter how broad, God is Able to deliver you.

A place of bondage - Exodus 13:14
"And it shall be when thy son asketh thee in time to come, saying, What is this? that thou shalt say unto him, By strength of hand the LORD brought us out from Egypt, from the house of bondage:"

Wherever you are, no matter the place, God is Able to deliver you.

A specific place - Exodus 13:16
"And it shall be for a token upon thine hand, and for frontlets between thine eyes: for by strength of hand the LORD brought us forth out of Egypt."

Whatever or whoever specifically has you in bondage today, God is Able to deliver you by the strength of His hand. **Remember to thank Him for His deliverance, even before it arrives.**

Bible Reading
Leviticus 19-20 | Luke 7

02.26 | February 26

His Foresight.

Exodus 14:1-2
"And the LORD spake unto Moses, saying, Speak unto the children of Israel, that they turn and encamp before Pihahiroth, between Migdol and the sea, over against Baalzephon: before it shall ye encamp by the sea."

The children of Israel had finally been released from bondage in Egypt. God had led them through the way of the wilderness of the Red Sea.
Exodus 13:18

They had faithfully followed the pillar of cloud by day and pillar of fire by night.
Exodus 13:21-22

The Lord then gave Moses further specific instructions for them to follow.
"…turn and encamp…"
He directed them to turn away from the land they had set out to obtain.
This did not make logical sense, so doubt and fear took over.
Exodus 14:12

The Lord knew what He was doing, but He did not reveal His plan to them. They were instructed to pitch their tents by the sea… the Red Sea. God placed them by the very place where He would soon deliver them; yet, they were unaware of His divine providence and protection that was about to take place. Imagine if they had given up and refused to follow His direction that day?

Sometimes, the Lord will direct us down a path that does not make any sense to us at the time. He wants us to trust Him by faith and simply follow Him. It is often right before deliverance comes that our flesh wants to throw in the towel the most. The devil wants us to quit when we are so close to victory. The Lord knew that sea beside them would soon be divided into walls of water so that they could walk across on dry ground. They did not know any of what was about to take place, but He did. He sees what we don't. **The Lord has foresight for what lies ahead.**
Exodus 14:13
"…Fear ye not, stand still, and see the salvation of the LORD, which he will shew to you to day…"

Do not quit today, Christian.
Deliverance is on the way.

Bible Reading
Leviticus 21-22 | Luke 8

February 27 | 02.27

Exodus 14:15
"And the LORD said unto Moses, Wherefore criest thou unto me? speak unto the children of Israel, that they go forward:"

Forward implies movement.
Yes, there are times when we should stand still and let God move; but sometimes, we stay still longer than God intended. Sometimes we are too comfortable, so we sit still and claim to be waiting on or for Him. Sometimes we know in our hearts that He already told us to take a step of faith and trust Him, but we are too fearful to leave our comfort zone.

We cannot go forward unless we are willing to listen, go, and follow the Lord's instructions.
Hebrews 11:8
"By faith Abraham, when he was called to go out into a place which he should after receive for an inheritance, obeyed; and he went out, not knowing whither he went."

Obedience is crucial to moving forward.
Disobedience causes us to go backward.

We cannot go forward by doubt or fear.
Ezra 10:4
"Arise; for this matter belongeth unto thee: we also will be with thee: be of good courage, and do it."

Listen to the testimony of Paul in regards to moving forward:
2 Corinthians 8:10-12
"And herein I give my advice: for this is expedient for you, who have begun before, not only to do, but also to be forward a year ago. Now therefore perform the doing of it; that as there was a readiness to will, so there may be a performance also out of that which ye have. For if there be first a willing mind, it is accepted according to that a man hath, and not according to that he hath not."

Don't wait and end up regretting that you didn't start earlier.
Be willing to start today.
Move forward by faith.

Bible Reading
Leviticus 23-24 | Luke 9

02.28 | February 28

The Word Divides Our Problems.

Exodus 14:16
"But lift thou up thy rod, and stretch out thine hand over the sea, and divide it: and the children of Israel shall go on dry ground through the midst of the sea."

Moving forward by faith is not the end of journey, it is the beginning.
Moses and the children of Israel were at a dead end. Their enemies were pursuing them from behind, and the Red Sea was before them.

It seemed as if they had nowhere to turn… but God.
Ever been there?

The Lord had instructed Moses through His Word of what he was supposed to do. Just as He does for us through the Word of God each and every time we open our Bibles.

Exodus 14:21
"And Moses stretched out his hand over the sea; and the LORD caused the sea to go back by a strong east wind all that night, and made the sea dry land, and the waters were divided."

The Lord made a way when there seemed there was no way, because He is the Way.

The solution to their problem was found
in their obedience to His Word.

2 Timothy 2:15
"Study to shew thyself approved unto God, a workman that needeth not to be ashamed, rightly dividing the word of truth."

**It is only when we rightly divide the Word
that the Word can divide our problems.**

If we choose to take the Scripture for what we want It to mean, we only allow for misunderstanding and confusion. God is not the Author of either of those.

**Our Answer is waiting within the pages of the Word,
because He is the Answer.**

Ask Him to guide you in the Truth today,
and watch Him begin to divide that problem that is before you.

Bible Reading
Leviticus 25-26 | Luke 10

February 29 | 02.29

The Midst Of The Sea.

Exodus 14:22
"And the children of Israel went into the midst of the sea upon the dry ground: and the waters were a wall unto them on their right hand, and on their left."

In the midst of our sea, we can walk on dry ground to deliverance when we trust that He is our only Hope and allow Him to direct us through.

Imagine the walls of water that were on either side of the children of Israel that day. Perhaps they could see ocean life through those walls like we would experience at an aquarium; yet, there were no windows installed to hold the water back, God Almighty did that for them. Perhaps they could touch the walls of water, yet it did not cause any to splash on the ground. Their feet were dry as they walked. Isn't that just like the Lord, that in the midst of our sea He calms us to where we do not even feel the effects of the water around us. We would drown if He did not hold the waters back.

Oftentimes, we focus on the miracle which resulted in the deliverance of the children of Israel, and we should; but sometimes we neglect the Truth of the Egyptians coming into the midst of the sea as well.

Exodus 14:23
"And the Egyptians pursued, and went in after them to the midst of the sea, even all Pharaoh's horses, his chariots, and his horsemen."

Their enemies pursued them even in the midst of the sea. People can be so ruthless that they even persecute us in the midst of our sea.

Exodus 14:27
"And Moses stretched forth his hand over the sea, and the sea returned to his strength when the morning appeared; and the Egyptians fled against it; and the LORD overthrew the Egyptians in the midst of the sea."

The Lord will defeat our enemies in the midst of our sea, and may even use the sea itself to do so after we have walked across on dry ground.

Exodus 14:31
"And Israel saw that great work which the LORD did upon the Egyptians: and the people feared the LORD, and believed the LORD, and his servant Moses."

**May the seas of life be used to cause us
to fear the Lord and believe on Him.**

Bible Reading
Leviticus 27 | Luke 11

03.01 | March 1

Resort & Rest.

Exodus 15:27
"And they came to Elim, where were twelve wells of water, and threescore and ten palm trees: and they encamped there by the waters."

After a storm, there is often a peaceful calm that encompasses the sea that once was raging. The disciples witnessed this first hand after Jesus spoke peace to the wind and the waves that rocked their boat. The children of Israel did not have a raging sea after they walked across on dry ground safely to the other side of their problem. Imagine though, when the walls of water came down and *"the sea returned to his strength"*, how the waves must have rippled the sea that was once divided. When the waves subsided, the sea was once again peaceful.

What a reminder of how God speaks peace to our hearts after a storm or when we reach the other side of our Red Sea.

Moses and the children of Israel began to sing songs of praise unto the Lord for the victory that He had triumphantly and gloriously provided. After traveling though the wilderness of Shur, and then Marah, where there was no water for them to drink. The Lord miraculously provided for them once again. He is Faithful. They then came to Elim, the land of wells of water and 70 palm trees. A peaceful resort for them to rest in all the Lord had done for them. When we go on vacation, we often choose to surround ourselves with palm trees. Imagine the children of Israel looking up at those 70 palm trees. What a comfort they must have felt after He had provided and came through for them once again.

Resort in Him - Psalm 92:12
"The righteous shall flourish like the palm tree: he shall grow like a cedar in Lebanon."

Rest in Him - Psalm 1:3
"And he shall be like a tree planted by the rivers of water, that bringeth forth his fruit in his season; his leaf also shall not wither; and whatsoever he doeth shall prosper."

After the Lord gives the victory, remember to praise Him and then take time to resort and rest in Him.

Psalm 71:3
"Be thou my strong habitation, whereunto I may continually resort: thou hast given commandment to save me; for thou art my rock and my fortress."

Bible Reading
Numbers 1-2 | Luke 12

March 2 | 03.02

Prove It.

1 Thessalonians 5:21
"Prove all things; hold fast that which is good."

How can we *"hold fast to that which is good"* if we do not have a way to distinguish whether something is good or not?

The answer is in the first three words of the verse.
"Prove all things"
We must prove everything by examining
whether something is genuine or true.

Acts 17:11
"These were more noble than those in Thessalonica, in that they received the word with all readiness of mind, and searched the scriptures daily, whether those things were so."

Everything in our lives must be proved by the Word of God.
If the Word says it is right, it is right.
If the Word says it is wrong, it is wrong.

Regardless if the world today says otherwise, the Word holds the Truth and must be our Final Authority for all things.

2 Timothy 3:16-17
"All scripture is given by inspiration of God, and is profitable for doctrine, for reproof, for correction, for instruction in righteousness: That the man of God may be perfect, throughly furnished unto all good works."

**We can only prove all things
as we renew our mind through the Word of God.**

Romans 12:2
"And be not conformed to this world: but be ye transformed by the renewing of your mind, that ye may prove what is that good, and acceptable, and perfect, will of God."

Search the Scriptures today, and hold fast to that which is good.
Prove all things by the Word.

Bible Reading
Numbers 3-4 | Luke 13

March 3

Acts 27:3
"And the next day we touched at Sidon. And Julius courteously entreated Paul, and gave him liberty to go unto his friends to refresh himself."

Paul was a prisoner at this point, and was given the opportunity to go to his friends to refresh himself. This tells us Paul had the type of friends who were refreshing.

When people mean a lot to us, we miss them when we are away from them. What can we do while we wait until we see them again? Pray for them! When we pray for others, it not only allows us to see the Lord moving in their life in answer to our prayers, but it can also refresh us.

There are few things more refreshing than an ice cold drink of water after working on a hot summer day. When we are tired and thirsty, just a drink of cold water seems to revitalize us to finish our task.

When we are tired and weary, we need refreshment.

Proverbs 25:25
"As cold waters to a thirsty soul, so is good news from a far country."

Sometimes, we need spiritual and emotional refreshment just as much as a physical drink of cold water.

Psalm 63:1-3
"O God, thou art my God; early will I seek thee: my soul thirsteth for thee, my flesh longeth for thee in a dry and thirsty land, where no water is; To see thy power and thy glory, so as I have seen thee in the sanctuary. Because thy lovingkindness is better than life, my lips shall praise thee."

When we are spiritually drained, there is only one Source of strength to which we can come to be refreshed. The Word of God is where we can renew our minds and find the help that we need.

Romans 12:2
"And be not conformed to this world: but be ye transformed by the renewing of your mind, that ye may prove what is that good, and acceptable, and perfect, will of God."

Whatever refreshment you are in need of today, there is thirst quenching Water available through the Word of God.

Bible Reading
Numbers 5-6 | Luke 14

March 4 | 03.04

The Source Of Refreshment

Proverbs 25:13
"As the cold of snow in the time of harvest, so is a faithful messenger to them that send him: for he refresheth the soul of his masters."

Solomon likens a faithful messenger to that which refreshes the soul.
Proverbs 25:25
"As cold waters to a thirsty soul, so is good news from a far country."

Good News = The Gospel
God has given us the Gospel, and as His children we are sent as His messengers to tell the world the Good News. When we faithfully proclaim the Gospel of Jesus Christ, not only do we ourselves find refreshment, but imagine how refreshing our obedience to His commission is to the Lord!

Matthew 28:19-20
"Go ye therefore, and teach all nations, baptizing them in the name of the Father, and of the Son, and of the Holy Ghost: Teaching them to observe all things whatsoever I have commanded you: and, lo, I am with you alway, even unto the end of the world. Amen."

Sharing the Gospel is refreshing.
Not only to those who need to hear the Truth of the Gospel, but it will refresh our hearts when we remember what He did for us. He is the Water of Life, and all those that come to Him will never be turned away thirsty.

Revelation 21:6
"And he said unto me, It is done. I am Alpha and Omega, the beginning and the end. I will give unto him that is athirst of the fountain of the water of life freely."

**He is the Source of Refreshment we need,
and that we need to share with others.**
Psalm 42:1-2
"As the hart panteth after the water brooks, so panteth my soul after thee, O God. My soul thirsteth for God, for the living God: when shall I come and appear before God?"

How thirsty are we for Him today?
The longer we go without a drink, the more we need refreshment. When our body is dehydrated, there is a craving for water that is instilled in us by our Creator. He gave us the ability to be thirsty. When our time with Him declines, our soul begins to thirst for Him.

Bible Reading
Numbers 7-8 | Luke 15

03.05 | March 5

Before Goliath.

1 Samuel 17:4
"And there went out a champion out of the camp of the Philistines, named Goliath, of Gath, whose height was six cubits and a span."

This man was not like any other man. He was a giant, standing about 9 feet tall. He seemed to be stronger than any other man, and was definitely eager to fight.

1 Samuel 17:8-9
"And he stood and cried unto the armies of Israel, and said unto them, Why are ye come out to set your battle in array? am not I a Philistine, and ye servants to Saul? choose you a man for you, and let him come down to me. If he be able to fight with me, and to kill me, then will we be your servants: but if I prevail against him, and kill him, then shall ye be our servants, and serve us."

King Saul and all Israel that heard those words were sore afraid and fled from Goliath. They were so fearful of his size and strength, no one wanted to face off against him. But when David heard Goliath's words, he had a different perspective.

1 Samuel 17:26
"And David spake to the men that stood by him, saying...for who is this uncircumcised Philistine, that he should defy the armies of the living God?"

1 Samuel 17:32
"And David said to Saul, Let no man's heart fail because of him; thy servant will go and fight with this Philistine."

David was told by King Saul that he was not able to go up against Goliath because he was too young. There were many reasons why David could not fight under his own power, but David did not plan on going into the battle alone.

Before there was ever a Goliath, there was a stone prepared.
Whatever battle lies before you today, remember that God has made a way to bring the victory. Disregard the critics and their many reasons that you are not able. **Just like David, you are not in this battle alone.** Choose to approach each day and each situation in faith that the Lord will deliver you. He has prepared a Stone to defeat the enemy that stands before you.

Bible Reading
Numbers 9-10 | Luke 16

March 6 | 03.06

Finding Grace In The Brook.

1 Samuel 17:40
"And he took his staff in his hand, and chose him five smooth stones out of the brook, and put them in a shepherd's bag which he had, even in a scrip; and his sling was in his hand: and he drew near to the Philistine."

On his way to the battlefield, David found five smooth stones in the brook. It was in that valley that he found the tools he needed for the battle that was ahead. With his staff in hand, he set out in faith that the Lord would fight Goliath for him. We know the rest of the story. David chose a stone, slang it toward Goliath, and smote the Philistine in his forehead killing him instantly. But why did David choose five smooth stones, when clearly he only needed one?

*"And he took his staff in his hand,
and chose him five smooth stones out of the brook"*

Throughout the Scriptures, the number five routinely points us to the grace of God. The account of the battle of David and Goliath is no different. In the middle of the Valley of Elah there was a brook, and it was there, with his staff in his hand that the Lord had David choose five smooth stones to take to the fight.

We can find grace in the brooks of our lives.

When we think we cannot go on...When the battle is too hard to fight on our own...When we are weary from the journey, there is grace.

His grace brings salvation.
Titus 2:11-12
"For the grace of God that bringeth salvation hath appeared to all men, Teaching us that, denying ungodliness and worldly lusts, we should live soberly, righteously, and godly, in this present world;"

His grace enables us.
1 Corinthians 15:10
"But by the grace of God I am what I am: and his grace which was bestowed upon me was not in vain; but I laboured more abundantly than they all: yet not I, but the grace of God which was with me."

His grace is sufficient for every battle we face.
2 Corinthians 12:9
"And he said unto me, My grace is sufficient for thee: for my strength is made perfect in weakness. Most gladly therefore will I rather glory in my infirmities, that the power of Christ may rest upon me."

Bible Reading
Numbers 11-12 | Luke 17

03.07 | March 7

Pearls Of Promise.

1 Peter 4:12-13
"Beloved, think it not strange concerning the fiery trial which is to try you, as though some strange thing happened unto you: But rejoice, inasmuch as ye are partakers of Christ's sufferings; that, when his glory shall be revealed, ye may be glad also with exceeding joy."

A natural pearl is formed when an irritant, sometimes a grain of sand or parasite, works its way inside a living creature that dwells in a shell…like an oyster, mussel, or clam. As a defense mechanism, the irritant is coated by a protective fluid inside the shell. Layer after layer of this coating is placed upon it, until a lustrous pearl is formed. This process can take six months to several years to take place.

The struggles we face in our day to day lives are like that irritant that comes within the shell of the living creature. **Without the pain and irritation, there would be no pearl.** Have you ever looked back at how the Lord used what started out as a painful experience, and now He has turned it into something beautiful?

We all have pearls in our lives that He has created.
God has a purpose and a plan when He allows trials and tribulations to come into our lives. Think of this time last year… how has your life changed?

A year ago, we had no idea what trials lied ahead of us. Some of us have lost loved ones. Some of us had to move to a new location. Some of us have been betrayed by people we love. Some of us have been left empty handed. Some of us have had to re-evaluate our priorities. Some of us have had to start over. Some can look back on the trials now; but some of us are still right in the middle of them, waiting for God to intervene.

The trials and irritants we face can force us to cling to the Pearls of Promise we find within the pages of the Word of God. Those familiar verses that we are so quick to quote to someone when they need them, yet so often we neglect them when we ourselves need them the most.

Look up these verses in your Bible:
Romans 8:18, Philippians 4:19, 2 Corinthians 4:17
Romans 8:28, Psalm 28:7

Thank Him today for the Pearls of Promise in His Word.

Bible Reading
Numbers 13-14 | Luke 18

March 8 | 03.08

Without The Promises.

2 Peter 3:9
"The Lord is not slack concerning his promise, as some men count slackness; but is longsuffering to us-ward, not willing that any should perish, but that all should come to repentance."

There are many many more Pearls of Promise within the Word of God, but those verses from yesterday are just a few that we can cling to in times of trouble. But imagine…What if you did not have those promises to cling to? What if the Truth of those Words did not apply to you? There would be nothing but gloom and despair. You would have no hope.

Sadly, that is the reality of every person that does not know Him.
Let that sink in…Your family member. Your coworker. Your friend. Your cashier. Your waitress. Your nurse. Your bank teller. Your neighbor. That person you hold the door open for. That person sitting beside you. Every person we pass by…If they do not know the Lord Jesus Christ, that is their condition at this moment.

For those of us who know Him…He is our Hope. He is our Anchor. He is our Peace. He is our Strength. He is everything we need.

But Who is He to them?
He is waiting to be their Saviour. He is not willing that any of them perish, but it is up to us to tell them about Him. We have been given the responsibility of sharing the Gospel with everyone around us.

They cannot believe in Him if they have not heard about Him.
Romans 10:14
"How then shall they call on him in whom they have not believed? and how shall they believe in him of whom they have not heard? and how shall they hear without a preacher?"

May this give us the desire to want to tell others about Him.
Ask the Lord to help you be a witness for Him today.
He can give you the strength and courage to be bold in your faith.

Walk across the street to invite a neighbor to church. Pass out a Gospel tract. Write a note to that person on your heart. Call that friend. Text that family member and tell them that not only you love them, but God loves them too. **Whatever the Lord lays on your heart, decide today to have the faith to obey His leading.** Allow Him to use you for His glory today to reach someone who is without the Promises that come from knowing Him.

Bible Reading
Numbers 15-16 | Luke 19

03.09 | March 9

A Limited Time.

Colossians 4:5
"Walk in wisdom toward them that are without, redeeming the time."

Black Friday is known for the deals that can only be found the day after Thanksgiving each year. These "unbelievable savings" disappear when the store closes or the calendar changes to Saturday. The deals expire simply because they are only available for a limited time.

Picture an hourglass. When it's turned over, the sand begins to trickle down into the other chamber, and the clock starts. At some point, the sand runs out, and the time is over.

We know the days we are living in are evil, but God's Word tells us to redeem the time we have left.
Ephesians 5:16
"Redeeming the time, because the days are evil."

Our hourglass of time is drawing to an end. Only the Lord knows when our time will be up, but the truth is that one day there will not be any more opportunities.

There are only two things that really matter before our time runs out. Those of us that are saved, because we have placed our faith in what Jesus Christ has done for us, we are to *"Walk in wisdom toward them that are without…"*

The time we have to reach others is running out.
At some point, there will not be any more opportunities to reach someone with the Gospel. Those tracts are not reaching anyone while they sit in the tract rack or are hidden in our purses.

Someone's eternity may depend on our obedience to share the Gospel with them.

The time to get saved is running out.
Maybe you've had religion for years, but deep down you know something isn't right. Perhaps you can quote the Romans Road, but you've never truly applied it to yourself. We can know all the right answers, but if we have never personally placed our faith in what Jesus Christ did for us on the cross, then we only have religion and not a relationship with Him. If you feel uneasy during every invitation, maybe it's time to consider if you truly know Him. Soon there will be no more opportunities to confess and believe on what Jesus has done. The sands of time are running fast.

Bible Reading
Numbers 17-18 | Luke 20

The Choice Of Whosoever.

Revelation 20:15
"And whosoever was not found written in the book of life was cast into the lake of fire."

There is a Judgment Day coming for everyone.
The Word of God warns us all about this Truth.

Hebrews 9:27
"And as it is appointed unto men once to die, but after this the judgment:"

We are appointed to die, and to be judged by God. **Where we will be judged is dependent upon our choice of where we will spend eternity.** The saved will appear before Him at the Judgment Seat of Christ, whereas the lost will be at the Great White Throne of Judgment.

2 Corinthians 5:10
"For we must all appear before the judgment seat of Christ; that every one may receive the things done in his body, according to that he hath done, whether it be good or bad."

Revelation 20:11
"And I saw a great white throne, and him that sat on it, from whose face the earth and the heaven fled away; and there was found no place for them."

The ungodly may scorn and scoff at their forthcoming judgment, but that will not excuse them from their impending appointment. We all have an appointment to keep.

Everyone is a Whosoever, but which Whosoever will you be?

John 3:16
"For God so loved the world, that he gave his only begotten Son, that whosoever believeth in him should not perish, but have everlasting life."

Revelation 20:15
"And whosoever was not found written in the book of life was cast into the lake of fire."

Make your choice now, before you do not have a choice.

If you have already made this decision, consider those around you who have not trusted Christ. Will you tell them before its too late?

Make the choice today to share the love of Christ and His glorious Gospel with Whosoever you can.

Bible Reading
Numbers 19-20 | Luke 21

03.11 | March 11

Psalm 88:9
"Mine eye mourneth by reason of affliction: LORD, I have called daily upon thee, I have stretched out my hands unto thee."

Affliction can cause us to be just as the Psalmist was with our hands stretched out to the Lord begging Him to intervene on our behalf. Sometimes we have no other choice, but to cry and call out to Him for help.

Psalm 143:6
"I stretch forth my hands unto thee: my soul thirsteth after thee, as a thirsty land. Selah."

But if affliction is what it takes to cause us to cry and call out to Him is it not worth the pain? Is it not worth the turmoil if it causes us to know Him more?

Exodus 1:12
"But the more they afflicted them, the more they multiplied and grew..."

If we remember the purpose of affliction, perhaps we would be more thankful for it.

Psalm 119:71
"It is good for me that I have been afflicted; that I might learn thy statutes."

Anything that causes us to know and apply the Word of God more, is something for which we should be thankful. The attitude of the Psalmist in this verse is what we should all desire for our own lives.

When we are afflicted, we have a choice to make.

Affliction can make us run to the Word of God for comfort and understanding, or it can cause us to run from the Scriptures. If we seek direction from anywhere else, we will only be left empty handed and disappointed. But if we choose to allow affliction to drive us to the Truth of the Scriptures, we will find the true purpose for the trial we are facing.

Psalm 94:19
"In the multitude of my thoughts within me thy comforts delight my soul."

Allow the Word of God to be your comfort in affliction today, and every day.

Bible Reading
Numbers 21-22 | Luke 22

God Sees, Hears & Knows.

Exodus 3:7
"And the LORD said, I have surely seen the affliction of my people which are in Egypt, and have heard their cry by reason of their taskmasters; for I know their sorrows;"

Affliction may seem to begin with someone else's decision or treatment of us, but God always has a purpose. Just as He did for Joseph, He has a plan for the pain.

Genesis 50:20
"But as for you, ye thought evil against me; but God meant it unto good, to bring to pass, as it is this day, to save much people alive."

The affliction that the children of Israel faced in Egypt was also not in vain. God had a plan all along. He was watching, listening, and waiting. As Moses stood before the burning bush, God told him there upon that holy ground that He not only had a plan for them, but He also has a plan for us today.

God Sees.
"And the LORD said, I have surely seen the affliction of my people"

God Hears.
"and have heard their cry"

God Knows.
"for I know their sorrows"

Whatever you are facing today, God sees, hears and knows. Affliction will not last forever, though when we are in the midst of it, it certainly feels like it will. Take comfort in the fact that God has a plan in and through our affliction.

Exodus 3:8
"And I am come down to deliver them..."

God will deliver us in His timing.
Trust Him today, even in the midst of affliction.

Bible Reading
Numbers 23-24 | Luke 23

03.13 | March 13

A Spiritual Rut.

Psalm 51:3
"For I acknowledge my transgressions: and my sin is ever before me."

It's hard to admit being in a spiritual rut when you know you are in fact the reason for being there in the first place. Acknowledging that your sinful choice(s) placed you in there is the most difficult. Taking ownership of your iniquity is the starting line for heading in the right direction.

The moment we stop and realize that we have caused ourselves to be right where we are is when we begin to understand the need to turn around… to repent.

Revelation 2:5
"Remember therefore from whence thou art fallen, and repent, and do the first works; or else I will come unto thee quickly, and will remove thy candlestick out of his place, except thou repent."

Stopping is one thing, but progress is not made until our direction changes. Repentance begins with the desire to change the state of our heart. **A spiritual U-turn is where our new walk starts.** We have to make the choice to turn on the blinker of our spiritual vehicle and not just change lanes, but completely make a 180 back toward where we left our fellowship with God. He didn't move, because He never changes. When we find ourselves in the wilderness of sin, it is because we chose to leave the comfort and care of the Shepherd.

When we decide to repent and turn ourselves back toward Him, we find that our Heavenly Father is right there with open arms welcoming us Home. His mercy has new meaning when we realize what we truly deserve for our sin. **He is Faithful and Just to forgive us, all we have to do is confess to Him that we are wrong.**

1 John 1:9
"If we confess our sins, he is faithful and just to forgive us our sins, and to cleanse us from all unrighteousness."

The moment we take ownership and admit our guilt, His mercy takes over and is simultaneously followed by His grace. Not only do we not get what we truly deserve, but we also find that He bestows blessings upon us that we definitely do not deserve. His mercy and grace are overwhelming, and all of this is simply because we are His children. Why? The only answer that comes close is simply because He loves us. **Turn back to Him today.**

Bible Reading
Numbers 25-26 | Luke 24

March 14 | 03.14

The Domino Effect.

1 Timothy 4:12
"Let no man despise thy youth; but be thou an example of the believers, in word, in conversation, in charity, in spirit, in faith, in purity."

Dominos is one of those games that can be played in a variety of ways. Sure, there are official rules on how to play the game as the inventor intended, but the dominos can also be used to build a new version of Stonehenge, a house or a fort. There is at least one more thing they can be used for, and perhaps everyone's favorite thing to do with dominos is line them up side by side in a line so that when one is knocked down the rest fall in sequence.

There is an effect to the cause of the first domino falling down that affects each of the other dominos nearby. Our testimony and influence is not much different than those lined up dominos.

There are people around us that are and will be affected by our choices.
Too often we operate seemingly unaware of how
the consequences of our actions affect more than just ourselves.

What we endorse, they will endorse.
**What we do in moderation,
they will most likely do in practice.**
Whether positive or negative, the result is the same.

Think about it in your own life. Who influenced you the most? Are your actions and thoughts now comparable to them? How does the examples you have followed line up with the example Christ set for us?

1 Corinthians 11:1
"Be ye followers of me, even as I also am of Christ."

Philippians 3:17
*"Brethren, be followers together of me,
and mark them which walk so as ye have us for an ensample."*

We are all a domino effect of those we have followed, and by the same comparison we are creating a domino effect to those who are following us.

What domino effect are you leaving behind?

Bible Reading
Numbers 27-28 | Mark 1

03.15 | March 15

Sought Means.

Luke 5:18
"And, behold, men brought in a bed a man which was taken with a palsy: and they sought means to bring him in, and to lay him before him."

Jesus had entered into Capernaum, and word got out that the Word was in the house. So many people gathered together to hear Him that there was no more room for people to come inside. There were four men that were determined to get their sick friend to Jesus so that he could be healed.

Luke 5:19
"And when they could not find by what way they might bring him in because of the multitude, they went upon the housetop, and let him down through the tiling with his couch into the midst before Jesus."

They had tried everything, and when nothing worked, they *"sought means"* that had never been done before. They literally climbed up on top of the house and tore the roof off so they could let down their friend on his bed where Jesus was. They were willing to do whatever was necessary to get their friend to Jesus. Their faith resulted in his healing.

Mark 2:5
"When Jesus saw their faith, he said unto the sick of the palsy, Son, thy sins be forgiven thee."

What are we willing to do in order to bring our friends to Jesus?
Could it be said of us today
that we have *"sought means"* to reach those we love with the Gospel?

**Sometimes we have to think outside the box
of how we can share the Gospel with others.**

Send them a card.
Give them a call.
Write them a letter.
Take them for a cup of coffee.
Bring them supper.
Pass out those tracts.
Wear that shirt.

Get creative.
Be willing to do whatever it takes
to reach somebody with the Gospel.

Bible Reading
Numbers 29-30 | Mark 2

March 16 | 03.16

Come.

Revelation 22:17
*"And the Spirit and the bride say, Come.
And let him that heareth say, Come. And let him that is athirst come.
And whosoever will, let him take the water of life freely."*

Come is simply a one word invitation that implies movement to a particular place or person. We see it several times throughout the Scriptures.

Noah & The Ark - Genesis 7:1
"And the LORD said unto Noah, Come thou and all thy house into the ark; for thee have I seen righteous before me in this generation."

God told Noah and his house to come into the ark which was the means of their salvation and a picture of ours.

Jesus For Salvation - John 6:37
"All that the Father giveth me shall come to me; and him that cometh to me I will in no wise cast out."

Throughout the Scriptures, the Message is the same.
All must come by faith to Jesus for salvation, and only Him.

John 14:6
"Jesus saith unto him, I am the way, the truth, and the life: no man cometh unto the Father, but by me."

He is still waiting with open arms to receive whosoever will come to Him through faith in Him alone. In the last chapter of the Bible, we find that the Message is still *"whosoever will".*

We are commanded to go and share the Gospel with others.
**When we give them the Truth of the Gospel
we are simply inviting them to come to Jesus.**

Isaiah 1:18
"Come now, and let us reason together, saith the LORD: though your sins be as scarlet, they shall be as white as snow; though they be red like crimson, they shall be as wool."

**When we come to Jesus,
it ought to make us want to invite others to come to Him too.**

Bible Reading
Numbers 31-32 | Mark 3

03.17 | March 17

Get Your Hands Up.

Exodus 17:11
"And it came to pass, when Moses held up his hand, that Israel prevailed: and when he let down his hand, Amalek prevailed."

Amalek had come to fight with Israel. Moses instructed Joshua to choose men and go out to fight with Amalek, and he would stand on top of the hill with the Rod of God in his hand. Joshua did just as he was told, and Moses, Aaron and Hur went up on top of the hill. When Moses held up his hand, Israel was winning, when he put down his hand, Amalek was winning.

Throughout the Scriptures, Amalek is a picture of the flesh, and the Rod of God is a picture of the Word of God. With this in mind, imagine the scene of this account.

When we put down the Word of God, and try to fix things on our own, the flesh will prevail.

Romans 8:6-8
"For to be carnally minded is death; but to be spiritually minded is life and peace. Because the carnal mind is enmity against God: for it is not subject to the law of God, neither indeed can be. So then they that are in the flesh cannot please God."

When when have our hands up, holding onto the Word of God, the Lord will give the victory.

How many times have we brought our situation to the Lord, lifting our hands off of it while claiming a promise from the Word of God and suddenly felt peace that it was out of our hands and into His?

Isaiah 26:3
"Thou wilt keep him in perfect peace, whose mind is stayed on thee: because he trusteth in thee."

Romans 5:1
"Therefore being justified by faith, we have peace with God through our Lord Jesus Christ:"

Get your hands up today while holding onto the Word of God!

Bible Reading
Numbers 33-34 | Mark 4

March 18 | 03.18

Trust & Trace.

Esther 2:17
"And the king loved Esther above all the women, and she obtained grace and favour in his sight more than all the virgins; so that he set the royal crown upon her head, and made her queen instead of Vashti."

The Book of Esther may not contain the Name of God, but we can see His sovereign hand throughout every page. What a picture of how the Lord is always working behind the scenes for our good and His glory!

Esther 4:14
"...who knoweth whether thou art come to the kingdom for such a time as this?"

Mordecai encouraged Esther to seize the opportunity that she had been given to be an instrument of the providencial hand of God. She chose to be bold and full of courage for the task that was before her.

As we walk by faith, we are trusting the Lord to order our steps and direct our paths as we more forward.

Trust Him.
Proverbs 3:5-6
*"Trust in the LORD with all thine heart;
and lean not unto thine own understanding.
In all thy ways acknowledge him, and he shall direct thy paths."*

We can also look back at the times in our lives that seemed uncertain and trace His hand because we chose to trust Him by faith each step of the way.

Trace Him.
Psalm 37:23
*"The steps of a good man are ordered by the LORD:
and he delighteth in his way."*

Think about the *"for such a time as this"* moments in your life. You may not have fully understood what He had in store, yet you chose to trust Him and follow His direction. Now you can look back and trace His hand through each and every situation.

Choose to trust Him and trace Him through your life today.

Bible Reading
Numbers 35-36 | Mark 5

03.19 | March 19

Choosing To Suffer.

Hebrews 11:25-26
*"Choosing rather to suffer affliction with the people of God,
than to enjoy the pleasures of sin for a season;
Esteeming the reproach of Christ greater riches than the treasures in
Egypt: for he had respect unto the recompence of the reward."*

Every day we make choices.
Few things in life are not the consequence of some choice
that either we have made, or someone has made for us.

Trusting the Lord is a choice.
Serving the Lord is a choice.
Yet, often times,
both of those involve also choosing to suffer affliction.

2 Timothy 3:12
"Yea, and all that will live godly in Christ Jesus shall suffer persecution."

Moses chose to suffer.
He knew that the rewards of suffering affliction for the Lord
far outweighed any pleasures that only last for a season.

Affliction is directly related to growth.
Imagine all that Moses would have missed
if he had chosen to stay in Egypt.

Hebrews 11:27
*"By faith he forsook Egypt, not fearing the wrath of the king:
for he endured, as seeing him who is invisible."*

If we desire to grow in grace,
we often can only do so by choosing to suffer affliction.

What choice does the Lord want you to make today?

Romans 8:18
*"For I reckon that the sufferings of this present time
are not worthy to be compared with the glory
which shall be revealed in us."*

Bible Reading
Deuteronomy 1-2 | Mark 6

March 20 | 03.20

Growing Pains.

Romans 8:18
"For I reckon that the sufferings of this present time are not worthy to be compared with the glory which shall be revealed in us."

As children, we all experienced physical growing pains as we grew in height and size. As parents, we feed our child milk so they can grow, while knowing that doing so will cause some pain for their own good. These same principles can be applied to our spiritual growth as children of God.

1 Peter 2:2
"As newborn babes, desire the sincere milk of the word, that ye may grow thereby:"

We grow as we spend more time in the Word of God.
However with growth, comes pain.

Matthew 16:24
"Then said Jesus unto his disciples, If any man will come after me, let him deny himself, and take up his cross, and follow me."

Suffering is part of following Him.
The very symbol of Christianity implies that suffering is part of being a Christian. The cross reminds us of the suffering of our Saviour, while also reminding us of the cross we must bear in order to follow Him. Yet, amongst the suffering, there are rewards.

Mark 8:35
"For whosoever will save his life shall lose it; but whosoever shall lose his life for my sake and the gospel's, the same shall save it."

There is joy in suffering for His glory.
Whatever pain we experience is all for a purpose.

James 1:2-4
"My brethren, count it all joy when ye fall into divers temptations; Knowing this, that the trying of your faith worketh patience. But let patience have her perfect work, that ye may be perfect and entire, wanting nothing."

He desires to do a work in and through us for His glory.
Choose to be thankful
for the growing pains today.

Bible Reading
Deuteronomy 3-4 | Mark 7

03.21 | March 21

Choices.

Mark 8:34-35
"And when he had called the people unto him with his disciples also, he said unto them, Whosoever will come after me, let him deny himself, and take up his cross, and follow me. For whosoever will save his life shall lose it; but whosoever shall lose his life for my sake and the gospel's, the same shall save it."

This statement was part of Jesus' response to the people after Peter had rebuked Him for explaining that the Son of Man must suffer many things as part of His Father's plan. While his intentions may have been good, Peter tried to hinder Christ from suffering the very purpose of why He came. Jesus then explained the requirements of being a true disciple.

"let him deny himself"
Choose His will instead.
In order to do so, we must choose to deny ourselves. We are either feeding the flesh or the Spirit. It is either our will or His.

"take up his cross"
Choose to suffer for His glory.
A cross symbolizes suffering and affliction, which in our lives often means trials. We can either let our trials define us or refine us for His glory.

"and follow me"
Choose to follow Him.
Following Him will lead to pain and suffering, yet we have His promise that doing so will save our lives. He left us an example to follow.

1 Peter 2:21
"For even hereunto were ye called: because Christ also suffered for us, leaving us an example, that ye should follow his steps:"

We are only His disciples when we choose these things in this order. Each requirement builds off the one before.

**Every denial of ourselves,
every cross we bear,
every step we take in following Him
is for the purpose of conforming us to His image.**

Bible Reading
Deuteronomy 5-6 | Mark 8

March 22 | 03.22

Matthew 27:46
*"And about the ninth hour Jesus cried with a loud voice, saying,
Eli, Eli, lama sabachthani? that is to say,
My God, my God, why hast thou forsaken me?"*

Jesus Christ asked this question while He was on the cross at Calvary. He questioned His Father simply asking why. It is not as if Jesus did not know the reason He was upon the cross that day. Jesus never asked a question that He did not already know the answer.

**Perhaps He asked this question
to show us it is okay for us to ask the same.**

There have been many to say that it is wrong to ask God why things happen in our lives. However, if Jesus Christ Himself asked *"why"*, how much more do we ask or think it?

Hebrews 4:15
*"For we have not an high priest which cannot be touched
with the feeling of our infirmities; but was in all points tempted
like as we are, yet without sin."*

Jesus never sinned, so it cannot be a sin to ask God why.
Many times we find ourselves in situations that we do not understand why things have happened the way they have. We need to remind ourselves that sometimes, we are not supposed to know.

Isaiah 55:8-9
"For my thoughts are not your thoughts, neither are your ways my ways, saith the LORD. For as the heavens are higher than the earth, so are my ways higher than your ways, and my thoughts than your thoughts."

We can rest in the fact that when we do not understand,
and are asking "why?"... He knows.

He has everything under control.
He will never leave us. He will never forsake us.

Hebrews 13:5
*"Let your conversation be without covetousness;
and be content with such things as ye have: for he hath said,
I will never leave thee, nor forsake thee."*

Bible Reading
Deuteronomy 7-8 | Mark 9

03.23 | March 23

Acts 4:12
"Neither is there salvation in any other: for there is none other name under heaven given among men, whereby we must be saved."

Most people desire to have a good name among those who know them. While it is important to maintain a good testimony, whatever reputation we have on our own has only temporary value. Proverbs 22:1

We can have a good name by choosing a Name much better than our own, the Name above every name, the Name Of Jesus.

His Name has purpose.
Matthew 1:21
"And she shall bring forth a son, and thou shalt call his name JESUS: for he shall save his people from their sins."

His Name brings life to all who believe on Him.
John 20:31
"But these are written, that ye might believe that Jesus is the Christ, the Son of God; and that believing ye might have life through his name."

His Name brings healing.
Acts 3:6
"Then Peter said, Silver and gold have I none; but such as I have give I thee: In the name of Jesus Christ of Nazareth rise up and walk."

His Name will cause every knee to bow before Him.
Philippians 2:9-11
"Wherefore God also hath highly exalted him, and given him a name which is above every name: That at the name of Jesus every knee should bow, of things in heaven, and things in earth, and things under the earth; And that every tongue should confess that Jesus Christ is Lord, to the glory of God the Father."

The Name of Jesus Christ makes a difference.
There is power in His Name. There is provision in His Name. There is protection in His Name. We are saved by His Name. We are secured by His Name. We are supplied by His Name.

When we believe on His Name, we choose Him.
By choosing Him, we obtain an inheritance that money cannot buy.

Bible Reading
Deuteronomy 9-10 | Mark 10

March 24 | 03.24

Our Whole Duty.

Ecclesiastes 12:13
"Let us hear the conclusion of the whole matter: Fear God, and keep his commandments: for this is the whole duty of man."

This is our purpose in life, or our *"whole duty"*.
It begins with the fear of God, which is where wisdom begins.

Proverbs 9:10
"The fear of the LORD is the beginning of wisdom: and the knowledge of the holy is understanding."

Proverbs 4:7
"Wisdom is the principal thing; therefore get wisdom: and with all thy getting get understanding."

The main thing for us to find is wisdom. The best thing for us, and superior to us, is wisdom. God gave us the opportunity to have wisdom when He gave us His Son, Jesus Christ. He is the Word and He is Wisdom.

He is the Beginning and the Ending.
He sees what we do not see. He knows how our situation will end before it even begins.

Revelation 1:8
"I am Alpha and Omega, the beginning and the ending, saith the Lord, which is, and which was, and which is to come, the Almighty."

He is the First and the Last.
We cannot find anyone or anything before Him or after Him that will satisfy our thirsty soul.

Revelation 22:13
"I am Alpha and Omega, the beginning and the end, the first and the last."

He is Preeminent.
In Him we live, move and have our being. Everything about us is dependent upon Him. We must allow Him to have His proper place within our lives.

Colossians 1:17-18
"And he is before all things, and by him all things consist. And he is the head of the body, the church: who is the beginning, the firstborn from the dead; that in all things he might have the preeminence."

Our whole duty in life is to fear Him and obey His Word.

Bible Reading
Deuteronomy 11-12 | Mark 11

03.25 | March 25

Built By Wisdom.

Proverbs 14:1
*"Every wise woman buildeth her house:
but the foolish plucketh it down with her hands."*

What we build upon is of great importance to the testimony of our lives. Jesus Christ taught this Truth at the end of His Sermon on the Mount. After all of the life changing things He told the people, He saved this parable for last. He begins with the reminder that Wisdom begins by hearing His Word.

Matthew 7:24-25
*"Therefore whosoever heareth these sayings of mine, and doeth them,
I will liken him unto a wise man, which built his house upon a rock:
And the rain descended, and the floods came, and the winds blew,
and beat upon that house; and it fell not: for it was founded upon a rock."*

**When we hear the Word of God and choose to build our lives
upon the Rock of Ages, we are secure in Him despite the storms.**

On the contrast, those who reject and neglect His Word will live in foolishness. Their lives are like a house built upon the sand, which cannot withstand the same storm that the wise survive.

The Wisdom of the Word makes the difference.

Matthew 7:26-27
*"And every one that heareth these sayings of mine, and doeth them not,
shall be likened unto a foolish man, which built his house upon the sand:
And the rain descended, and the floods came, and the winds blew, and
beat upon that house; and it fell: and great was the fall of it."*

We have the choice today
of what we will build our lives upon:
the wisdom of the world or the Wisdom of the Word.

**Live so that others will see
that your life is built by Wisdom.**

Bible Reading
Deuteronomy 13-14 | Mark 12

March 26 | 03.26

Bold As A Lion.

Proverbs 28:1
*"The wicked flee when no man pursueth:
but the righteous are bold as a lion."*

There are no coincidences within the Word of God. Every Word is there for a specific purpose. Every phrase and description is Divinely inspired for specific reasons. Lions are known as the King of the Jungle due to their immense strength and courage. Under the inspiration of the Holy Spirit, Solomon depicts boldness as the characteristic of a lion. This is the first mention of being bold; and refers to a sense of security for the righteous believer.

The Strength of the Lion

Through Christ we have the strength to accomplish anything that is set before us. We need only submit our weakness to Him.

Philippians 4:13
"I can do all things through Christ which strengtheneth me."

The Courage of the Lion

With Christ by our side, we can have not only courage, but good courage. There is no need to fear because He will never forsake us.

Deuteronomy 31:6
*"Be strong and of a good courage, fear not, nor be afraid of them:
for the LORD thy God, he it is that doth go with thee;
he will not fail thee, nor forsake thee."*

How can we be bold as a Lion?

We must spend time with Jesus.
Acts 4:13

The boldness of Peter and John shows us that any of God's children can boldly speak and stand for Him. The people around them could tell that they had spent time with Jesus. Could the same be said of us?

We must speak to Jesus so that we can boldly speak of Him.
Acts 4:31

Because they prayed, God showed up in a great way. He empowered them to speak the Truth boldly, and the place was shaken where they were.

Ask the Lord to make you bold as a Lion today.

Bible Reading
Deuteronomy 15-16 | Mark 13

03.27 | March 27

Tolerance.

Isaiah 5:20-21
"Woe unto them that call evil good, and good evil; that put darkness for light, and light for darkness; that put bitter for sweet, and sweet for bitter! Woe unto them that are wise in their own eyes, and prudent in their own sight!"

In the politically correct society we live in, we often strive not to offend those around us. Such a culture has created a tolerance for just about anything.

Proverbs 17:15
"He that justifieth the wicked, and he that condemneth the just, even they both are abomination to the LORD."

Tolerance is simply justifying sin and condemning that which is right. The Word of God clearly says that it is an abomination to the Lord to do so. He is disgusted when we justify what is wrong or make excuses for our sin.

Proverbs 6:16-19
"These six things doth the LORD hate: yea, seven are an abomination unto him: A proud look, a lying tongue, and hands that shed innocent blood, An heart that deviseth wicked imaginations, feet that be swift in running to mischief, A false witness that speaketh lies, and he that soweth discord among brethren."

Are we willing to offend God in order not to offend someone else?
What a high price to pay in order to be tolerant of those around us.

Proverbs 17:16
"Wherefore is there a price in the hand of a fool to get wisdom, seeing he hath no heart to it?"

Wisdom cannot be bought by money, but it does require sacrifice.
Jesus paid the price for us to have Wisdom
when He gave His life on Calvary.

God simply wants us to ask Him for Wisdom.
What a pity it is that we often fail to ask Him.

James 1:5
"If any of you lack wisdom, let him ask of God, that giveth to all men liberally, and upbraideth not; and it shall be given him."

Bible Reading
Deuteronomy 17-18 | Mark 14

March 28 | 03.28

An Appointment.

Hebrews 9:27
*"And as it is appointed unto men once to die,
but after this the judgment:"*

Judgment Day is coming…and not the Arnold Schwarzenegger kind.
The Word of God warns us about this Truth.
We are appointed to die, and to be judged by God.

**Where we will be judged is dependent upon our choice
of where we will spend eternity.**

God's children will appear before Him at the Judgment Seat of Christ, and the unsaved will be at the Great White Throne.

2 Corinthians 5:10
*"For we must all appear before the judgment seat of Christ;
that every one may receive the things done in his body,
according to that he hath done, whether it be good or bad."*

Revelation 20:11
"And I saw a great white throne, and him that sat on it, from whose face the earth and the heaven fled away; and there was found no place for them."

The ungodly may scorn and scoff at their forthcoming judgment, but that will not excuse them from their impending appointment.

We all have an appointment to keep.
Romans 10:13
*"For **whosoever** shall call upon the name of the Lord shall be saved."*

Revelation 20:15
*"And **whosoever** was not found written in the book of life
was cast into the lake of fire."*

Every single person will be one of these two whosoevers. **Make your choice now, before you do not have a choice of where you will spend eternity.**

If you have already made this decision,
consider those around you who still have an appointment awaiting them.

Will you tell them before it's too late?
Make the choice today to share the love of Christ
and His glorious Gospel.

Bible Reading
Deuteronomy 19-20 | Mark 15

03.29 | March 29

The Purpose Of Things.

Philippians 1:12
*"But I would ye should understand, brethren,
that the things which happened unto me have fallen out
rather unto the furtherance of the gospel;"*

Paul wrote the Book of Philippians while he was in prison. It would be very easy to think that Paul's bondage would hinder the spread of the Gospel. He was bound, unable to go out and reach others. Yet, he understood that there was a purpose far greater than if he was free to roam about with the Romans.

Philippians 1:13-14
"So that my bonds in Christ are manifest in all the palace, and in all other places; And many of the brethren in the Lord, waxing confident by my bonds, are much more bold to speak the word without fear."

His situation caused others to be bold in his absence. They saw how Paul handled the things that happened to him, and it encouraged them to speak the Word without fear.

Does your faith make others bolder?
Our testimony has an effect on those around us.
How we handle day-to-day situations tell as much,
if not more, about our faith as when the storms arrive.

Sometimes we may feel as if we are bound, unable to do much for Christ; but our testimony can cause others to speak in places we may never reach.

2 Timothy 2:9
"Wherein I suffer trouble, as an evil doer, even unto bonds; but the word of God is not bound."

His Word cannot be imprisoned.
Regardless of our circumstance, His Word can still be sent out
to reach others with the Gospel of Jesus Christ.

Whatever you face today, His Word is not bound.
God has a plan, and He is still in control.

**Take comfort today that the purpose of things
that happen to us is to further the Gospel.**

Bible Reading
Deuteronomy 21-22 | Mark 16

March 30 | 03.30

Keep Thy Heart.

Proverbs 4:23
"Keep thy heart with all diligence; for out of it are the issues of life."

Some have called this the theme verse for the Book of Proverbs, for our wisdom depends on the state of our hearts.

Deuteronomy 4:9
"Only take heed to thyself, and keep thy soul diligently, lest thou forget the things which thine eyes have seen, and lest they depart from thy heart all the days of thy life: but teach them thy sons, and thy sons' sons;"

The condition of our hearts affects every thing that we do.
All of our actions depend on what resides within our hearts.

How we speak… Proverbs 4:24
"Put away from thee a froward mouth, and perverse lips put far from thee."

What we look at… Proverbs 4:25
*"Let thine eyes look right on,
and let thine eyelids look straight before thee."*

Where we go… Proverbs 4:26-27
*"Ponder the path of thy feet, and let all thy ways be established.
Turn not to the right hand nor to the left: remove thy foot from evil."*

We must guard our hearts in order to keep our actions in check by being transformed and renewed through the Scriptures.
Romans 12:2
"And be not conformed to this world: but be ye transformed by the renewing of your mind, that ye may prove what is that good, and acceptable, and perfect, will of God."

The Word of God discerns both our thoughts and the intentions that lie within our hearts.
Hebrews 4:12
"For the word of God is quick, and powerful, and sharper than any twoedged sword, piercing even to the dividing asunder of soul and spirit, and of the joints and marrow, and is a discerner of the thoughts and intents of the heart."

Allow the Word of God to pierce the hardness of your heart, and enable wise actions to be displayed. The power of the Word of God can change your heart today and every day.

Bible Reading
Deuteronomy 23-24 | Acts 1

03.31 | March 31

Life Found In The Word.

John 6:63
"It is the spirit that quickeneth; the flesh profiteth nothing: the words that I speak unto you, they are spirit, and they are life."

Persecution can make us feel like the life has been taken out of us; but we can find renewed life each day through the Word of God.

Psalm 119:88
"Quicken me after thy lovingkindness; so shall I keep the testimony of thy mouth."

His Word gives us life.
When we feel defeated, His Word revives us.
When we feel empty, His Word sustains us.
When we feel needy, His Word provides for us.

Ephesians 2:4-7
"But God, who is rich in mercy, for his great love wherewith he loved us, Even when we were dead in sins, hath quickened us together with Christ, (by grace ye are saved;) And hath raised us up together, and made us sit together in heavenly places in Christ Jesus: That in the ages to come he might shew the exceeding riches of his grace in his kindness toward us through Christ Jesus."

He wants us to know we can have eternal life through Him.

1 John 5:11-13
"And this is the record, that God hath given to us eternal life, and this life is in his Son. He that hath the Son hath life; and he that hath not the Son of God hath not life. These things have I written unto you that believe on the name of the Son of God; that ye may know that ye have eternal life, and that ye may believe on the name of the Son of God."

He does all of this, because He loves us.
Romans 5:1-5

God loves us so much that He not only gave His Son for us, but He also preserved His Word for us.

He wants us to know we have life through His Son, and we can renew our minds each day through His Word.

Bible Reading
Deuteronomy 25-26 | Acts 2

Abide In Truth.

John 15:4
"Abide in me, and I in you. As the branch cannot bear fruit of itself, except it abide in the vine; no more can ye, except ye abide in me."

What does it mean to abide? Webster tells us…to bear patiently, to endure without yielding, to wait for and accept without objection, to remain stable or fixed in a state. These definitions seem to suggest abiding beside or under something, however if we look at the verse closer, Jesus said *"Abide in me, and I in you."* If we are to bear anything, He must dwell in us and we in Him. We can only endure without yielding to our flesh if we submit ourselves unto Him. **He is the Way, the Truth, the Life, and the Vine.**

Picture a branch on its own…is it alive or dead? Every branch we have ever seen by itself has died, or is dying, simply because it left the Vine, its Source of Life. More branches cannot be produced if a branch is no longer connected to the Vine. How are we any different? The moment we attempt to live in our own strength, the decline begins. We may not feel a change for a few hours, or maybe even days, but the difference is already there.

Our spiritual life begins to wither and decay the moment we leave the Vine.
John 15:6
"If a man abide not in me, he is cast forth as a branch, and is withered…"

Fruit is impossible without Him.
John 15:5
"I am the vine, ye are the branches: He that abideth in me, and I in him, the same bringeth forth much fruit: for without me ye can do nothing."

Jesus Christ spoke these words on His way to the Garden of Gethsemane. He knew this illustration would soon be seen by His disciples. The vines and branches of every tree within the Garden were a reminder of Him and this truth.

Without Him, we have no fruit.
In Him, we have the opportunity to bring forth much fruit.
Much fruit brings glory to God.
John 15:8
"Herein is my Father glorified, that ye bear much fruit; so shall ye be my disciples."
Much or none…the choice is ours. **Abide in Him today, and every day.**

Bible Reading
Deuteronomy 27-28 | Acts 3

04.02 | April 2

The Word Came.

John 1:1
*"In the beginning was the Word, and the Word was with God,
and the Word was God."*

The longest chapter in the Word of God is Psalm 119. Of the 176 verses, only a few are without a reference to the Word. Is it any coincidence that the longest chapter focuses on the Word Itself? Absolutely not.

"In the beginning…"
The Gospel according to John begins with the same three words that Genesis does. The Book of John begins by explaining that the Word was not only also in the beginning with God, but in fact the Word was God.

John 1:3
*"All things were made by him;
and without him was not any thing made that was made."*

The Word made everything.
All that was created was made by the Word of God.

In Him was and is Life.
John 1:4
"In him was life; and the life was the light of men."

Life is given to all who believe in Him.
John 1:12
*"But as many as received him, to them gave he power
to become the sons of God, even to them that believe on his name:"*

The Word came.
John 1:14
*"And the Word was made flesh, and dwelt among us,
(and we beheld his glory, the glory as of the only begotten of the Father,)
full of grace and truth."*

He came for one purpose.
The Word of God…the Son of God…Jesus Christ, came so that one day some 33 years later, He could die on a cross for the sins of the world. Three days and three nights later, the Word rose again. His victorious resurrection enables us to receive the free Gift of salvation…Him.

The Word came, died and rose again so that we could live.
Romans 10:8-9

Bible Reading
Deuteronomy 29-30 | Acts 4

Full Of Grace And Truth.

John 1:14
*"And the Word was made flesh, and dwelt among us,
(and we beheld his glory, the glory as of the only begotten of the Father,)
full of grace and truth."*

The Word was made flesh.
He came as a baby wrapped in swaddling clothes, yet He was still the King of Kings and Lord of Lords.

Luke 1:32-33
*"He shall be great, and shall be called the Son of the Highest:
and the Lord God shall give unto him the throne of his father David:
And he shall reign over the house of Jacob for ever;
and of his kingdom there shall be no end."*

The Word dwelt among us.
He came and was rejected by His own people, yet all who receive Him by faith become His children.

John 1:11-12
*"He came unto his own, and his own received him not.
But as many as received him, to them gave he power
to become the sons of God, even to them that believe on his name:"*

The Word was full of grace.
He came, and it is no wonder the Scripture tells us specifically that He is full of grace, for by grace we are saved.

Ephesians 2:8-9
"For by grace are ye saved through faith; and that not of yourselves: it is the gift of God: Not of works, lest any man should boast."

The Word was full of truth.
He came and was full of truth, because He is the Truth.

John 17:17
"Sanctify them through thy truth: thy word is truth."

He was full. God knows we are empty until we receive Him.
We cannot know grace or truth without Him.

Bible Reading
Deuteronomy 31-32 | Acts 5

04.04 | April 4

The Way.

John 14:6
*"Jesus saith unto him, I am the way, the truth, and the life:
no man cometh unto the Father, but by me."*

This was Jesus' answer to a question Thomas asked Him.

John 14:5
*"Thomas saith unto him, Lord, we know not whither thou goest;
and how can we know the way?"*

**This same question is being asked today
as people seek to find the way to Heaven.**

Thomas did not ask for a way, he asked for *"the way"*.
There is only One Way.

The first mention of the phrase *"the way"* is found in Genesis when Adam and Eve are driven out of the Garden of Eden.

Genesis 3:24
*"So he drove out the man; and he placed at the east of the garden of Eden
Cherubims, and a flaming sword which turned every way,
to keep the way of the tree of life."*

The tree of life is a picture of Jesus Christ.

Matthew 3:3
*"For this is he that was spoken of by the prophet Esaias, saying,
The voice of one crying in the wilderness, Prepare ye the way of the Lord,
make his paths straight."*

The first time we find *"the way"* in the New Testament it is also a reference to Him from Isaiah about John the Baptist bearing witness of Jesus.
Jesus said…*"I am the way".*

In order to know the Way, we must know Him.

1 John 5:20
*"And we know that the Son of God is come,
and hath given us an understanding, that we may know him that is true,
and we are in him that is true, even in his Son Jesus Christ.
This is the true God, and eternal life."*

**When we know Him, we not only know the Way,
but also the Truth and the Life.**

Bible Reading
Deuteronomy 33-34 | Acts 6

April 5 | 04.05

The Truth.

John 8:32
"And ye shall know the truth, and the truth shall make you free."

This verse is often quoted on its own; however, it is a finishing clause to the previous verse.

John 8:31
*"Then said Jesus to those Jews which believed on him,
If ye continue in my word, then are ye my disciples indeed;"*

**In order to know the Truth,
we must continue in His Word; for He is the Word.**

We cannot be His disciples without first believing on Him as Saviour. The word *"continue"* here, refers to cleaving or holding fast to something, or in this case, Someone.

John 8:31-32
*"Then said Jesus to those Jews which believed on him,
If ye continue in my word, then are ye my disciples indeed;
And ye shall know the truth, and the truth shall make you free."*

There is so much to glean from the conditional promises found within the Word of God.
"If…then…"

If we choose to believe on Him, we are His disciples.
His disciples know Him as the Truth.
"…and the truth shall make you free."

The context of this chapter is Jesus Christ conversing with the group of Pharisees which wished to stone the woman caught in the act of adultery. They were convicted by their own conscience, yet not by the Word of God.

John 8:36
"If the Son therefore shall make you free, ye shall be free indeed."

Knowing the Truth brings freedom.

Bible Reading
Joshua 1-2 | Acts 7

04.06 | April 6

The Life.

John 11:25-26
"Jesus said unto her, I am the resurrection, and the life: he that believeth in me, though he were dead, yet shall he live: And whosoever liveth and believeth in me shall never die. Believest thou this?"

Lazarus was dead. His sisters were mourning over the loss of their brother. Mary and Martha had faith that if only Jesus had been there before Lazarus died, He could have healed him. What they did not realize was that Jesus would in fact heal their brother, but through a greater miracle. One that would bring more people unto Himself.

In the storms of our lives, God rarely, if ever, answers exactly like we hoped He would. Oftentimes, He has a greater purpose that can only be brought to pass in ways that only He understands…for His ways are higher than our ways.

Jesus raised Lazarus from the dead, because He is the Resurrection and the Life. He brought Lazarus physical healing in this passage, but one day later Lazarus would die physically again.

Jesus is the Life, because He is the only One to have resurrected once and for all. **When we believe in Him, we find life…everlasting life.**

John 3:16
"For God so loved the world, that he gave his only begotten Son, that whosoever believeth in him should not perish, but have everlasting life."

Believing in Jesus is more than just believing He exists and is the Son of God. There is a difference in knowing about someone, and actually knowing them.

Knowing of or about Jesus is religion.
Knowing Jesus is about a relationship with Him.

We are all asked the same question:
John 11:26
"…Believest thou this?"
May our response be the same as Martha's was that day.
John 11:27
"She saith unto him, Yea, Lord: I believe that thou art the Christ, the Son of God, which should come into the world."

He gives life to all who believe in Him.

Bible Reading
Joshua 3-4 | Acts 8

April 7 | 04.07

A Picture Of Jesus.

Acts 8:35
"Then Philip opened his mouth, and began at the same scripture, and preached unto him Jesus."

We are not told exactly what Philip said in preaching Jesus unto the Eunuch that day; but we are told from what Scripture he began.

Isaiah 53:7-8
"He was oppressed, and he was afflicted, yet he opened not his mouth: he is brought as a lamb to the slaughter, and as a sheep before her shearers is dumb, so he openeth not his mouth. He was taken from prison and from judgment: and who shall declare his generation? for he was cut off out of the land of the living: for the transgression of my people was he stricken."

Throughout Isaiah 53, there are many references to our Lord and Saviour, Jesus Christ. **Read through the entire chapter today, and look for Him.** He is that Tender Plant. He is the Root out of a dry ground. He was despised and rejected of men. He was and is acquainted with our grief. He is the only One that has truly borne our griefs and carried our sorrows.

Jesus was wounded for our transgressions, and bruised for our iniquities. It was our chastisement that was upon Him that day on Calvary. It is with His stripes we are healed, because each stripe He received brought forth His precious blood.

Ephesians 1:7
"In whom we have redemption through his blood, the forgiveness of sins, according to the riches of his grace;"

As Philip and the Eunuch went on their way, they came unto a certain water. The Eunuch asked what hindered him from being baptized. Philip's answer is removed from many of the modern translations today.

Acts 8:37
"And Philip said, If thou believest with all thine heart, thou mayest. And he answered and said, I believe that Jesus Christ is the Son of God."

It is our belief in Who Jesus is, and what He did for us, that brings salvation. **Baptism is the outward expression of what has taken place inside of us.** It is a picture of the death, burial, and resurrection of Jesus Christ, and it identifies us as believers in the Gospel of Jesus Christ.

He came. He died. He was buried. He is risen.
For us.

Bible Reading
Joshua 5-6 | Acts 9

04.08 | April 8

Wise To Give.

John 3:16
"For God so loved the world, that he gave his only begotten Son, that whosoever believeth in him should not perish, but have everlasting life."

God gave His Only Begotten Son so that we might have life, the Ultimate Example of giving. He did not withhold Himself from giving what He had to give. He gave so that we could also give, and He expects the same from us.

Proverbs 3:27-28
"Withhold not good from them to whom it is due, when it is in the power of thine hand to do it. Say not unto thy neighbour, Go, and come again, and to morrow I will give; when thou hast it by thee."

He wants us to give cheerfully.
2 Corinthians 9:7
"Every man according as he purposeth in his heart, so let him give; not grudgingly, or of necessity: for God loveth a cheerful giver."

The more we give, the more we will receive.
2 Corinthians 9:6
"But this I say, He which soweth sparingly shall reap also sparingly; and he which soweth bountifully shall reap also bountifully."

Luke 6:38
"Give, and it shall be given unto you; good measure, pressed down, and shaken together, and running over, shall men give into your bosom. For with the same measure that ye mete withal it shall be measured to you again."

We desire to receive; yet so often we neglect or even refuse to give.
We expect others to show us love and mercy, yet how often do we fail to extend the same grace in return?

Acts 20:35
"I have shewed you all things, how that so labouring ye ought to support the weak, and to remember the words of the Lord Jesus, how he said, It is more blessed to give than to receive."

God tells us time and time again that it is wise to give.
What are you giving today?

Bible Reading
Joshua 7-8 | Acts 10

April 9 | 04.09

The Light Of The World.

John 12:46
*"I am come a light into the world,
that whosoever believeth on me should not abide in darkness."*

We have the Light of Christ within us, and it is up to us to shine so that others may see the glorious Light of the Gospel.

Proverbs 4:18-19
"But the path of the just is as the shining light, that shineth more and more unto the perfect day. The way of the wicked is as darkness: they know not at what they stumble."

In the middle of the darkness, *"the path of the just"* can light the way; because this is not just any shining light, but the Light of the World.

John 8:12
"Then spake Jesus again unto them, saying, I am the light of the world: he that followeth me shall not walk in darkness, but shall have the light of life."

Darkness allows even the dimmest light to shine.
No matter how dark it may seem, we have the opportunity to allow Christ to shine through us so that others may see Him.

2 Corinthians 4:3-4
"But if our gospel be hid, it is hid to them that are lost: In whom the god of this world hath blinded the minds of them which believe not, lest the light of the glorious gospel of Christ, who is the image of God, should shine unto them. For we preach not ourselves, but Christ Jesus the Lord; and ourselves your servants for Jesus' sake. For God, who commanded the light to shine out of darkness, hath shined in our hearts, to give the light of the knowledge of the glory of God in the face of Jesus Christ."

We shine brightest when we hold up the Word of God.

Philippians 2:15-16
"That ye may be blameless and harmless, the sons of God, without rebuke, in the midst of a crooked and perverse nation, among whom ye shine as lights in the world; Holding forth the word of life; that I may rejoice in the day of Christ, that I have not run in vain, neither laboured in vain."

It is His Word that makes the difference.

Matthew 5:16
"Let your light so shine before men, that they may see your good works, and glorify your Father which is in heaven."

Shine the Light today, and every day.
Bible Reading
Joshua 9-10 | Acts 11

04.10 | April 10

The Foundation For Everything.

Psalm 138:2
*"I will worship toward thy holy temple, and praise thy name
for thy lovingkindness and for thy truth:
for thou hast magnified thy word above all thy name."*

There is a Name that is above all other names, the Name of Jesus.

Matthew 18:20
*"For where two or three are gathered together in my name,
there am I in the midst of them."*

John 14:13
*"And whatsoever ye shall ask in my name, that will I do,
that the Father may be glorified in the Son."*

John 20:31
*"But these are written, that ye might believe that Jesus is the Christ,
the Son of God; and that believing ye might have life through his name."*

Acts 4:12
*"Neither is there salvation in any other: for there is none other name
under heaven given among men, whereby we must be saved."*

Romans 10:13
"For whosoever shall call upon the name of the Lord shall be saved."

The Name of Jesus has power. We gather in His Name. We pray in His Name. We believe and have life through His Name. We find salvation through His Name. We praise His Name. Yet…the Holy Spirit used David to pen these Words:

Psalm 138:2
"…for thou hast magnified thy word above all thy name."

As much power as there is in the Name of Jesus Christ, the Lord magnifies His Word above His Name. Jesus Christ is the Word. We have the written Word preserved for our every need. Yet, how often do we neglect the very Source we need the most? The Lord has chosen to magnify His Word above His own Name, should we not also do the same?

His Word must be our foundation for everything. All we believe. All that we are. All that we do. All that we say. Everything and all things.

What is your foundation today?
If you are not standing upon the Word today, it's time to move.

Bible Reading
Joshua 11-12 | Acts 12

April 11 | 04.11

Turn To The Word.

Matthew 4:16-17
*"The people which sat in darkness saw great light;
and to them which sat in the region and shadow of death light is sprung up. From that time Jesus began to preach, and to say,
Repent: for the kingdom of heaven is at hand."*

The prophet Isaiah foretold that this Great Light would come.
The Light of the World chose to begin His preaching with one Word.
"Repent."

This word *"Repent"* means more than just changing your mind or turning away from something…it refers not only turning from, but also unto something…or rather in this case, Someone.

Jesus Christ spoke of turning from sin and unto Him.
The Word spoke the Word which pointed people to Himself.

Mark 1:15
"And saying, The time is fulfilled, and the kingdom of God is at hand: repent ye, and believe the gospel."

His purpose was for us to repent unto Him.
Not a select few or even many,
but He came so that all should come unto Him.

2 Peter 3:9
"The Lord is not slack concerning his promise, as some men count slackness; but is longsuffering to us-ward, not willing that any should perish, but that all should come to repentance."

After we are saved, repentance does not end. Those times when we have strayed away from Him, the same word applies. He is waiting for us to repent and return unto Him, restoring our fellowship with Him.

Revelation 2:5
"Remember therefore from whence thou art fallen, and repent, and do the first works; or else I will come unto thee quickly, and will remove thy candlestick out of his place, except thou repent."

Once we are saved, our relationship cannot change, but sin hinders our communion with Him. Psalm 66:18 If you do not know Him, *"Repent".* If you do know Him, but have strayed away, *"Repent".* Just as He showed us on Calvary, **He is waiting with open arms for His children to turn unto Him.**

Bible Reading
Joshua 13-14 | Acts 13

04.12 | April 12

The Hour Is Come.

John 13:1
"Now before the feast of the passover, when Jesus knew that his hour was come that he should depart out of this world unto the Father, having loved his own which were in the world, he loved them unto the end."

Throughout the New Testament we see several times where the Lord Jesus declares that His time has not yet come.

At the wedding in Cana of Galilee, Jesus tells his mother. John 2:3

When He was urged to go to the feast of the tabernacles. John 7:6

Although Jesus knew what lied ahead and all that would happen in order to fulfill His purpose, **He willingly waited until He knew it was time according to the will of His Father.**

John 12:23
"And Jesus answered them, saying,
The hour is come, that the Son of man should be glorified."

He knew when it was time, and what that entailed; all the while loving us unto the end. His hour was come.

John 17:1-2
"These words spake Jesus, and lifted up his eyes to heaven, and said, Father, the hour is come; glorify thy Son, that thy Son also may glorify thee: As thou hast given him power over all flesh, that he should give eternal life to as many as thou hast given him."

He would soon travel to the Garden of Gethsemane where He would be betrayed and taken away bound by the Jews. He allowed this because His mind was set on Calvary and those He would willingly give His life for as a ransom for many. **He was willing to suffer for us, are we willing to suffer for Him?** 1 Peter 4:14

Sometimes, we forget that God is glorified when we suffer persecution.
The days we are living in are what the Scriptures refer to as the last days.
2 Timothy 3:1,12,14-15

The hour is come that we are living in harsh days, and those who live godly in Christ Jesus shall suffer persecution. Yet, the hour is also come for us to continue in the things that we have learned through His Word. **Will we stand upon the Truth of the Word of God regardless of the consequences here on earth?** Galatians 6:9-10

Bible Reading
Joshua 15-16 | Acts 14

April 13 | 04.13

Betrayed.

Matthew 26:20-21
"Now when the even was come, he sat down with the twelve. And as they did eat, he said, Verily I say unto you, that one of you shall betray me."

When we suffer for His sake, the persecution we face makes us more like Jesus Christ. In between these two verses in Matthew, there is a beautiful scene of the humility and love of Christ that takes place found in John 13. After supper, Jesus took a bason of water and began to wash the feet of His disciples. The Saviour gave the Ultimate Example of leadership in serving others; so much so, He even washed the feet of the one He knew would betray Him.

John 13:18
"I speak not of you all: I know whom I have chosen: but that the scripture may be fulfilled, He that eateth bread with me hath lifted up his heel against me."

Each disciple had to lift up his heel in order to have his foot washed, but when Judas lifted his it was against Jesus in hostility. Christ knew this was so that Scripture was fulfilled.

Psalm 41:9
"Yea, mine own familiar friend, in whom I trusted, which did eat of my bread, hath lifted up his heel against me."

When Jesus foretold of this, the disciples began to question.
Matthew 26:22
Jesus knew exactly who it was.
John 13:26-27

Have you felt like you have been betrayed? Take comfort in the fact that the betrayal only makes us more like Christ. In Psalm 55, David speaks of being betrayed. He even goes so far as to say they took sweet counsel together within the house of God. But David chose to call upon God for deliverance instead of getting revenge; just as Jesus chose to drink the bitter cup of betrayal because He knew a greater purpose was at hand.

**If you feel betrayed today,
choose to respond by casting your burden upon the Lord.**
Psalm 55:22
Commit them to His care today.
Depend on Him to defend you.

Bible Reading
Joshua 17-18 | Acts 15

04.14 | April 14

God Intervened.

Romans 5:8
"But God commendeth his love toward us, in that, while we were yet sinners, Christ died for us."

This verse is quoted often. Many have memorized all 18 words. Yet, how much have we really taken in the Truth of what they describe?

"But God…"
Referring to the previous verses…Romans 5:6-7
God intervened.
He made a Way, where there was no way.

"commendeth his love"
God is Love and showed His love for humanity by giving Himself in the form of His Son, Jesus Christ, to die for the ungodly. Ephesians 2:7

"toward us"
As marvelous as the other 16 words are, these two are the most amazing of them all. **God loved us so much that He gave His only begotten Son for us.** Nothing can separate us from the love of God because He was willing to sacrifice Himself for us. There is no greater love than that. John 15:13

"in that, while we were yet sinners"
We are the reason. It was our sin that was laid upon Him.
Isaiah 53:6
"All we like sheep have gone astray; we have turned every one to his own way; and the LORD hath laid on him the iniquity of us all."

"Christ died for us."
Every nail that pierced His body…Every drop of blood He shed…
Every Word He said… was for us.
1 John 4:9-10

God loves us so much that our words cannot describe nor can our finite minds comprehend. He simply wants us to have faith in Him. If you do not know Him personally today, please do not wait any longer. You are not promised tomorrow, or even the rest of this day. Religion will not save you. Heritage will not save you. Heaven is reserved only for those who have by faith trusted in the Lord Jesus Christ and His payment for their sin.

Have you rejected His gift before?
Receive Him today.

Bible Reading
Joshua 19-20 | Acts 16

April 15 | 04.15

Make It Sure.

Matthew 27:65-66
*"Pilate said unto them, Ye have a watch: go your way,
make it as sure as ye can. So they went, and made the sepulchre sure,
sealing the stone, and setting a watch."*

After the body of Jesus was placed in the tomb which Joseph of Arimathaea had prepared, the chief priests and Pharisees were haunted by His words.
Matthew 17:22-23
Mark 10:33-34
Luke 9:22
John 2:19

They were desperate to do anything they possibly could to try and make sure what Jesus had prophesied would not happen. They were depending upon themselves. They even had an excuse prepared…they would blame it on the disciples stealing the body of Jesus.

Many today are depending upon themselves and their good works to get to Heaven. Many even have excuses prepared, just like the Pharisees. They try to make sure that their way will be sufficient enough.

John 14:6
*"Jesus saith unto him, I am the way, the truth, and the life:
no man cometh unto the Father, but by me."*

He is the Way, and the Only Way.
Nothing that we can do in and of ourselves can atone for our sin.
Only the blood of Jesus.

The Pharisees tried to make sure Jesus would not raise from the dead…
but He did.
May today be the day you make it sure in your life.
2 Peter 1:10

The Bible says we can know.
1 John 5:13
"These things have I written unto you that believe on the name of the Son of God; that ye may know that ye have eternal life, and that ye may believe on the name of the Son of God."

Make it sure today.
If you are not sure, please contact us.

Bible Reading
Joshua 21-22 | Acts 17

04.16 | April 16

Waiting For The Miracle.

Matthew 12:40
"For as Jonas was three days and three nights in the whale's belly; so shall the Son of man be three days and three nights in the heart of the earth."

When certain of the scribes and the Pharisees required a sign, Jesus spoke of the only sign given to an evil and adulterous generation…the sign of Jonah.

Jonah 1:17
"Now the LORD had prepared a great fish to swallow up Jonah. And Jonah was in the belly of the fish three days and three nights."

Sunday School teachers have often taught with flannelgraphs and now digital images of Jonah sitting and waiting inside the belly of that great fish. Can you imagine how the eleven disciples and all those that believed and followed Jesus felt during the three days and three nights of waiting?

Luke 23:56
"And they returned, and prepared spices and ointments; and rested the sabbath day according to the commandment."

All four of the Gospel records mention the preparation after Jesus Christ died. Preparation speaks of making ready or being prepared for what is ahead. They prepared for what was coming, then they waited for the miracle. **What a picture of where we are, or should be, today.**

Luke 12:37
"Blessed are those servants, whom the lord when he cometh shall find watching: verily I say unto you, that he shall gird himself, and make them to sit down to meat, and will come forth and serve them."

Our preparation is our salvation that we find by faith in Jesus Christ.
1 Peter 3:15
"But sanctify the Lord God in your hearts: and be ready always to give an answer to every man that asketh you a reason of the hope that is in you with meekness and fear:"

After we are prepared, we wait for His return.
While He is preparing a place for us. John 14:1-3

He is coming back… Are you prepared?
1 Corinthians 2:9
May we never be ashamed to share the Gospel while we wait.

Bible Reading
Joshua 23-24 | Acts 18

April 17 | 04.17

They Remembered.

Luke 24:8
"And they remembered his words,"

The Pharisees were haunted by the Words of Jesus, but His believers needed to be reminded that He said He would rise again in three days. When the women came to the sepulchre very early in the morning on the first day of the week, they were perplexed because His body was not there.

They forgot.
Perhaps out of shock, but still…
they neglected to remember what He had said would happen.

How often in our lives are we into the same state?
We get so perplexed over the circumstances we are in
that we forget what the Word of God says.

These women needed to be reminded,
so two angels spoke these words of comfort:
Luke 24:5-7
"…they said unto them, Why seek ye the living among the dead? He is not here, but is risen: remember how he spake unto you when he was yet in Galilee, Saying, The Son of man must be delivered into the hands of sinful men, and be crucified, and the third day rise again."

Mary Magdalene was the first to see
the Lord Jesus Christ after He had risen. Mark 16:9

She was commissioned by Christ to go and tell the Good News,
and she obeyed. John 20:17-18

Just like Mary Magdalene, we too have been given the opportunity to share the Gospel with others. Have we obeyed? What great blessings have we missed out on simply because we neglected to remember what Jesus said for us to do?

He is Risen.
His resurrection makes the Gospel of Jesus Christ the Good News.

1 Corinthians 15:17
"And if Christ be not raised, your faith is vain; ye are yet in your sins."

If He had not risen, there would be no Good News for us to share.
Share the Gospel with someone today, and every day.

Bible Reading
Judges 1 | Acts 19

04.18 | April 18

Lift Him Up.

John 12:32
"And I, if I be lifted up from the earth, will draw all men unto me."

What a promise from the Word Himself.
If we simply lift up Jesus, He will draw all men unto Him.

Is that not what the goal of every church service should be? May it not stop there. Every service, every song, every moment of our lives should have one purpose... to lift Him up!

Lift up the Name of Jesus!

Philippians 2:9-11
*"Wherefore God also hath highly exalted him,
and given him a name which is above every name:
That at the name of Jesus every knee should bow, of things in heaven,
and things in earth, and things under the earth; And that every tongue
should confess that Jesus Christ is Lord, to the glory of God the Father."*

When we lift up the Name of Jesus, the Name above all names, we are confessing that He is Lord, which brings glory to God the Father. There is no other name that compares to the Name of Jesus.

**The Name of Jesus should be the Foundation
for all we are and believe.**

2 Timothy 2:19
*"Nevertheless the foundation of God standeth sure, having this seal,
The Lord knoweth them that are his. And, Let every one
that nameth the name of Christ depart from iniquity."*

The Name of Jesus is the pathway to salvation.

Romans 10:13
"For whosoever shall call upon the name of the Lord shall be saved."

There is just something about the Name of Jesus!

Lift Him up today, and every day.

**Bible Reading
Judges 2-3 | Acts 20**

April 19 | 04.19

He Is Still Risen.

Luke 24:44
"And he said unto them, These are the words which I spake unto you, while I was yet with you, that all things must be fulfilled, which were written in the law of Moses, and in the prophets, and in the psalms, concerning me."

Praise God that Jesus was and is Who He said He was! He died for our sins, spent three days and three nights in the tomb, and then raised again victoriously on the third day defeating death, hell, and the grave.

His resurrection made the Gospel possible!
Without the resurrection, our faith would be in vain.
His resurrection has provided us the Free Gift of salvation,
if we would only believe in Him.
Romans 10:9
*"That if thou shalt confess with thy mouth the Lord Jesus,
and shalt believe in thine heart
that God hath raised him from the dead, thou shalt be saved."*

Crowds of people gather daily at the Garden Tomb outside of Jerusalem longing to see the fact that Christ is not in that grave with their own eyes. Some come searching for answers to believe, but many come already knowing the answer.

Matthew 28:6
*"He is not here: for he is risen, as he said.
Come, see the place where the Lord lay."*

We set aside a weekend every year to celebrate His sacrifice and resurrection, and we should. But the truth is…even the Tuesday after Easter He is STILL our Risen Saviour! Are we as enthused today as we were on Easter Sunday? Will we be less excited tomorrow to celebrate His resurrection? Next month? Six months? Every day is Easter.

*He lives, He lives, Christ Jesus lives today
He walks with me and talks with me
Along life's narrow way
He lives, He lives, Salvation to impart
You ask me how I know He lives?
He lives within my heart!*
Alfred H. Ackley

Bible Reading
Judges 4-5 | Acts 21

04.20 | April 20

Determined Doubt.

John 20:29
"Jesus saith unto him, Thomas, because thou hast seen me, thou hast believed: blessed are they that have not seen, and yet have believed."

After He arose, Jesus appeared to His disciples several times. He once stood in the midst of ten, and Thomas was not there. When he heard that Jesus had came, he chose not to believe simply because he had not seen Jesus himself.

John 20:25
"The other disciples therefore said unto him, We have seen the Lord. But he said unto them, Except I shall see in his hands the print of the nails, and put my finger into the print of the nails, and thrust my hand into his side, I will not believe."

Many people today have also chosen not to believe, simply because they cannot see Jesus themselves. Thomas went so far as to say four of the saddest words in all of Scripture…*"I will not believe"*. **He was determined in his disbelief.**

How many times in our lives have we refused to believe something simply because we did not witness it ourselves?

There is no faith in determined doubt.
Hebrews 11:1
"Now faith is the substance of things hoped for, the evidence of things not seen."

Faith in only that which is seen is a lack of faith.
The Bible is very clear on what that brings.
Romans 14:23

Without faith, it is impossible to please God.
Hebrews 11:6

Jesus explained this same Truth to Thomas after he finally believed when he had seen Him. Thomas' story is written within the pages of the The Gospel record according to John so that we may read them and believe. John 20:30-31

Seeing Jesus through the pages of the Word of God is a matter of faith.
Faith is what pleases God. Faith in salvation, yes, but we must have faith in every aspect of our lives as we walk with the Lord. Romans 1:17

Bible Reading
Judges 6-7 | Acts 22

Ye Shall Find.

John 21:6
"And he said unto them, Cast the net on the right side of the ship, and ye shall find. They cast therefore, and now they were not able to draw it for the multitude of fishes."

Simon Peter had decided that he was going to go fishing, and several of the disciples followed him. They all entered into the same ship, and that night they caught nothing.

John 21:4
"But when the morning was now come, Jesus stood on the shore: but the disciples knew not that it was Jesus."

They were focused on their own efforts…or lack thereof. So much so, that they were unaware that the Resurrected Saviour stood before them.

The unrecognizable Voice gave them specific instructions, and they obeyed. When the net was miraculously full of fish, John knew it had to be the Lord. Only He could provide such a multitude of fishes.

John 21:11
"Simon Peter went up, and drew the net to land full of great fishes, an hundred and fifty and three: and for all there were so many, yet was not the net broken."

With their own efforts and focus, they were left emptyhanded; yet, under the Lord's direction they had more than enough. **It was the direction of the Word of God that made the difference.** The same is true for us today… When we attempt to do the Lord's work under our own power, we too will be left emptyhanded. Any work done in our flesh is all in vain.

John 15:5
"I am the vine, ye are the branches: He that abideth in me, and I in him, the same bringeth forth much fruit: for without me ye can do nothing."

Alternatively, when we seek the Lord, and willfully follow His direction and allow Him to do the work through us, anything is possible.

Philippians 4:13
"I can do all things through Christ which strengtheneth me."

Choose to obey His Word today, and discover the same Truth as the disciples…*"ye shall find."*

Bible Reading
Judges 8-9 | Acts 23

04.22 | April 22

The Last Words.

Mark 16:15
"And he said unto them, Go ye into all the world, and preach the gospel to every creature."

In Christ's last Words before He ascended to Heaven, He commissioned His disciples to spread the Gospel through His power and not our own. **One day there will not be any more opportunities to share the Gospel.** Within this one verse are seven segments of the Great Commission to help us understand the responsibility He has given us. These segments also pose seven questions for us to consider how they apply to our lives. Remember that each of these Words are written in red, spoken by the Word Himself.

Go. A verb that requires action to take place. Go simply means to move from one place to another, to leave, to travel. **Who should go?**

Ye. Who was He talking to? His followers. Do you profess to be a Christian, a follower of Christ? Then this applies to you just as much as it did to those who heard the words from the Risen Saviour that day. **How are you involved in the Great Commission?**

Into. A preposition, meaning to express movement or action with the result that someone or something becomes enclosed or surrounded by something else. **What, where, or who does Christ tell us to go into?**

All the world. He wants us to go into all the world. Not only in our Jerusalem; not just in our Judaea; not just in our Samaria, but also unto the uttermost part of the earth. **Where do you share what He has done?**

Preach. How are we supposed to relay the Message? We are to preach, to publicly proclaim or teach; to earnestly advocate our belief. This is not limited to those called men of God who are preachers. This is to every Christian. **How are you proclaiming what Christ has done?**

The Gospel. What are we to preach? The death, burial, and resurrection of Jesus Christ…plus nothing, minus nothing. We cannot earn our way to Heaven. It is only by our belief and faith of how Jesus paid the price for our sin and rose victoriously from the grave on the third day. **What are you doing with the Gospel today?**

To every creature. He did not exclude anyone. There is not a person on the planet that does not need the Gospel. We have the Good News and yet we routinely keep it to ourselves. **Who is waiting for you to tell them?**

Bible Reading
Judges 10-11 | Acts 24

Matthew 4:19
"And he saith unto them, Follow me, and I will make you fishers of men."

Two words..."*Follow me*". These same two words are spoken repeatedly by the same Person throughout the New Testament. They were spoken as an invitation to join or come after Him. But more important was Who the people were invited to follow.

"Follow me"
He spoke of Himself.
He was, and is, Jesus.
The Son of God. God in the flesh. The Messiah. The Saviour.

These two words were more than just an invitation. Each time was, and is, an opportunity given to place faith in the One that said them. Nineteen times, within the pages of Scripture, Jesus uttered these two words. Six of those times, no other words were said with them. He simply said, *"Follow me"*.

Oftentimes we are not given an explanation as to why we are in a certain situation. God may have not purposefully brought it to pass, but regardless, He allowed it. **The situation you are facing today may feel unique to you, but He knows.** You may not be physically standing on the shore casting a net into the sea, but the Lord knows exactly where you are and what you are dealing with.

He is still speaking the same words to you today as He did to Peter and Andrew that day by the Sea of Galilee…*"Follow me"*.

Every storm, every valley, every virus, is just another opportunity to place faith in Him. **Are you willing to follow Him today?**

John 10:27
"My sheep hear my voice, and I know them, and they follow me:"

Trace His steps within the pages of the Word of God.
Allow Him to speak to your heart like no one else can.
Let Him speak peace to your troubled soul.

John 14:27
"Peace I leave with you, my peace I give unto you: not as the world giveth, give I unto you. Let not your heart be troubled, neither let it be afraid."

Bible Reading
Judges 12-13 | Acts 25

04.24 | April 24

Without Delay.

Matthew 4:20
"And they straightway left their nets, and followed him."

This was Peter and Andrew's response when Jesus said unto them, *"Follow me".* No explanation was given, they just decided to place faith in Who He was. The sons of Zebedee, James and John, had the same reaction when Jesus called them; and Scripture tells us they possibly gave up even more than the other brothers.

Matthew 4:22
"And they immediately left the ship and their father, and followed him."

Their faith to follow allowed them to see miracle after miracle that Jesus did as He went all about Galilee teaching and preaching. What if they had said no? Think of all they would have missed out on.

We read of two men, in Luke 9, that made excuses for not following.

Luke 9:59
"And he said unto another, Follow me. But he said, Lord, suffer me first to go and bury my father."

Luke 9:61
"And another also said, Lord, I will follow thee; but let me first go bid them farewell, which are at home at my house."

Jesus' response was clear and to the point.

Luke 9:62
"And Jesus said unto him, No man, having put his hand to the plough, and looking back, is fit for the kingdom of God."

What are you using as an excuse today?
Are you looking back while attempting to do the work of the Lord?

Regardless of what you have to leave or give up, it is worth it to follow Him. Decide today that you are done making excuses. Decide that waiting until the "right time" is just a delay from seeing the miracle.

Choose today to follow Him in faith without delay.

Hebrews 12:2
"Looking unto Jesus the author and finisher of our faith; who for the joy that was set before him endured the cross, despising the shame, and is set down at the right hand of the throne of God."

Bible Reading
Judges 14-15 | Acts 26

April 25 | 04.25

Ask For A Miracle.

Matthew 14:29
"And he said, Come. And when Peter was come down out of the ship, he walked on the water, to go to Jesus."

Peter not only had faith to follow Jesus, but he had faith to ask Jesus to do the impossible through him.

Matthew 14:28
"And Peter answered him and said, Lord, if it be thou, bid me come unto thee on the water."

Jesus walking on the water was a miracle in itself…but Peter had the audacity to ask the Lord if He would allow him to walk on the water too.

"Come."
One word from Jesus, spoken as a result of Peter's faith-filled request.

We often ask for Jesus to do a miracle in our lives, but have you ever asked Him to do one through you?

Peter walking on the water had nothing to do with his ability. God allowed his feet not to sink when he came down out of the boat. His eyes were fixed upon Jesus, because he knew he did not have the power within himself to do what he was doing.

The Scripture proves this by the fact that as soon as Peter took his eyes off Jesus and looked at the wind boisterous around him, he began to sink. Yet the moment he cried out amidst his fear, the Lord rescued him.

Matthew 14:31
"And immediately Jesus stretched forth his hand, and caught him, and said unto him, O thou of little faith, wherefore didst thou doubt?"

Discard the doubt today.
Keep your eyes on Jesus.

Mark 9:23
"Jesus said unto him, If thou canst believe, all things are possible to him that believeth."

Ask Him to do the impossible through you for His glory.

Bible Reading
Judges 16-17 | Acts 27

04.26 | April 26

Part Of A Miracle.

John 2:5
"His mother saith unto the servants, Whatsoever he saith unto you, do it."

The wise words of His mother were heard by the servants at the marriage in Cana of Galilee. Can you imagine their reaction? Perhaps confusion or maybe anticipation.

She obviously knew something they did not.
There were six waterpots of stone nearby.

John 2:7
"Jesus saith unto them, Fill the waterpots with water…"

The servants had a choice to make.
Do they ignore both Jesus and Mary's instructions
or choose to follow them?
"…And they filled them up to the brim."

Not only did they obey, they anticipated that something marvelous was about to take place. Why else would they have filled them to the brim?

If we want to see the impossible, we have to be willing to not only do what we are told, but to the best we can, and allow Him to take over.

Colossians 3:17
"And whatsoever ye do in word or deed, do all in the name of the Lord Jesus, giving thanks to God and the Father by him."

It is not our ability that matters, but rather our obedience.
How willing are you to obey whatever He says?

John 2:8
*"And he saith unto them, Draw out now,
and bear unto the governor of the feast. And they bare it."*

He allowed them to have a part in the miracle.

They had no part in performing it, but He gave them the opportunity to do more than just see something miraculous. They not only witnessed the impossible, but imagine the faces of six servants as each of them dipped into what was once clear water, and came out red like crimson. The miracle was in their hand.

**What might the Lord allow us to be a part of
if we were simply willing to allow Him to get the glory?**

Bible Reading
Judges 18-19 | Acts 28

April 27 | 04.27

A Silent Answer.

Luke 23:9
"Then he questioned with him in many words; but he answered him nothing."

Sometimes silence is best.
Christ showed us this example several times throughout the Scripture, most noticeably when He was on trial. He was questioned and accused; yet He wisely chose to remain silent. Herod had heard of the miracles that Jesus had done, and hoped to witness one himself. He questioned, but the response of Jesus spoke volumes.

He answered nothing.

Matthew 27:12-14
"And when he was accused of the chief priests and elders, he answered nothing. Then said Pilate unto him, Hearest thou not how many things they witness against thee? And he answered him to never a word; insomuch that the governor marvelled greatly."

He did not even open His mouth.
Just as Isaiah had wrote many years before.

Isaiah 53:7
"He was oppressed, and he was afflicted, yet he opened not his mouth: he is brought as a lamb to the slaughter, and as a sheep before her shearers is dumb, so he openeth not his mouth."

Silence is a wise response to both our critics and those who do us wrong.

Luke 23:13-14
"And Pilate, when he had called together the chief priests and the rulers and the people, Said unto them, Ye have brought this man unto me, as one that perverteth the people: and, behold, I, having examined him before you, have found no fault in this man touching those things whereof ye accuse him:"

We too can wisely choose to remain silent amidst the persecution.
Regardless of the false accusations or the suffering we endure, following Christ's example of silence is most often the wisest way we can respond.

Silent Wisdom is heard louder than any words we could ever say.

Bible Reading
Judges 20-21 | Romans 1

04.28 | April 28

Clean Through The Word.

John 15:3
"Now ye are clean through the word which I have spoken unto you."

The first step in solving a problem is admitting there is a problem.
Do we even realize when there is sin in our lives?

We cannot get rid of the sin that displeases the Lord unless we first acknowledge our sin.

Psalm 119:9
"Wherewithal shall a young man cleanse his way? by taking heed thereto according to thy word."

How can we cleanse our hearts?
By the Word of God.

John 15:1-2
"I am the true vine, and my Father is the husbandman. Every branch in me that beareth not fruit he taketh away: and every branch that beareth fruit, he purgeth it, that it may bring forth more fruit."

If we want a clean heart, we must take heed to His Word and allow Him to purge away the sin from our lives.

Do you desire a clean heart today?
Prayerfully ask the Lord to show you the sin that needs cleansed.

Psalm 51:10
"Create in me a clean heart, O God; and renew a right spirit within me."

A clean heart is only a confession away.
No earthly priest is required,
we can simply approach the throne of grace
to obtain mercy and find grace to help in time of need.

1 John 1:9
"If we confess our sins, he is faithful and just to forgive us our sins, and to cleanse us from all unrighteousness."

Bible Reading
Ruth 1 | Romans 2

April 29 | 04.29

Fruit That Remains.

John 15:16
"Ye have not chosen me, but I have chosen you, and ordained you, that ye should go and bring forth fruit, and that your fruit should remain: that whatsoever ye shall ask of the Father in my name, he may give it you."

Fruit that we buy from the produce section at the grocery store often does not last very long. If we leave an orange in the fruit basket for too long, mold begins to appear.

The fruit found through abiding in Christ never decays.
John 15:7
"If ye abide in me, and my words abide in you, ye shall ask what ye will, and it shall be done unto you."

This fruit is imperishable simply because it does not originate with us. We have no part in this fruit other than our obedience to do whatever He tells us.

Fruit that remains abideth forever.
John 15:4
"Abide in me, and I in you. As the branch cannot bear fruit of itself, except it abide in the vine; no more can ye, except ye abide in me."

Fruit that remains is everlasting.
John 6:27
"Labour not for the meat which perisheth, but for that meat which endureth unto everlasting life, which the Son of man shall give unto you: for him hath God the Father sealed."

Fruit that remains will not return void.
Isaiah 55:11
"So shall my word be that goeth forth out of my mouth: it shall not return unto me void, but it shall accomplish that which I please, and it shall prosper in the thing whereto I sent it."

He promises that when we give out His Word,
It will accomplish what He pleases.

That is fruit that remains.
We cannot bear fruit without Him.

Bible Reading
Ruth 2 | Romans 3

04.30 | April 30

Take No Thought.

Matthew 6:25
"Therefore I say unto you, Take no thought for your life, what ye shall eat, or what ye shall drink; nor yet for your body, what ye shall put on. Is not the life more than meat, and the body than raiment?"

Anxiety has become a common thing today.
Fear of the unknown or what could happen abounds.
This is not the way that God wants us to live.
Jesus Himself addressed the anxiety of His disciples.

Matthew 6:31-32
"Therefore take no thought, saying, What shall we eat? or, What shall we drink? or, Wherewithal shall we be clothed? (For after all these things do the Gentiles seek:) for your heavenly Father knoweth that ye have need of all these things."

There is no reason to be nervous today.
The Lord has everything under control.

Matthew 6:33
"But seek ye first the kingdom of God, and his righteousness; and all these things shall be added unto you."

**Our responsibility is to seek Him first,
then He will give us what we need.**

Matthew 6:34
"Take therefore no thought for the morrow: for the morrow shall take thought for the things of itself. Sufficient unto the day is the evil thereof."

There is no need to fear tomorrow, He already knows.
Nothing can affect God's children except that which He allows.
He filters every single thing according to His will for our lives.

Why should we worry then?
Paul admonished the church of Philippi of what they should worry about.

Philippians 4:6
"Be careful for nothing; but in every thing by prayer and supplication with thanksgiving let your requests be made known unto God."

Bible Reading
Ruth 3 | Romans 4

May 1 | 05.01

Matthew 6:30
"Wherefore, if God so clothe the grass of the field, which to day is, and to morrow is cast into the oven, shall he not much more clothe you, O ye of little faith?"

Notice the last two words…*"little faith"*. Only five times do we find these two words together within the pages of Scripture, and each time they are written in red…spoken by the Lord Jesus Christ.
Matthew 6:30; 8:26; 14:31; 16:8 & Luke 12:28

When we use the word little, we typically refer to the volume or mass of an object; but Jesus was not referring to the size of their faith.

Each time He speaks the words in reference to one subject…doubt. Two times He is on a mountain speaking to the multitudes. Two times He is in a ship on the stormy sea. One time He rebuked the disciples for neglecting to remember what He had done for them in the past. The miracles that they not only witnessed, but He wrought through their hands.

We can find ourselves doubting when we are on a spiritual mountain, in the middle of a storm, or simply when we forget all that He has done for us.

It was not about the size of faith, but rather their lack of faith.
Mark 4:40
"And he said unto them, Why are ye so fearful? how is it that ye have no faith?"

Jesus further proves this later in Matthew when He refers to having faith the size of a grain of mustard seed.
Matthew 17:20
"And Jesus said unto them…If ye have faith as a grain of mustard seed, ye shall say unto this mountain, Remove hence to yonder place; and it shall remove; and nothing shall be impossible unto you."

Have you ever seen a mustard seed?
It is not large in size whatsoever, in fact, it is tiny.

Any amount of faith in Him makes a difference.
Simply because of Who we place of faith in.

He did it before, and He will do it again.
May we have faith that He is always Faithful.

Bible Reading
Ruth 4 | Romans 5

05.02 | May 2

The Possession Of Faith.

Matthew 17:20
"And Jesus said unto them, Because of your unbelief: for verily I say unto you, If ye have faith as a grain of mustard seed, ye shall say unto this mountain, Remove hence to yonder place; and it shall remove; and nothing shall be impossible unto you."

Jesus chose to use the mustard seed, likely the smallest seed known to the Jews, as an illustration that even the smallest amount of faith in Him can make a difference.

"If ye have faith…"
Mustard seed faith is simply the possession of faith.

Mark 4:31-32
"It is like a grain of mustard seed, which, when it is sown in the earth, is less than all the seeds that be in the earth: But when it is sown, it groweth up, and becometh greater than all herbs, and shooteth out great branches; so that the fowls of the air may lodge under the shadow of it."

Seeds are meant to be planted.
We must sow our faith in order to reap what only He can provide.

Faith is simply our belief that He is Able even when we cannot see.

Hebrews 11:1
"Now faith is the substance of things hoped for, the evidence of things not seen."

The entire chapter of Hebrews 11 shows us that all things are possible through and by faith. If we have faith, we can see and experience the impossible.

Matthew 21:21
"Jesus answered and said unto them, Verily I say unto you, If ye have faith, and doubt not, ye shall not only do this which is done to the fig tree, but also if ye shall say unto this mountain, Be thou removed, and be thou cast into the sea; it shall be done."

We either have faith or we do not.
Scripture tells us over and over the difference faith makes.
He simply wants us to ask and believe.

Matthew 21:22
"And all things, whatsoever ye shall ask in prayer, believing, ye shall receive."

Bible Reading
1 Samuel 1-2 | Romans 6

May 3 | 05.03

The Practice Of Faith.

Mark 11:22
"And Jesus answering saith unto them, Have faith in God."

Before every season of Major League Baseball, all 30 teams head south to Spring Training for a few months. They have daily workouts with their coaches and teammates for a few weeks, and then play several unofficial games with opposing teams in order to get themselves ready for when it really counts. They practice before the game.

As Christians, it is vital that we practice our faith.
The practice of faith comes in two forms:
1. The actual application or use of faith.
2. The repetition of exercising faith regularly.

We must not only possess faith; we must practice it.
The practice of faith must always be directed to the Person of our faith.

Psalm 62:8
"Trust in him at all times; ye people, pour out your heart before him: God is a refuge for us. Selah."

Faith is trusting Him.
Faith is believing in Him.

We cannot please Him if we do not have faith.

Hebrews 11:6
"But without faith it is impossible to please him: for he that cometh to God must believe that he is, and that he is a rewarder of them that diligently seek him."

Our desire should be to please Him.
Faith not only pleases Him, it brings glory and honor to Him.
Practice your faith in Him today, and every day.

Bible Reading
1 Samuel 3-4 | Romans 7

05.04 | May 4

The Priority Of Faith

Matthew 6:33
"But seek ye first the kingdom of God, and his righteousness; and all these things shall be added unto you."

The entire chapter of Matthew 6 is the middle of what is commonly referred to as the Sermon on the Mount which Jesus preached unto the multitudes.

Many well-known verses come from the chapters which Jesus spoke upon the mountain that day. If you visit Israel, the place where this likely took place is near the Sea of Galilee and it is easy to imagine how the voice of Jesus sounded through the landscape. Did He need a mountain to make His voice heard? No, but He chose utilize His own creation that day to make His human voice louder for all to hear.

What does it mean to seek the kingdom of God?
The context of this passage is Jesus teaching His followers to not take any thought for their need of food, drink, or clothing. He also told them why they should not worry about those things.

Matthew 6:32
"(For after all these things do the Gentiles seek:) for your heavenly Father knoweth that ye have need of all these things."

The next verse He says what to do instead.
"But seek ye first the kingdom of God, and his righteousness"

He simply wanted them to have faith that He would provide.
Trusting in Him should not be the second, or third thing we do.
We are to first seek Him by faith.

Possessing and practicing faith is most effective when it is prioritized. Why do we often complicate things by trying everything else before we decide to trust Him? How much better would our lives be if we simply lived by faith? Therein lies the problem to the issues we face. To seek Him first is to have faith in Him before we worry about anything. Instead of prioritizing everything else, make Him your priority today. What a difference we would see in our day-to-day lives if only He was first.

Jesus told the multitudes what would happen
if they chose to seek Him first…
"…and all these things shall be added unto you."
Make faith in Him your priority today.

Bible Reading
1 Samuel 5-6 | Romans 8

May 5 | 05.05

Intercessory Faith.

Mark 2:5
*"When Jesus saw their faith, he said unto the sick of the palsy,
Son, thy sins be forgiven thee."*

There was once a day that when people heard Jesus was preaching, they would flood the house to hear the Truth. Multitudes would line the street in front of the door so much so that no one else could get in. This particular day, Jesus Himself was preaching the Word. Four men carried their friend sick of the palsy upon his bed. This man could not walk to Jesus on his own. They could not carry him through the door because of the crowd; yet, they refused to give up. **They were determined to get him to Jesus.**

Mark 2:4
*"And when they could not come nigh unto him for the press,
they uncovered the roof where he was: and when they had broken it up,
they let down the bed wherein the sick of the palsy lay."*

Luke's account of this scene tells us why they went to such extremes to help their friend. They knew there was only One Who could intervene. Luke 5:19

The sick man may have had faith that Jesus could heal him, but we are told what got the Lord's attention that day.

"When Jesus saw their faith…"
It was the faith of his friends that Jesus saw.
They were not focused on their own needs that day. Instead, they bound together to make a difference in their friend's life. He needed a miracle, and they knew that only Jesus could perform it.

Do we have faith to bring someone else to Jesus? Enough faith to resort to desperate methods in order to get them the help they need? Most likely their situation does not require you to scale the walls of a house, rip off the roof, and lower them down through the ceiling. What a picture of the true faith these men had in Who Jesus is and what He could do. Could the same be said of us? Are we willing to do whatever it takes, no matter how strange it may seem, for Jesus to see our faith that He can intervene in someone else's life?

Intercessory prayer can make a difference. But it is the faith behind those prayers for others that truly makes the difference. Intercede on someone's behalf asking God to do what only He can in their life. Prayer changes things. Faith makes the impossible possible. How's your intercessory faith?

Bible Reading
1 Samuel 7-8 | Romans 9

05.06 | May 6

Expecting Faith.

Matthew 9:28
"And when he was come into the house, the blind men came to him: and Jesus saith unto them, Believe ye that I am able to do this? They said unto him, Yea, Lord."

Jesus had just left Jarius' house where He healed his daughter. His fame was spreading abroad across the land. People were talking about Who Jesus is, and what miracles He was performing. Isn't it interesting that the next people mentioned were two blind men? They obviously had never seen Jesus, but they must have heard about Him. Much like us today.

Matthew 9:27
"And when Jesus departed thence, two blind men followed him, crying, and saying, Thou Son of David, have mercy on us."

They sought His help and healing,
without ever laying eyes upon Him.
That is faith.

The question Jesus asked them, is often the same question that He asks of us. *"Believe ye that I am able to do this?"*
Our belief in Him determines the state of our faith.

Imagine the two blind men speaking in unison, *"Yea, Lord."*
Matthew 9:29
"Then touched he their eyes, saying, According to your faith be it unto you."

Their faith became sight…literally.
What is your expectation of Him today?
He will meet you there.
"According to your faith be it unto you."

Imagine if the two blind men had answered,
"Maybe, Lord." Or, *"No, Lord."*
They would have remained blind.
If we believe He is Able to provide what we need, He will.
If doubt exists, we are likely to miss out.
Expecting faith waits with anticipation of what He has planned.
What are you expecting Him to do today?
"According to your faith be it unto you."
God will meet you at your expectation of Him.
Bible Reading
1 Samuel 9-10 | Romans 10

Finding Faith.

Matthew 10:39
*"He that findeth his life shall lose it:
and he that loseth his life for my sake shall find it."*

Losing something rarely means finding it. Finding something rarely means losing it. Yet, this is exactly how Jesus compares our lives in light of the temporal and the eternal.

If we dare to live for ourselves, we are sure to lose it all someday.
Matthew 6:19
"Lay not up for yourselves treasures upon earth, where moth and rust doth corrupt, and where thieves break through and steal:"

**If we are willing to surrender our lives for His sake,
we will find rewards that will last for eternity.**
Matthew 6:20-21
"But lay up for yourselves treasures in heaven, where neither moth nor rust doth corrupt, and where thieves do not break through nor steal: For where your treasure is, there will your heart be also."

The Lord Jesus reiterated this truth in Matthew, Mark, Luke and John. In Mark, He expounds on further reasoning to lose our lives…the Gospel.
Mark 8:35-36
"For whosoever will save his life shall lose it; but whosoever shall lose his life for my sake and the gospel's, the same shall save it. For what shall it profit a man, if he shall gain the whole world, and lose his own soul?"

Even if we gain the whole world here, is it worth it?
No amount of riches, fame, or glory can compare to one day with Him.

Laying even one reward at His feet will surpass
any joy that the things of this world may bring us.

Finding faith is our willingness to lose anything or anyone for Him.
Philippians 3:7
*"But what things were gain to me,
those I counted loss for Christ."*

Find your faith today.

Bible Reading
1 Samuel 11-12 | Romans 11

05.08 | May 8

Stretching Faith.

Matthew 12:13
"Then saith he to the man, Stretch forth thine hand. And he stretched it forth; and it was restored whole, like as the other."

This man's right hand was withered. His hand was dry, and deprived of what it needed to function. He did not even ask for Jesus to help him. **But Jesus saw His need.**

The Pharisees watched carefully to see if Jesus would heal the man on the Sabbath, that they might accuse Him for being unlawful. They had an agenda.

Mark 3:4
"And he saith unto them, Is it lawful to do good on the sabbath days, or to do evil? to save life, or to kill? But they held their peace."

Luke 6:10
"And looking round about upon them all, he said unto the man, Stretch forth thy hand. And he did so: and his hand was restored whole as the other."

The man obeyed what Jesus told him to do, in faith that something would happen. He received the healing he needed, and the Pharisees that watched missed their opportunity to believe.

Sometimes when the Lord works a miracle in our lives, those who observe it will choose jealousy over joy. May this never stop us from stretching out our hands in faith that He has a greater purpose for our lives. Throughout the Scriptures, the Lord had people stretch out their hands before He would do something.

Exodus 14:16
"But lift thou up thy rod, and stretch out thine hand over the sea, and divide it: and the children of Israel shall go on dry ground through the midst of the sea."

Moses was told to lift up his rod and stretch out his hand. When he did this in faith, the Lord made a way where there was no way before.

Whatever your need… Whatever your problem…
Stretch out your hand toward Him today.
Psalm 143:6
"I stretch forth my hands unto thee: my soul thirsteth after thee, as a thirsty land. Selah."

Bible Reading
1 Samuel 13-14 | Romans 12

May 9 | 05.09

Searching Faith.

John 5:39
"Search the scriptures; for in them ye think ye have eternal life: and they are they which testify of me."

Have you ever played a word search? A box of letters evenly spaced, some arranging words that are found in a legend. The object of the game is to find the words listed in the legend within the box of letters. Some circle the words, some highlight. Each word that is found is crossed off the list with a sense of accomplishment. Some frantically try to find the words as fast as they can. Some sit peacefully, peering over each letter to see if it corresponds with the one next to it. Regardless of the method used, the goal is the same… to find a word.

How similar this concept is in comparison to how we should approach the Scriptures. The difference being, of course, that when we read our Bible, we are not to search for just any word…but the Word.

John 1:1,14
"In the beginning was the Word, and the Word was with God, and the Word was God… And the Word was made flesh, and dwelt among us, (and we beheld his glory, the glory as of the only begotten of the Father,) full of grace and truth."

When you read the Bible do you look for Jesus?
He is found on every page.
Sometimes hidden within the wording, but He is there.
He said so Himself.

John 5:39
"Search the scriptures; for in them ye think ye have eternal life: and they are they which testify of me."

If we just casually read to mark a check box on our to-do list, we are sure to miss Him. Yet, anytime we search for Him by faith, we are sure to find Him.

Jeremiah 29:13
"And ye shall seek me, and find me, when ye shall search for me with all your heart."

Search for Him today, and every day.

Bible Reading
1 Samuel 15-16 | Romans 13

05.10 | May 10

Luke 7:50
"And he said to the woman, Thy faith hath saved thee; go in peace."

The Pharisees had seen Jesus heal people of many different types of physical infirmities. Then one day, a woman in the city heard that Jesus was in Simon's house. She had a reputation of being a sinner.

When she knew that Jesus was eating at the Pharisee's house, she knew this was her chance to meet Him. She brought with her an alabaster box of ointment.

Luke 7:37
"And, behold, a woman in the city, which was a sinner, when she knew that Jesus sat at meat in the Pharisee's house, brought an alabaster box of ointment,"

Instead of just giving Jesus the gift she brought, she stood behind Him weeping. Then she began to wash His feet with her tears and wipe them dry with her hair. Before she put the ointment on, she kissed His feet in adoration of Who He was.

**This woman knew her condition,
and she knew that Jesus was the Only Answer.**

Luke 7:48
"And he said unto her, Thy sins are forgiven."

There is no record of her saying a word until after Jesus forgave her. No words were needed.

Her faith in Him was all that mattered.
She wept over Who she knew He is, and her sorrow for her sin.
Her tears and service toward Him showed her sincerity.

Saving faith in Jesus resulted in her forgiveness and salvation.
The same can happen to anyone who chooses to believe on Him today.

Bible Reading
1 Samuel 17-18 | Romans 14

May 11 | 05.11

Ask The Question.

Acts 9:6
"And he trembling and astonished said, Lord, what wilt thou have me to do? And the Lord said unto him, Arise, and go into the city, and it shall be told thee what thou must do."

Saul of Tarsus also had a reputation. He was known for persecuting the disciples by breathing out threatenings and slaughter against them. When he came near Damascus, there was suddenly a light from heaven shining round about him. Jesus Christ spoke to Him from this Great Light.

Acts 9:4
"And he fell to the earth, and heard a voice saying unto him, Saul, Saul, why persecutest thou me?"

Can you imagine such a great Light suddenly appearing before you? If you have ever met Jesus by faith, the Light of the Gospel shined in your heart as you trusted in Him.

Saul acknowledged Who He is even in his first question.

Acts 9:5
"And he said, Who art thou, Lord? And the Lord said, I am Jesus whom thou persecutest: it is hard for thee to kick against the pricks."

His next response to Jesus is a question that we should all ask.
"Lord, what wilt thou have me to do?"

After Saul encountered Jesus, he immediately asked Him what he was to do. If only we all had the willingness to ask the same question. The Lord did not leave Saul to figure it out for himself. He immediately gave him instructions that Saul was to carry out in faith that Jesus knew what was best.

**He provides us with our instructions,
but often we are too fearful to even ask the question.**
Fear of what He may want us to do.
Fear of what people will say or think.
Fear of…[fill in the blank].

The Lord is actually the One Who makes us willing to serve Him,
yet He also gives us the choice of doing so.
Are you willing today?
Set aside the fear of the unknown. Instead, follow the same instructions.
"Arise, and go into the city, and it shall be told thee what thou must do."

Bible Reading
1 Samuel 19-20 | Romans 15

05.12 | May 12

The Sweetness Of Friendship.

Proverbs 27:9
*"Ointment and perfume rejoice the heart:
so doth the sweetness of a man's friend by hearty counsel."*

A sweet fragrance brings delight to a weary heart. Likewise, a friend can bring sweetness to our lives unlike any thing we have in ourselves alone.

Rejoicing in friendship.
David & Jonathan
1 Samuel 23:16-18

"And Jonathan Saul's son arose, and went to David into the wood, and strengthened his hand in God. And he said unto him, Fear not: for the hand of Saul my father shall not find thee; and thou shalt be king over Israel, and I shall be next unto thee; and that also Saul my father knoweth. And they two made a covenant before the LORD: and David abode in the wood, and Jonathan went to his house."

We need friends who will strengthen us when we are weak, and rejoice with us over what God is doing in our lives. There is no room for jealousy within true friendship. We are to bear one another's burdens as well as celebrate the work of the Lord in us and through us.

Rejoicing in friendly counsel.
David & Nathan
2 Samuel 12:7

"And Nathan said to David, Thou art the man. Thus saith the LORD God of Israel, I anointed thee king over Israel, and I delivered thee out of the hand of Saul;"

We need friends who will counsel us according to the Word of God. Whether we need direction or correction, any advice or rebuke given to us by a friend must be founded upon Biblical principles. A friend who expresses concern for our situation or behavior out of love, should not be turned away. Their compassionate guidance can make a difference in our lives if we will take heed to their friendly counsel.

Who is bringing a sweet aroma to your life today?
Thank the Lord for the friends you have,
and ask Him to help you be the best friend you can be to them.

Bible Reading
1 Samuel 21 | Romans 16

May 13 | 05.13

A Testimony Of Faith.

Matthew 14:36
"And besought him that they might only touch the hem of his garment: and as many as touched were made perfectly whole."

Jesus and the disciples had just stepped off the ship and onto the land of Gennesaret. This was the same ship in which Peter had come down out of when he momentarily walked on the water. When the men of Gennesaret knew that Jesus was in town, they sent word into all the country and brought unto Him all that were diseased and in need of healing.

"And besought him that they might only…"
They had faith that if they were only able to do one thing, they could be healed. All they desired to do was touch the hem of His garment.

Where did they get such an idea?
Matthew 9:20-21
"And, behold, a woman, which was diseased with an issue of blood twelve years, came behind him, and touched the hem of his garment: For she said within herself, If I may but touch his garment, I shall be whole."

The testimony of the Woman With An Issue Of Blood
had spread into their land.
She had came in the press behind Him,
desperately seeking just a touch of the hem of His garment.

Matthew 9:22
"But Jesus turned him about, and when he saw her, he said, Daughter, be of good comfort; thy faith hath made thee whole. And the woman was made whole from that hour."

Her faith in Jesus had an effect on many others.
We do not know how many were healed that day in Gennesaret, but the Scripture says many were. She had tried everything else and spent all she had in trying to find a cure. What if she had doubted that He could heal her twelve-year infirmity?

She brought people to Jesus that she likely had never met.
Her testimony gave them the faith to believe that if He could heal her, He could heal them too.

What effect does your testimony have on the faith of others?

Bible Reading
1 Samuel 22 | 1 Corinthians 1 | 141

05.14 | May 14

Silenced By Fear.

John 7:11
"Then the Jews sought him at the feast, and said, Where is he?"

In the chaos of our world today, many seem to be asking the same question. Where is Jesus? The people who were looking for Him were not His disciples. Yet, the disciples neglected to share the Answer to the question. Perhaps they did not know the Answer.

The people of the Jews were murmuring amongst themselves concerning Him. Some said He was a good man. Others disagreed.

The saddest part was that His disciples stayed silent.

John 7:13
"Howbeit no man spake openly of him for fear of the Jews."
**Their silence was driven by fear
of what other people would think of them.**

How similar to our circumstances today!
People are searching for Jesus, yet they do not know where to find Him.

Perhaps because we, His disciples, have stayed silent for so long.
We are often silent out of fear of what others will think of us.

Somehow it has become more important what others think about us, instead of what they think of Him.

The circumstances are still the same today
as they were when the disciples went up to the feast.
They were unaware that Jesus was there them.

John 7:10
"But when his brethren were gone up, then went he also up unto the feast, not openly, but as it were in secret."

He was watching to see what they would say, how they would answer the question of the Jews that sought Him, *"Where is he?"*

He is watching to see how we will handle the same question.
Will we stay silent out of fear…or will we choose to proclaim the Answer?

Refuse to be silenced by fear today.

Bible Reading
1 Samuel 23 | 1 Corinthians 2

May 15 | 05.15

2 Kings 4:8
"And it fell on a day, that Elisha passed to Shunem, where was a great woman; and she constrained him to eat bread. And so it was, that as oft as he passed by, he turned in thither to eat bread."

A happenstance is known to be a circumstance that happens by chance. We see what some may call a Biblical "happenstance" in a town called Shunem, where a great woman constrained Elisha to eat bread. She faithfully fed him each time he passed by. Three times within all the pages of Scripture is this phrase *"it fell on a day"* found, and all within the same chapter.

2 Kings 4:8 - Was it a happenstance that Elisha passed through Shunem that first time? No, the Lord ordered his steps to where this great woman was so that he could be fed.

2 Kings 4:11 - Was it a happenstance that this great woman and her husband felt the need to provide Elisha a place to stay when he came? No, the Lord burdened their hearts and used them to provide his need of shelter and rest. Elisha desired to do something for this great woman for the kindness she had shown to him. His servant, Gehazi, realized that she had no child, and her husband was old. Elisha then prophesied that in a certain season, according to the time of life, she would embrace a son. Exactly what he said happened.

2 Kings 4:18 - The child had a health issue. His father arranged for the son to be sent to his mother. She knew who to ask for help. The rest of chapter 4 tells how the Lord used Elisha to heal her son, all because the woman had faith that He could. Was it a happenstance that the child went out to his father in the field, just when he needed help? No, the Lord placed him just where he needed to be in order for him to receive the help he needed.

Nothing we do is by happenstance. While it may be a fun word to say, when you think about it, there is no such thing. Our lives are a testimony of how God cares for His children. If we look back, we can trace His hand through every storm, mountain top, and valley. This should encourage us to look ahead in faith of what He will do, instead of fearful of what could possibly happen. **God directs all things, and there are no coincidences with Him.** Look for His hand of provision and direction in every moment.

The more you look for Him, the more you will find Him.

Bible Reading
1 Samuel 24-25 | 1 Corinthians 3

05.16 | May 16

Psalm 84:10
*"For a day in thy courts is better than a thousand.
I had rather be a doorkeeper in the house of my God,
than to dwell in the tents of wickedness."*

If the Spring of 2020 taught us anything, may it be that we should never lose our longing to be in the House of the Lord.

Psalm 84:2
*"My soul longeth, yea, even fainteth for the courts of the LORD:
my heart and my flesh crieth out for the living God."*

Psalm 27:4
*"One thing have I desired of the LORD, that will I seek after;
that I may dwell in the house of the LORD all the days of my life,
to behold the beauty of the LORD, and to enquire in his temple."*

**As children of God, even our worst days are better
than the best days of those who do not know Him.**

Once we have trusted Christ by grace through faith in His finished work on Calvary, we have no reason to fear the future. Instead, we can praise Him today and for all eternity around His throne in Heaven.

For those who die without knowing Him, they will spend eternity in the Lake of Fire separated from God forever.

The Psalmist wrote that he would *"rather be a doorkeeper in the house of my God, than to dwell in the tents of wickedness."* He understood how much better it is to be a servant for Him than to be served like a king. He simply wanted to be near the presence of God.

**Once we have tasted the goodness of the Lord,
how can we desire anything else?**

Psalm 34:8
*"O taste and see that the LORD is good:
blessed is the man that trusteth in him."*

A day with Him is simply better than a thousand without Him.

Bible Reading
1 Samuel 26-27 | 1 Corinthians 4

May 17 | 05.17

When I Heard These Words.

Nehemiah 1:4
"And it came to pass, when I heard these words, that I sat down and wept, and mourned certain days, and fasted, and prayed before the God of heaven,"

It has often been said that one phone call can change your life. Sometimes its unsettling news from a doctor or being made aware that someone you love has passed away. Maybe its news of a job promotion or of some unexpected blessing that God provided just when you needed it.

In Nehemiah's case, the news he heard was devastating. He immediately sat down and wept as a result and ended up mourning for days. His sorrow caused him to fast and pray unto the God of Heaven.

Have you ever reacted this way to news you received?
The next seven verses contain Nehemiah's prayer unto the Lord.

Nehemiah 1:11
"O Lord, I beseech thee, let now thine ear be attentive to the prayer of thy servant, and to the prayer of thy servants, who desire to fear thy name: and prosper, I pray thee, thy servant this day, and grant him mercy in the sight of this man. For I was the king's cupbearer."

What if we went to the Lord in prayer about our current situation as Nehemiah did about his?

He pleaded for God to intervene, not just for him, but for the children of Israel. He admitted his sin before Him. He acknowledged what the Lord had said before, then he begged for the Lord to grant His people mercy.

If we ever needed to pray this way before, we need it today.
Our hearts are often consumed with dread, doubt and despair as we look around at our surroundings.

The same God that Nehemiah served, is the One we serve and can go to today in prayer. He has not changed. He is still willing to have mercy upon His people, if only we will ask.

"…when I heard these words…"

What is your reaction today?
May the Word of God prick our hearts today for our need of Him.

Bible Reading
1 Samuel 28-29 | 1 Corinthians 5

05.18 | May 18

So I Prayed.

Nehemiah 2:4
*"Then the king said unto me, For what dost thou make request?
So I prayed to the God of heaven."*

The king noticed there was a change in Nehemiah's countenance, and asked why. His feelings were written all over his face. Can you relate?

Nehemiah 2:3
"And said unto the king, Let the king live for ever: why should not my countenance be sad, when the city, the place of my fathers' sepulchres, lieth waste, and the gates thereof are consumed with fire?"

His sorrow was rooted in despair that his home place was destroyed. The king asked what he needed.

Nehemiah's immediate reaction is a reminder that we should all apply to our lives. Instead of ranting or even weeping for help, he once again chose to pray. He was a man of prayer. In a time of sorrow, he prayed. In a time of opportunity, he prayed. The king basically offered to do whatever he needed, and instead of using that to his advantage, he sought the Lord for direction.

Psalm 18:6
*"In my distress I called upon the LORD, and cried unto my God:
he heard my voice out of his temple, and my cry came before him,
even into his ears."*

Nehemiah could have asked the king to send help to his hometown; but instead, the Lord directed Nehemiah to ask if he could go himself to help.

Nehemiah 2:5
*"And I said unto the king, If it please the king, and if thy servant have found favour in thy sight, that thou wouldest send me unto Judah,
unto the city of my fathers' sepulchres, that I may build it."*

He had a desire to serve the Lord by serving people.
When he came to town, he led by example.
"...come, and let us build up the wall of Jerusalem..."
And it all started by him immediately seeking the Lord's direction.

Seek the Lord's direction in prayer today. He may direct you to build up some wall in His kingdom or it may be as simple as building up a friend by encouraging them in their walk with Him.

Bible Reading
1 Samuel 30-31 | 1 Corinthians 6

May 19 | 05.19

Rise Up And Build.

Nehemiah 2:18
"Then I told them of the hand of my God which was good upon me; as also the king's words that he had spoken unto me. And they said, Let us rise up and build. So they strengthened their hands for this good work."

The saying "teamwork makes the dream work" is shown first hand in the Book of Nehemiah. He led the people by example as they worked together to rebuild the walls of Jerusalem. Nehemiah told them of how God had directed him, and how he believed that the hand of God was upon him.

"Let us rise up and build."
Some chose to support him and work together with him toward the purpose. These faithful supporters even chose to strengthen their hands for the work. This had to have encouraged Nehemiah as he followed the Lord. Then there were others that reacted differently...

Nehemiah 2:19
"But when Sanballat the Horonite, and Tobiah the servant, the Ammonite, and Geshem the Arabian, heard it, they laughed us to scorn, and despised us, and said, What is this thing that ye do? will ye rebel against the king?"

Some laughed, scorned and even despised those who were purposing themselves to do what the Lord had for them.

When we seek the Lord's direction, follow Him by faith, and purpose within ourselves to carry out whatever task He has given, we too will see people react in different ways. **Faith to follow the Lord often results in Him filtering out some things and people.** We can choose to ignore the Lord working things out for our good and His glory, or we can trust that He knows best.

Nehemiah 2:20
"Then answered I them, and said unto them, The God of heaven, he will prosper us; therefore we his servants will arise and build: but ye have no portion, nor right, nor memorial, in Jerusalem."

Nehemiah's response to his critics should encourage us that the work must continue even when we are facing opposition. Oftentimes, opposition is just a sign that God is up to something.

Regardless of where or who your opposition comes from, choose to continue the work that God has given you to do. He will make a way for His work to prosper. **Trust Him today, and allow Him to do a work in and through you.**

Bible Reading
2 Samuel 1-2 | 1 Corinthians 7

05.20 | May 20

Nevertheless.

Nehemiah 4:9
"Nevertheless we made our prayer unto our God, and set a watch against them day and night, because of them."

The work had begun despite the opposition. The wall was being built in sections, but all by the same team. The more they worked, the more opposition they faced. What may have been a justified reason to quit became the fuel to press on.

Nehemiah 4:6
"So built we the wall; and all the wall was joined together unto the half thereof: for the people had a mind to work."

Nehemiah faithfully took their situation to the Lord in prayer. All the while, Sanballat and his conspirators came together to fight against and hinder the work that was being done in Jerusalem. Regardless of the persecution he faced, Nehemiah was determined to pray for God to intervene. Rather than attempt to handle the adversaries, he chose to allow God to fight for them. Nehemiah 4:15

There were builders and there were burden bearers. Each of them had a part in what God was doing through them. They had one hand in the work and held a weapon with the other hand. What a picture of how we should work today. **Take the Sword in your hand and work with the other.**

Hebrews 4:12
"For the word of God is quick, and powerful, and sharper than any twoedged sword, piercing even to the dividing asunder of soul and spirit, and of the joints and marrow, and is a discerner of the thoughts and intents of the heart."

The Word of God is both our Weapon and our Comfort in the great work that He has for us to do.
Nehemiah 4:19-21
"...The work is great and large, and we are separated upon the wall, one far from another. In what place therefore ye hear the sound of the trumpet, resort ye thither unto us: our God shall fight for us. So we laboured in the work..."

Allow His Word to strengthen your hands and encourage you to continue on in the work, regardless of the opposition.
Our God fights for us just the same today. *"Nevertheless..."*

Bible Reading
2 Samuel 3-4 | 1 Corinthians 8

May 21 | 05.21

A Great Work.

Nehemiah 6:3
"And I sent messengers unto them, saying, I am doing a great work, so that I cannot come down: why should the work cease, whilst I leave it, and come down to you?"

Making the work that God has given you to do a priority in your life does not mean you are prideful. Some have taken Nehemiah's statement, *"I am doing a great work"*, to mean that he was filled with pride. Quite the contrary. He simply spoke the truth. The work he was involved in was a God-given task, and he took that seriously.

Ecclesiastes 9:10
"Whatsoever thy hand findeth to do, do it with thy might; for there is no work, nor device, nor knowledge, nor wisdom, in the grave, whither thou goest."

He was filled with sincerity. He was also stedfast in his determination to keep his focus on the purpose at hand, instead of any distraction that was thrown at him.

Nehemiah 6:9
"For they all made us afraid, saying, Their hands shall be weakened from the work, that it be not done. Now therefore, O God, strengthen my hands."

Paul encouraged labourers to follow the same principles.

1 Corinthians 15:58
"Therefore, my beloved brethren, be ye stedfast, unmoveable, always abounding in the work of the Lord, forasmuch as ye know that your labour is not in vain in the Lord."

Our enemy will try to distract us from the great work the Lord has given us to do in any way he can. *"…why should the work cease…?"*

Disregard any excuse the devil tries to tempt you with in order to distract you from your God-given purpose…to give Him glory.

Nehemiah 6:15-16
"So the wall was finished… And it came to pass, that when all our enemies heard thereof, and all the heathen that were about us saw these things, they were much cast down in their own eyes: for they perceived that this work was wrought of our God."

Everything we do should point others to Him.

Bible Reading
2 Samuel 5-6 | 1 Corinthians 9

05.22 | May 22

Attentive Unto The Book.

Nehemiah 8:3
"And he read therein before the street that was before the water gate from the morning until midday, before the men and the women, and those that could understand; and the ears of all the people were attentive unto the book of the law."

The street was flooded with people as far at the eye could see. They all came with one purpose, all with the same request. The people requested that the Book of the Law of Moses be brought by Ezra so he could read to them.

Nehemiah 8:5-6
"And Ezra opened the book in the sight of all the people; (for he was above all the people;) and when he opened it, all the people stood up: And Ezra blessed the LORD, the great God. And all the people answered, Amen, Amen, with lifting up their hands: and they bowed their heads, and worshipped the LORD with their faces to the ground."

What attention and reverence they had for the Book! Though the Words of the Law made them mourn and weep, Ezra encouraged them to not allow their sorrow to overcome their joy.

Nehemiah 8:10
"Then he said unto them, Go your way, eat the fat, and drink the sweet, and send portions unto them for whom nothing is prepared: for this day is holy unto our Lord: neither be ye sorry; for the joy of the LORD is your strength."

Our joy and strength are dependent upon our attention to the Word of the Lord. Consider today the people all across the world that do not have a copy of the Scriptures. While most of us have multiple full copies sitting on shelves within our homes, there are people who would give anything they have to even have a partial.

The children of Israel flooded the street that day thirsty to hear the Word, and yet sometimes we regulate the Bible to just another app on our smart phones. **May we renew our attentiveness to the Book each and every day.**

Romans 12:2
"And be not conformed to this world: but be ye transformed by the renewing of your mind, that ye may prove what is that good, and acceptable, and perfect, will of God."

Bible Reading
2 Samuel 7-8 | 1 Corinthians 10

May 23 | 05.23

Because Of All Of This.

Nehemiah 9:38
"And because of all this we make a sure covenant, and write it; and our princes, Levites, and priests, seal unto it."

Because…a prelude of an explanation of the reason for something. Sometimes we have to explain why we choose to do or not to do a particular thing. Sometimes we are asked to give a reason.

1 Peter 3:15
"But sanctify the Lord God in your hearts: and be ready always to give an answer to every man that asketh you a reason of the hope that is in you with meekness and fear:"

In Nehemiah 9, we find the children of Israel assembled and fasting. They had separated themselves for specific purposes…to confess their sins, to read from the Book of the Law of the LORD, and ultimately to worship Him. The Levites stood upon the stairs and began to cry out to the LORD their God with a loud voice.

Nehemiah 9:6
"Thou, even thou, art LORD alone; thou hast made heaven, the heaven of heavens, with all their host, the earth, and all things that are therein, the seas, and all that is therein, and thou preservest them all; and the host of heaven worshippeth thee."

Throughout the rest of the chapter, we find them dwelling on what they knew that the Lord had done amongst them. *"And because of all this…"*

Have you ever looked back upon your life and purposefully remembered all that the Lord has done for you? No doubt He has been just as faithful, merciful, and patient with us as He was with the children of Israel.

Perhaps today you too can choose to thank Him for all that He has done. *"And because of all this…"*

The people made a covenant that day, the princes, Levites, and priests sealed it. They purposed both individually within themselves, and as a whole people. *"…to walk in God's law, which was given by Moses the servant of God, and to observe and do all the commandments of the LORD our Lord, and his judgments and his statutes;"* Nehemiah 10:29

When you think about all the Lord has done for you, does it not make you want to also renew your covenant to walk with Him?
"And because of all this…"

Bible Reading
2 Samuel 9-10 | 1 Corinthians 11

05.24 | May 24

Forsake Not The House Of God.

Nehemiah 10:39
"For the children of Israel and the children of Levi shall bring the offering of the corn, of the new wine, and the oil, unto the chambers, where are the vessels of the sanctuary, and the priests that minister, and the porters, and the singers: and we will not forsake the house of our God."

When the people of Israel renewed their covenant after the walls were rebuilt, they summarized their renewed dedication with nine strong words.
"…we will not forsake the house of our God."

This phrase is directly linked to a familiar verse
found in the New Testament.

Hebrews 10:25
*"Not forsaking the assembling of ourselves together,
as the manner of some is; but exhorting one another:
and so much the more, as ye see the day approaching."*

In the day the writer of Hebrews pinned these Words under the inspiration of the Holy Spirit, there were some whose manner, or habit, it was to forsake the assembly of the church.

If it was happening then, how much more is it happening today?
The Truth of the verse is just as true today as it was then.

Instead of forsaking, we are admonished to exhort one another
while assembling.

The church of the living God is ultimately the people; yet, we are still told to assemble together. Maybe because He knows that sometimes we forget how important it is to do so.

In the times of our lives when we do forsake the house of our God,
is there not a noticeable difference in our day-to-day lives?

Something is missing when we do not assemble together.

Bible Reading
2 Samuel 11-12 | 1 Corinthians 12

So Much The More.

Hebrews 10:25
*"Not forsaking the assembling of ourselves together,
as the manner of some is; but exhorting one another:
and so much the more, as ye see the day approaching."*

If God says something once, it makes it True. The times when He repeats Himself should cause us to look for even more Truth for us to learn. When a phrase is repeated in the Scripture, there is likely a Truth connecting the corresponding verses. *"so much the more"*

In Hebrews, the Scriptures tell us to assemble together even more frequently as we see the day approaching. What day? His Second Coming, and that day is coming soon. Two other times the phrase is mentioned in a similar way, both referring to the Good News being spread that Jesus was healing the infirmities of the people. Mark 7:36 & Luke 5:15

What a picture of how we can share the Good News with others that Jesus still saves! **He is the Free Gift of eternal life to all who come to Him by faith.**

The only other time we see the phrase is found when Jesus heals a blind man near Jericho. This time it is not mentioned in reference to His fame spreading abroad, but rather to the man being healed of his blindness.

Luke 18:39
"And they which went before rebuked him, that he should hold his peace: but he cried so much the more, Thou Son of David, have mercy on me."

This man pleaded and begged Jesus to heal him, and was rebuked by those around him for his faith. But that did not stop or quiet the man. He cried even louder…*"so much the more"*. The blind man immediately received his healing, and chose to follow Jesus, glorifying God.

**We too were once blinded in our sin,
in need of receiving the sight that only salvation brings.**

"so much the more"
Every time the phrase is found
within the pages of Scriptures it points to Jesus.
There is so much more when it comes to Him.

Bible Reading
2 Samuel 13-14 | 1 Corinthians 13

05.26 | May 26

That Which Brings Joy.

1 John 1:1
"That which was from the beginning, which we have heard, which we have seen with our eyes, which we have looked upon, and our hands have handled, of the Word of life;"

He was and is from the beginning.

John 1:1
"In the beginning was the Word, and the Word was with God, and the Word was God."

We have heard Him through ears of faith as we hear the Words of God.

Romans 10:17
"So then faith cometh by hearing, and hearing by the word of God."

We have seen Him through eyes of faith as the Light shines through the pages of the Word of God.

2 Corinthians 4:6
"For God, who commanded the light to shine out of darkness, hath shined in our hearts, to give the light of the knowledge of the glory of God in the face of Jesus Christ."

He is the Word of Life which we are privileged and blessed to be able to hold in our hands.

Philippians 2:16
"Holding forth the word of life; that I may rejoice in the day of Christ, that I have not run in vain, neither laboured in vain."

Because we have heard and seen Him, we must desire to declare Him unto others so that they too can know Him.

1 John 1:3
"That which we have seen and heard declare we unto you, that ye also may have fellowship with us: and truly our fellowship is with the Father, and with his Son Jesus Christ."

What joy there is in knowing Him!
Real joy can radiate from us simply because He lives in us.

1 John 1:4
"And these things write we unto you, that your joy may be full."

Bible Reading
2 Samuel 15-16 | 1 Corinthians 14

May 27 | 05.27

This Then Is The Message.

1 John 1:5
"This then is the message which we have heard of him, and declare unto you, that God is light, and in him is no darkness at all."

The media today seems to have their own news cycle, whether there is truth to it or not. They need ratings to survive, so whatever will get the most attention is the story of the hour. Nearly every story is filled with negativity in an effort to incite fear in the hearts of their viewers.

Fear is a powerful tool.
It brings darkness all around us and within us.

2 Timothy 1:7
"For God hath not given us the spirit of fear; but of power, and of love, and of a sound mind."

God has not given us a spirit of fear, so if we are fearful and afraid it did not come from Him.

Darkness creates more opportunities for the Light to shine brighter. The message we have heard of Him can bring Light to the darkness, because He is the Light. There is no darkness at all in Him.

1 John 1:6-7
"If we say that we have fellowship with him, and walk in darkness, we lie, and do not the truth: But if we walk in the light, as he is in the light, we have fellowship one with another, and the blood of Jesus Christ his Son cleanseth us from all sin."

Does our message bring Light or darkness to those around us?

Are we shining the Light of the glorious Gospel
by sharing it with others?

Or do we choose to hide it?

Declare the message of Hope in the darkness today.
There is hope in Jesus.

Tell someone about Him so that they can see their need for Him.

Bible Reading
2 Samuel 17-18 | 1 Corinthians 15

05.28 | May 28

For The Master's Use.

2 Timothy 2:21
"If a man therefore purge himself from these, he shall be a vessel unto honour, sanctified, and meet for the master's use, and prepared unto every good work."

Have you ever considered what it means to use something?
Use: to take, hold or deploy as a means of accomplishing a purpose or achieving a result; to employ.

When a pencil or pen is used, pressure must be applied.
When a toaster is used, heat is generated.
Think of other objects…what is required for them to work?

We often hear the phrase of someone desiring to be *"used by the Lord"*, perhaps never considering what it truly entails. Many desire for the Lord to use them, yet how many are willing to endure what it takes to be used?

If our faith is to be trusted, it must first be tested.
Oftentimes, the Lord allows pressure to be applied to His servants. Sometimes, our faith must be tried with fire.

1 Peter 1:7
"That the trial of your faith, being much more precious than of gold that perisheth, though it be tried with fire, might be found unto praise and honour and glory at the appearing of Jesus Christ:"

Many wear the symbol of a cross to express their faith, yet how many are willing to die for the cause of Christ? The cross implies death. Jesus died on the Cross of Calvary for our sins, and we must be willing to take up our cross and follow Him by dying to ourselves.

Luke 9:23
"And he said to them all, If any man will come after me, let him deny himself, and take up his cross daily, and follow me."

If we are to be *"meet for the master's use"*, we must be willing to purge out anything that dishonors Him, while sanctifying ourselves unto Him. It is only then that we can be used by Him and *"prepared unto every good work."*

Do you desire to be used by Him?
Prepare today.

Bible Reading
2 Samuel 19-20 | 1 Corinthians 16

May 29 | 05.29

Out Of Them All.

2 Timothy 3:10-11
"But thou hast fully known my doctrine, manner of life, purpose, faith, longsuffering, charity, patience, Persecutions, afflictions, which came unto me at Antioch, at Iconium, at Lystra; what persecutions I endured: but out of them all the Lord delivered me."

Timothy fully understood what Paul had went through. This knowledge could have caused Timothy to desire to stray away from the faith because he had seen what cost was involved.

*"…what persecutions I endured:
but out of them all the Lord delivered me."*

But for every persecution and affliction of Paul that Timothy witnessed, he also got to see the Lord's provision and deliverance.

2 Timothy 3:12
"Yea, and all that will live godly in Christ Jesus shall suffer persecution."

We must expect to be hated and despised, because Jesus was.
Because He faced persecution and afflictions, so must His disciples.

**But with the persecution and affliction,
we can also expect Him to deliver us out of them all.**

Psalm 34:1-4
*"I will bless the LORD at all times:
his praise shall continually be in my mouth.
My soul shall make her boast in the LORD:
the humble shall hear thereof, and be glad.
O magnify the LORD with me,
and let us exalt his name together.
I sought the LORD, and he heard me,
and delivered me from all my fears."*

**Take comfort that He is Faithful to hear us
when we call upon Him.**

If you feel persecuted or afflicted today, seek the Lord.
Deliverance from all your fears is found in Him.

Bible Reading
2 Samuel 21-22 | 2 Corinthians 1

05.30 | May 30

Crumbs.

Matthew 15:27
"And she said, Truth, Lord: yet the dogs eat of the crumbs which fall from their masters' table."

Chocolate chip cookies. Brownies. Homemade banana bread. Hungry yet? These and many other delicious foods often leave crumbs behind when they are eaten. Crumbs are usually residue that is left from something consumed, and are not enough to make an entire meal. In fact, crumbs are usually just discarded as serving no further purpose.

Yet…crumbs were enough for the Syrophenician Woman. She cried unto Jesus to have mercy upon her and heal her daughter; but at first, Jesus answered her not a word. Apparently, she then cried unto His disciples, trying to get their attention, and they desired to send her away. Then she persisted again with Jesus…yet this time, she approached Him differently.

Matthew 15:25
"Then came she and worshipped him, saying, Lord, help me."

She worshipped Him first…then asked for His help.
The Book of Mark tells us that she fell at his feet. This got His attention.

The Syrophenician Woman believed that even crumbs from the table of Jesus could make a difference.
Jesus called her a woman of great faith.

Later in the New Testament,
we find that Jesus calls Himself the Bread of Life.

John 6:35
"And Jesus said unto them, I am the bread of life: he that cometh to me shall never hunger; and he that believeth on me shall never thirst."

Think of that Truth in reference to the testimony of the Syrophenician Woman…in her great faith she was satisfied with just crumbs from Him. **Would you be satisfied with crumbs of Him today?** Yet the Truth is, He does not offer His children crumbs…He offers all of Himself.

Crumbs of Scripture can transform your life by faith today in His Word.
When we look for Crumbs, He gives us the Whole Loaf.

Bible Reading
2 Samuel 23-24 | 2 Corinthians 2

Recalled.

Lamentations 3:21
"This I recall to my mind, therefore have I hope."

What do you make a habit of recalling to your mind? Memories, mistakes, misfortunes… or provision, protection, and peace?

Jeremiah purposefully dwelt on what God had done…and in the context of this chapter within the Book of Lamentations, he spent the previous 20 verses remembering his affliction and the wrath of God upon his life.

Lamentations 3:19-20
"Remembering mine affliction and my misery, the wormwood and the gall. My soul hath them still in remembrance, and is humbled in me."

His life was not a bed of roses, but Jeremiah realized that his weakness only allowed the Lord's strength to shine through the darkness. That was reason enough for him to have hope. Despite his circumstances, some of which he brought upon himself, he understood that God had a purpose.

He knew that God could use what he endured for His glory.
This is similar to Paul's perspective of his thorn in the flesh.

2 Corinthians 12:8-10
"For this thing I besought the Lord thrice, that it might depart from me. And he said unto me, My grace is sufficient for thee: for my strength is made perfect in weakness. Most gladly therefore will I rather glory in my infirmities, that the power of Christ may rest upon me. Therefore I take pleasure in infirmities, in reproaches, in necessities, in persecutions, in distresses for Christ's sake: for when I am weak, then am I strong."

Recall to your mind today what the Lord has done in your life in the past that can give you hope today.

Psalm 119:81
"My soul fainteth for thy salvation: but I hope in thy word."

Remind yourself through the Scriptures, for in Them we can find hope.

Bible Reading
1 Kings 1-2 | 2 Corinthians 3

06.01 | June 1

The Cost Of Silence.

Matthew 21:27
"And they answered Jesus, and said, We cannot tell. And he said unto them, Neither tell I you by what authority I do these things."

Jesus asked them a question. Instead of giving the answer, they chose to reason with themselves as to what would be the best answer.

Matthew 21:25-26
"The baptism of John, whence was it? from heaven, or of men? And they reasoned with themselves, saying, If we shall say, From heaven; he will say unto us, Why did ye not then believe him? But if we shall say, Of men; we fear the people; for all hold John as a prophet."

If they answered one way, they knew He would rebuke them.
If they answered the other way, they feared the people's reaction.

They could have spoken the truth, but they chose differently.

"We cannot tell."
Though they uttered three words, they really said nothing at all.

Their silence caused them to miss out on hearing from Jesus.
"Neither tell I you…"

Consider how applicable this situation is to our lives today.

When we are called to give an answer, do we speak the Truth or reason with ourselves as to what answer would be in our best interest?

The chaotic situations arising in our world today are causing some to give an answer for our faith. The persecutions that we have heard for years would eventually come have begun to arrive.

Will we stay silent?
Will we speak words that really say nothing at all?
Or will we choose to use such a time as this to speak the Truth?

Sometimes, the cost of silence is far too great.

Bible Reading
1 Kings 3-4 | 2 Corinthians 4

Hope In Him.

Lamentations 3:24
"The LORD is my portion, saith my soul; therefore will I hope in him."

The object of our hope determines the result.
If we hope in people, we are sure to be disappointed.
If we hope in an organization, we are likely to be left emptyhanded.

But if we hope in the Lord…
There is no ending to the sentence above.

The result of hoping in Him is endless.

Are you waiting in Him today?
Are you expecting Him to do what only He can?

That is placing our *"hope in him"*.

When we rest and depend on Him, there is no telling what He has in store.
It is those times when we neglect to do so, that we truly miss out on what He could have done.

Psalm 31:24
"Be of good courage, and he shall strengthen your heart, all ye that hope in the LORD."

He is our strength.
He is our stay.
He is where we find encouragement.
He is our comfort.
He is our help.

He is our hope.

Psalm 42:5
*"Why art thou cast down, O my soul?
and why art thou disquieted in me? hope thou in God:
for I shall yet praise him for the help of his countenance."*

**When everything and everyone else fail us,
He is Faithful.**

Bible Reading
1 Kings 5-6 | 2 Corinthians 5

06.03 | June 3

Methods Of Waiting.

Lamentations 3:25-26
*"The LORD is good unto them that wait for him,
to the soul that seeketh him. It is good that a man should both hope
and quietly wait for the salvation of the LORD."*

Waiting is a strength of very few people.
Our humanity often prevents us from being patient.
We want what we want, and we want it now.
Microwaves, drive-thrus, and *"instant"* anything
are blatant reminders of this fact.

"It is good that a man should both hope and quietly wait…"
Notice the adjective used to describe how it is good for us to wait.
Quietly? It almost seems like too much to ask.

Our words tend to be many while we wait.
Somehow, we have been conditioned to believe that if we vocalize our opinion and disdain about how long something takes it will instantly speed up the process. However, this is simply not how the Lord intends for His children to behave.

Psalm 37:7
*"Rest in the LORD, and wait patiently for him:
fret not thyself because of him who prospereth in his way,
because of the man who bringeth wicked devices to pass."*

Patiently and quietly.
If only we would learn to live out these methods of waiting.
Doing so would demonstrate the grace of God to those around us.
Has He not been so gracious to patiently and quietly wait on us?

Isaiah 30:18
*"And therefore will the LORD wait, that he may be gracious unto you,
and therefore will he be exalted, that he may have mercy upon you:
for the LORD is a God of judgment: blessed are all they that wait for him."*

Others see how we handle waiting.
Our testimony is at stake when we refuse to patiently and quietly wait.
When we quietly wait with grace,
we are promised to experience the goodness of the Lord.
It is good to both *"hope and quietly wait"* for Him,
simply because He is Good.

Bible Reading
1 Kings 7-8 | 2 Corinthians 6

June 4 | 06.04

Trust Not Traps.

Proverbs 29:25
*"The fear of man bringeth a snare:
but whoso putteth his trust in the LORD shall be safe."*

Fearfulness of what others will do or think of us is often used as an excuse while we wait. The Lord calls this a snare…a trap or cause of injury.

Traps have bait to lure their prey into destruction.
Mice want the cheese or peanut butter,
yet when they receive it they are met with their demise.

Does that not sound like how our enemy tries to allure us into sin by the very thing our flesh craves?
Psalm 91:2-3
*"I will say of the LORD, He is my refuge and my fortress: my God;
in him will I trust. Surely he shall deliver thee
from the snare of the fowler, and from the noisome pestilence."*

**The Lord is Able to deliver us
from any snare the devil places in our path,
but the choice is ours of whether to trust Him to do so.**

Proverbs 30:5
*"Every word of God is pure:
he is a shield unto them that put their trust in him."*

There is safety in trusting Him.
Why would we want to delay our deliverance?

Proverbs 18:10
*"The name of the LORD is a strong tower:
the righteous runneth into it, and is safe."*

Run to Him today.

Bible Reading
1 Kings 9-10 | 2 Corinthians 7

06.05 | June 5

Marvel Not.

Ecclesiastes 5:8
"If thou seest the oppression of the poor, and violent perverting of judgment and justice in a province, marvel not at the matter: for he that is higher than the highest regardeth; and there be higher than they."

There may be what seem like injustices in this world, yes. However, far too often we neglect to remember or realize that nothing happens that God does not allow. **Every single thing is filtered by Him.**

When we witness such things,
we can choose to wisely process what we see.
"…marvel not at the matter…"
Do not be astounded. Do not be dumbfounded.
Do not be stunned or surprised.

When we allow ourselves to marvel over what seems like an injustice, we forget that God must have a purpose. Oppressors may be high, but He is higher.

Do not be afraid.
Isaiah 41:10
"Fear thou not; for I am with thee: be not dismayed; for I am thy God: I will strengthen thee; yea, I will help thee; yea, I will uphold thee with the right hand of my righteousness."

Do not doubt Him.
Proverbs 3:5
*"Trust in the LORD with all thine heart;
and lean not unto thine own understanding."*

Marvel not at the things of this world, for we are not of this world.
1 John 3:13
"Marvel not, my brethren, if the world hate you."

We will be hated for Who we know.
John 15:19
*"If ye were of the world, the world would love his own:
but because ye are not of the world, but I have chosen you out of the world, therefore the world hateth you."*

Marvel not at the hate; instead, choose to marvel at Him.

Bible Reading
1 Kings 11-12 | 2 Corinthians 8

While It Is Day.

John 9:4
"I must work the works of him that sent me, while it is day: the night cometh, when no man can work."

Jesus passed by and saw a man blind from birth. His disciples asked why he was born blind, and Jesus explained the purpose behind his aliment.

John 9:3
"Jesus answered, Neither hath this man sinned, nor his parents: but that the works of God should be made manifest in him."

Blindness is all around us.
Every human being born into this world has inherited the same disease.

2 Corinthians 4:4
"In whom the god of this world hath blinded the minds of them which believe not, lest the light of the glorious gospel of Christ, who is the image of God, should shine unto them."

We must work. The only other option is disobedience and dishonor. If we choose to sit idle while there is work to still be done, we not only do Him a disservice for all that He has done for us, but we are sure to miss out on many blessings He has in store.

Ecclesiastes 9:10
"Whatsoever thy hand findeth to do, do it with thy might; for there is no work, nor device, nor knowledge, nor wisdom, in the grave, whither thou goest."

His work in us. It is not our works that matter, but rather His work that He does in and through us. We cannot heal blinded eyes, but He can. It is simply our responsibility to tell the blind Who can make them see.

"...while it is day..."
The night is coming when we can no longer work for Him.

The sun is setting on the days remaining. **We must walk toward them that are without the Truth.**

Colossians 4:5
"Walk in wisdom toward them that are without, redeeming the time."

How will we use the time we have now? Peter and John were faced with the same decision we have before us, and they chose to refuse to be silenced.

Acts 4:20
"For we cannot but speak the things which we have seen and heard."

Bible Reading
1 Kings 13-14 | 2 Corinthians 9

06.07 | June 7

Mightier Than The Waves.

Psalm 93:4
"The LORD on high is mightier than the noise of many waters, yea, than the mighty waves of the sea."

Many resort to beaches around the world for rest and relaxation. The salty breeze and sand beneath their toes offer solace as the roaring of the waves soothe the noise within them.

What a reminder the coasts are of the Almighty Creator that made them!

It is not the ambiance of being on the shore that brings peace and rest to our hearts, but rather the One Who created us. Sometimes the noise within us and around us becomes so great and overpowering that we know we must break away for a little while. Instead of seeking comfort from His creation, we, as His children, have the Creator Himself to speak peace to our raging souls.

No matter the storm, He can speak peace.
Psalm 89:9
"Thou rulest the raging of the sea: when the waves thereof arise, thou stillest them."

The Psalmist used the raging waters as an example of the power and might of the Lord, and later in the New Testament we see that Truth demonstrated by Jesus Himself.

Mark 4:39
"And he arose, and rebuked the wind, and said unto the sea, Peace, be still. And the wind ceased, and there was a great calm."

Three words spoken by the Word made all the difference.
He is mightier than the waves.

Peace comes despite the wind and waves when we rest in Him.

Isaiah 26:3
"Thou wilt keep him in perfect peace, whose mind is stayed on thee: because he trusteth in thee."

Bible Reading
1 Kings 15-16 | 2 Corinthians 10

June 8 | 06.08

Weigh It Against The Truth.

Proverbs 20:10
*"Divers weights, and divers measures,
both of them are alike abomination to the LORD."*

A variety of messages only leads to confusion, often in an attempt to disguise the Truth.

1 Corinthians 14:33
*"For God is not the author of confusion,
but of peace, as in all churches of the saints."*

The Truth must be consistently seen in all that we say and do.
Though our methods may be different,
our Message must remain the same.
Proverbs 11:1
*"A false balance is abomination to the LORD:
but a just weight is his delight."*

Consider a pair of scales. In order to create a balance, the weight must be the same on both sides. A true balance is achieved when the exact amount of weight is placed on either side of the scale so that the platforms align perfectly.

**The devil seeks to confuse the minds of those seeking God
by multiplying sources that claim to speak the Truth.**
All roads of religion do not lead to Heaven.
It is only by the blood of Jesus Christ that we will reach the gates of pearl.

A false doctrine and the Truth do not weigh the same.
Where there is no Truth, there is no salvation, relationship, or eternal life.

The devil desires to deceive us into believing that a false doctrine is the Truth. If our belief does not stand upon the Truth of the Word of God, we have no Truth at all.

What the Bible says is wrong, is wrong.
What the Bible says is right, is right.
There are no gray areas when weighing Truth and error.
There cannot be a balance when things do not weigh the same.
Proverbs 16:11
*"A just weight and balance are the LORD'S:
all the weights of the bag are his work."*
Weigh everything against the Truth of the Word of God today.

Bible Reading
1 Kings 17-18 | 2 Corinthians 11

06.09 | June 9

Come & Rest.

Matthew 11:28
"Come unto me, all ye that labour and are heavy laden, and I will give you rest."

Vacation season is upon us. Summer is almost here. Many will soon resort to beaches or mountains to find solace and peace for a season.

Labourers need their rest.
Mark 6:31
"And he said unto them, Come ye yourselves apart into a desert place, and rest a while: for there were many coming and going, and they had no leisure so much as to eat."

Jesus Christ was an advocate for coming apart and resting awhile. In fact, He led by example in purposefully taking time away from people to rest.

The verse today is referred to frequently, and often quoted with the remaining two verses of the chapter.

Matthew 11:29-30
"Take my yoke upon you, and learn of me; for I am meek and lowly in heart: and ye shall find rest unto your souls. For my yoke is easy, and my burden is light."

Jesus invites labourers to come unto Him. The invitation is for those who labour. This means more than punching a clock or spending eight hours behind a desk at the office. This is labouring with a burden. A burden for others. A burden for souls. We also find that those who labour will find themselves *"heavy laden"*, when the burden is nearly too much to bear alone. The solution to our heavy laden-ness is to simply come to Him.

"Come unto me..."
What comfort there is in coming to Him!
A Resource and Solution that we neglect far too often.
Along with the Solution, there is a promise.
"...and I will give you rest."

We could try to define exactly what is meant by *"rest"* here, but no definition would be sufficient...for He is everything we could possibly need.

"...and I will give you _____."

The rest found in Him is better than a blank check... no value can be placed on it. If you are weary and burdened down today from your labour, He is still inviting. *"Come unto me...I will give you rest."*

Bible Reading
1 Kings 19-20 | 2 Corinthians 12

June 10 | 06.10

Promises To Give.

Joshua 1:3
*"Every place that the sole of your foot shall tread upon,
that have I given unto you, as I said unto Moses."*

All throughout the Word of God we find promises of conditional blessings. These are where God has promised something, if we will simply do what He says. How simple, yet our humanity often complicates our response.

Three verses into the Book of Joshua, we find the Lord promising Joshua that He has given the children of Israel the land. He even specifies that every place they step is the land which He has given them.

They had not stepped one foot upon this promised land.
"Every place that the sole of your foot shall tread upon…"

Yet the Lord said He had already given it to them.
"…that have I given unto you, as I said unto Moses."

It was up to them to have faith to walk on and claim the promise.
God gives, but it is up to us to receive His promises by faith in Him.

John 3:16
*"For God so loved the world, that he gave his only begotten Son,
that whosoever believeth in him should not perish,
but have everlasting life."*

Luke 6:38
*"Give, and it shall be given unto you; good measure, pressed down, and shaken together, and running over, shall men give into your bosom. For with the same measure that ye mete withal
it shall be measured to you again."*

Psalm 37:4
*"Delight thyself also in the LORD;
and he shall give thee the desires of thine heart."*

He has promised many things.
He is waiting for us to have the faith to receive them.

What are we missing out on
simply because we have not done what He asked?

Bible Reading
1 Kings 21-22 | 2 Corinthians 13

06.11 | June 11

Promises To Abide.

Joshua 1:5
*"There shall not any man be able to stand before thee
all the days of thy life: as I was with Moses, so I will be with thee:
I will not fail thee, nor forsake thee."*

Joshua had a new chapter in his life that included new responsibilities. He was commissioned to go forth and lead others. Can you imagine the weight on Joshua's shoulders as he heard this? His flesh must have swelled in pride only to be crippled by fear. How could he do this on his own?

The Lord comforted Joshua by giving him
the same promise He gave to Moses.

Deuteronomy 31:6
*"Be strong and of a good courage, fear not, nor be afraid of them:
for the LORD thy God, he it is that doth go with thee;
he will not fail thee, nor forsake thee."*

The Lord never leaves, fails or forsakes His children.
**Over and over again this same promise is shown
through the testimonies of the children of the Lord.**
As He was with Moses…
Exodus 13:21-22
As He was with Joshua…
Joshua 1:9
As He was with David…
1 Chronicles 28:20
As He was with Israel…
Isaiah 41:10

As He was with _____…
…so He will be with us.

**How many examples of His faithfulness do we need
in order to believe what He says?**

Hebrews 13:5
*"Let your conversation be without covetousness;
and be content with such things as ye have: for he hath said,
I will never leave thee, nor forsake thee."*

He promises to abide with His children.

Bible Reading
2 Kings 1-2 | Galatians 1

June 12 | 06.12

Promises To Hear.

Psalm 40:1
*"I waited patiently for the LORD;
and he inclined unto me, and heard my cry."*

Have you ever been talking with someone and you know they do not hear you? Perhaps they heard your voice, but it is obvious they are not listening to your words. Whether stranger, friend or family, this happens from time to time in our daily conversations because we are all flesh. Sometimes distractions get in the way.

But there is One…He is never too busy. He is never distracted. He is never not listening. (Yes, double negative, but its true.)

He hears us. So much so that over and over again we see this promise throughout His Word. He reminds us that He will hear us, if only we will call upon Him. He hears our call, our cries, our complaints, our burdens, our rants, and even our ramblings.

Psalm 3:4
*"I cried unto the LORD with my voice,
and he heard me out of his holy hill. Selah."*

Psalm 18:6
*"In my distress I called upon the LORD, and cried unto my God:
he heard my voice out of his temple, and my cry came before him,
even into his ears."*

Psalm 34:4
"I sought the LORD, and he heard me, and delivered me from all my fears."

Jonah 2:2
"And said, I cried by reason of mine affliction unto the LORD, and he heard me; out of the belly of hell cried I, and thou heardest my voice."

He hears us. Simply because He cares for His children. Every promise within the pages of Scripture are rooted in the fact that He loves and cares for us. The promises that He hears us should cause us to desire to call upon Him.

Jeremiah 33:3
"Call unto me, and I will answer thee, and shew thee great and mighty things, which thou knowest not."

In order for Him to answer, He must first hear our call.

Bible Reading
2 Kings 3-4 | Galatians 2

06.13 | June 13

Promises To Endure.

Exodus 18:23
"If thou shalt do this thing, and God command thee so, then thou shalt be able to endure, and all this people shall also go to their place in peace."

Endurance does not come naturally or automatically. It is a skill that must be learned and earned through diligence and hard work. We cannot put on a pair of brand-new running shoes and go run 26.2 miles to earn a sticker for the back of our vehicle when we have not ran even a block in five years. It simply does not work that way. God did not create our bodies to automatically handle such pressure or strain. If we desire to run a marathon, we must train and prepare. The same is true in our spiritual lives. As we walk with the Lord on a daily basis, He enables within us an endurance to withstand the race set before us.

Paul endured, and the Lord delivered him.
2 Timothy 3:11

Abraham patiently endured.
Hebrews 6:15

What an example of how we should wait...yet so often we choose to be impatient while we bear the trial we are facing. Although there are many examples throughout the pages of Scripture of how the Lord can enable us to endure what comes our way, there is One Who is truly the Ultimate Example.

Hebrews 12:1-2
"Wherefore seeing we also are compassed about with so great a cloud of witnesses, let us lay aside every weight, and the sin which doth so easily beset us, and let us run with patience the race that is set before us, Looking unto Jesus the author and finisher of our faith; who for the joy that was set before him endured the cross, despising the shame, and is set down at the right hand of the throne of God."

We can endure whatever comes before us, simply because He chose to endure the cross for us. **The key to enduring is choosing to willingly obey what God commands.** The Lord promised Moses that if he would do that, He would enable him to endure, and give them peace. There is peace available to us as He enables us to endure whatever may come...if only we will first choose to do what the Word of God says.

Bible Reading
2 Kings 5-6 | Galatians 3

June 14 | 06.14

We Have Heard.

Joshua 2:10
"For we have heard how the LORD dried up the water of the Red sea for you, when ye came out of Egypt; and what ye did unto the two kings of the Amorites, that were on the other side Jordan, Sihon and Og, whom ye utterly destroyed."

They say news travels fast. This is especially true in our modern-day world with all the technology we have at our fingertips. Something can happen across the globe, and we will likely receive a notification about it in a matter of minutes. News begins to travel in one of two ways. Those who experienced it, and those who witnessed it.

How did Rahab hear of the Lord drying up the Red Sea for the children of Israel?
This news traveled fast and had an effect on those who heard it.
Joshua 2:11
"And as soon as we had heard these things, our hearts did melt, neither did there remain any more courage in any man, because of you: for the LORD your God, he is God in heaven above, and in earth beneath."

When the Lord does something miraculous, that news should be spread faster than any media broadcast cycle. Notice how Rahab phrased her statement about knowing what the Lord had done:
"we have heard how the Lord… _____ …for you"
Consider for a moment what would be applicable for you to put in that blank. For You.
Have people heard what the Lord has done for you?
If we were to take a notepad and begin writing out every single thing the Lord has done for us, there would not be enough paper at our disposal to do so. Why? Because that is how much He loves us.

The love of God is inexhaustible and unexplainable. Every single thing He does for us is out of that love. Yes, it begins with our salvation…but it does not stop there. Salvation is only the beginning of our story. His love brings purpose to our lives, and when we yield ourselves to Him there is no telling what He has in store. Rahab had heard what the Lord had done for the two spies, and her faith in that He could do the same for her changed her life as well.

What have people heard that the Lord has done for you?
Start telling them today. It could change their life too.

Bible Reading
2 Kings 7-8 | Galatians 4

06.15 | June 15

Uncharted Territory.

Joshua 3:4
"Yet there shall be a space between you and it, about two thousand cubits by measure: come not near unto it, that ye may know the way by which ye must go: for ye have not passed this way heretofore."

Unprecedented times cause us to react in one of two ways…fight or flight. We can choose to stay and venture by faith through the unknown, or we can run and hide away in fear. They had not been in this place or situation before. Joshua was used of the Lord to lead the children of Israel after the death of Moses. His response to uncharted territory is an example of how we should also conduct ourselves in uncertain times.

Joshua 3:5
"And Joshua said unto the people, Sanctify yourselves: for to morrow the LORD will do wonders among you."

His first two words made all the difference. He knew that they must set themselves apart to seek the Lord and allow Him alone to lead them. The people followed Joshua because He followed the Lord. The Lord blessed his leadership because he was solely focused on what the Lord would have them to do and where He wanted them to go.

Joshua 3:7
"And the LORD said unto Joshua, This day will I begin to magnify thee in the sight of all Israel, that they may know that, as I was with Moses, so I will be with thee."

The Lord was with Him.
Joshua yielded himself to the Lord,
which allowed Him to do great things in and through him.

*"…Sanctify yourselves:
for to morrow the LORD will do wonders among you."*

**When we are in uncharted territory,
may we realize there is opportunity for the Lord to do great things.**

Bible Reading
2 Kings 9-10 | Galatians 5

June 16 | 06.16

Take To Serve.

Exodus 10:26
"Our cattle also shall go with us; there shall not an hoof be left behind; for thereof must we take to serve the LORD our God; and we know not with what we must serve the LORD, until we come thither."

In 1907, Baden-Powell, an English soldier, devised the Scout motto: Be Prepared. He wrote that to Be Prepared means "you are always in a state of readiness in mind and body to do your duty." More than a century later, preparedness is still a cornerstone of Scouting.

Moses was leading the children of Israel to be prepared for whatever lied ahead. *"…for thereof must we take to serve the LORD our God; and we know not with what we must serve the LORD, until we come thither."* **He was preparing to take with them whatever may be necessary to serve and worship the Lord.**

"take to serve"…Be Prepared…Consider this motto in reference to our walk with the Lord…we should always Be Prepared for what He has in store.
But how can we do that?

Seek To Be Prepared
Psalm 34:10
*"The young lions do lack, and suffer hunger:
but they that seek the LORD shall not want any good thing."*

Study To Be Prepared
2 Timothy 2:15
"Study to shew thyself approved unto God, a workman that needeth not to be ashamed, rightly dividing the word of truth."

Submit To Prepared
Romans 12:1
"I beseech you therefore, brethren, by the mercies of God, that ye present your bodies a living sacrifice, holy, acceptable unto God, which is your reasonable service."

The most important aspect of being ready to serve Him is yielding unto Him. If we try to accomplish anything in our own strength or abilities, it will return void and be fruitless. John 15:4

It is Him working in and through us that makes a difference in eternity.
We need only prepare ourselves to allow Him to do so.

Bible Reading
2 Kings 11-12 | Galatians 6

06.17 | June 17

1 Corinthians 2:10
*"But God hath revealed them unto us by his Spirit:
for the Spirit searcheth all things, yea, the deep things of God."*

Like a shining thread woven intricately in a remnant of tapestry, two words are frequently found together throughout the pages of Scripture. These two words are without a doubt intentionally placed in many verses all throughout both the Old and New Testaments…perhaps to continually remind us of the Truth that is found within them.

"But God…"

Two words, and just six letters…yet unending mercy and grace.

Search the Scriptures to find the Truths connected to these two words.
He intervenes. He protects. He directs. He promotes. He abides. He redirects. He delivers. He provides. He defends. He interjects. He redeems. He fights. He strengthens. He judges. He overthrows. He rebukes. He prepares. He forgives. He reproves. He knows. He heals. He loves. He confounds. He reveals. He gives. He destroys. He calls. He mediates. He forbids. He tries. He quickens.

He is Faithful.
1 Corinthians 10:13
*"There hath no temptation taken you but such as is common to man:
but God is faithful, who will not suffer you to be tempted above
that ye are able; but will with the temptation also make a way to escape,
that ye may be able to bear it."*

He is Merciful.
Ephesians 2:4-5
*"But God, who is rich in mercy, for his great love wherewith he loved us,
Even when we were dead in sins, hath quickened us together with Christ,
(by grace ye are saved;)"*

Every moment, every circumstance, every sweet and every bitter situation, He is working for our good and His glory. No matter how dark, God has a purpose. No matter how bright, God has a plan.

"But God…"
Let Him intervene in your life today.

Bible Reading
2 Kings 13-14 | Ephesians 1

June 18 | 06.18

By Him.

Colossians 1:16-17
*"For by him were all things created, that are in heaven,
and that are in earth, visible and invisible, whether they be thrones,
or dominions, or principalities, or powers: all things were created by him,
and for him: And he is before all things, and by him all things consist."*

**Every time that God intervenes in our lives
it should be a reminder of Who He is.**
"…by him…"
His actions speak for themselves, but He is the only One Who's Words truly speak louder than His actions. In His Word, we learn Who He is, what He has already done, what He is doing right now, and what He has promised He will do.

His Word always makes the difference.
It continually tells us Who He is.

He is Creator.
Every part of God's creation was created by Him.
John 1:3
*"All things were made by him; and without him
was not any thing made that was made."*

God spoke and things appeared. Every intricate detail of His creation, including us, was put into place the moment He uttered the Words. What power He displayed by simply speaking! Almighty power…which only comes from Him.

"…by him…"
All throughout the Scriptures, we can see His presence dwelling with His children. Every example that is left for us within the pages of the Word of God is there to remind us of Who He is and how only *"…by him…"* can things happen.

The same Almighty power that created the earth in which we live, the same Almighty power that breathed the breath of life into Adam and created the Woman from his rib…is available to us today through His Word.

What has He created in your life?
Allow every circumstance to remind you of Who He is.

Bible Reading
2 Kings 15-16 | Ephesians 2

06.19 | June 19

In Him.

Colossians 1:19-20
*"For it pleased the Father that in him should all fulness dwell;
And, having made peace through the blood of his cross,
by him to reconcile all things unto himself; by him, I say,
whether they be things in earth, or things in heaven."*

If there were a Table of Contents for the Bible, it would not be best listed as the 66 Books within the Canon of Scriptures; but rather just One Word…
Jesus.

"…in him…"
All the fulness of the Godhead bodily dwells in Him.
He was and is God in the flesh.
The Word.

In Him there is Peace.
In Him there is Salvation.
In Him there is _____.

Everything we could possibly need is found in Him.

Colossians 1:18
*"And he is the head of the body, the church:
who is the beginning,
the firstborn from the dead;
that in all things he might have the preeminence."*

**Everything is found in Him
so that He might have preeminence in every thing.**
Is He first in your life today?

He is the Answer to our questions.
He is the Reason for our existence.
He is…

Are you searching for something?
Find it in Him.

Bible Reading
2 Kings 17-18 | Ephesians 3

June 20 | 06.20

For Him.

Hebrews 9:28
"So Christ was once offered to bear the sins of many; and unto them that look for him shall he appear the second time without sin unto salvation."

He was there when God spoke the World into existence.
He was the Method God used…the Word.

Colossians 1:16
"For by him were all things created, that are in heaven, and that are in earth, visible and invisible, whether they be thrones, or dominions, or principalities, or powers: all things were created by him, and for him:"

He was and is the Reason.
"…for him…"

What is your reason for doing anything?
Self-glorification, self-preservation, self-motivation… notice what all three of those begin with…self. Most of the time, what we do has selfish motives. Sad to admit, but no less true.

He should always be our Reason.
"…for him…"

Are you working for Him today?
Colossians 3:23-24
"And whatsoever ye do, do it heartily, as to the Lord, and not unto men; Knowing that of the Lord ye shall receive the reward of the inheritance: for ye serve the Lord Christ."

Are you looking for Him today?
Titus 2:13-14
"Looking for that blessed hope, and the glorious appearing of the great God and our Saviour Jesus Christ; Who gave himself for us, that he might redeem us from all iniquity, and purify unto himself a peculiar people, zealous of good works."

Everything should be "…*for him*…"

Bible Reading
2 Kings 19-20 | Ephesians 4

06.21 | June 21

An Unlawful Choice.

Esther 4:14
"For if thou altogether holdest thy peace at this time, then shall there enlargement and deliverance arise to the Jews from another place; but thou and thy father's house shall be destroyed: and who knoweth whether thou art come to the kingdom for such a time as this?"

When we venture into uncharted territory by faith, there inevitably comes a point where we must make another decision of whether to continue on or abandon the mission.

Sometimes, what the Lord leads us to do goes against the rules.
Esther told Mordecai it was unlawful for her to do what he suggested.

Esther 4:11
If she did what he asked, she would literally have to risk her life. Mordecai knew the danger before he charged her to go in unto the king, but he had faith that God would intervene. Esther could either hold her peace and miss the opportunity for God to use her to protect His people, or carry on in faith that He would direct and provide.

"…who knoweth whether thou art come to the kingdom for such a time as this?"
The time is now.

We make choices throughout every day of whether or not we will allow the Lord to use us for His glory. Sometimes we yield to Him, and sometimes we miss out on what He had planned.

Missing out may give us safety, but is it worth missing the rewards He has in store? The rewards that are not for a trophy shelf, but are what we will cast at His feet. The rewards are not for us, they are for Him.

Choose today to follow the Word of the Lord, and nothing else.
Allow Him to direct your path.
Yield to His direction, no matter where it may take you.

Colossians 3:23-24
"And whatsoever ye do, do it heartily, as to the Lord, and not unto men; Knowing that of the Lord ye shall receive the reward of the inheritance: for ye serve the Lord Christ."

No task is too small or too great if it is for His glory.

Bible Reading
2 Kings 21-22 | Ephesians 5

June 22 | 06.22

Willing To Perish.

Esther 4:16
"Go, gather together all the Jews that are present in Shushan, and fast ye for me, and neither eat nor drink three days, night or day: I also and my maidens will fast likewise; and so will I go in unto the king, which is not according to the law: and if I perish, I perish."

Esther was willing to do what was not only unlawful, but deadly. She knew the consequences, but the life of her people was at stake.

Esther 4:14
"…who knoweth whether thou art come to the kingdom for such a time as this?"

God had placed her there for a reason.
Have you ever considered that God has you where you are right now for a specific purpose?

She encouraged others to contribute, because she knew she could not to do this on her own. They fasted for her while she fasted in faith that He would provide.

Sometimes, we must use extraordinary measures to seek the Lord and His provision.
Mark 9:29
"And he said unto them, This kind can come forth by nothing, but by prayer and fasting."

She had faith to do what she could. "…and so will I go…"
She was willing to die for her faith. "…and if I perish, I perish."
Whatever happened, she knew God had a plan.
She only desired to follow Him. On the third day, Esther put on her royal apparel, and stood in the court of the king in faith that God would intervene. Esther 5:2

God's timing is everything. He knows who, what, when, where, and how something or someone is needed.
Esther's faith enabled her to be used by the Lord in such a special way; but she is not the only one He desires to use for His glory.

God has you where you are for such a time as this.
There are no coincidences to what you are facing.
Seek the Lord for guidance, and when He directs…yield to Him, regardless of the consequences.

Bible Reading
2 Kings 23-25 | Ephesians 6

06.23 | June 23

Confidence.

Philippians 3:4
"Though I might also have confidence in the flesh. If any other man thinketh that he hath whereof he might trust in the flesh, I more:"

The Apostle Paul knew that if anyone could have a reason to have confidence in their flesh, it was him. He understood that some would expect him to depend on his past. Philippians 3:5-6

But Paul chose to leave all of that behind for One purpose.
Philippians 3:7
"But what things were gain to me, those I counted loss for Christ."
He gave it all up for Him.
Nothing in his past, no matter how grand,
was comparable to knowing Christ.
Philippians 3:8
"Yea doubtless, and I count all things but loss for the excellency of the knowledge of Christ Jesus my Lord: for whom I have suffered the loss of all things, and do count them but dung, that I may win Christ,"

He was willing to lose, and even suffer, if it meant getting closer to Him.
Phlippians 3:9
"And be found in him, not having mine own righteousness, which is of the law, but that which is through the faith of Christ, the righteousness which is of God by faith:"

What is our confidence in today?
Who we know? Where we live? What church we attend?
What profession we have?

All of that is confidence in the flesh. If we choose to trust in the flesh, we will be continually, and eventually completely, disappointed. Instead, we can choose to place our confidence only in Him, even if that means He has to rewrite our entire story.

Philippians 3:10-11
"That I may know him, and the power of his resurrection, and the fellowship of his sufferings, being made conformable unto his death; If by any means I might attain unto the resurrection of the dead."

Losing everything in order to know Him is always worth it.
"…that I may win Christ, And be found in him…That I may know him…"

Bible Reading
1 Chronicles 1-2 | Philippians 1

June 24 | 06.24

Forgetting Those Things.

Philippians 3:13-14
"Brethren, I count not myself to have apprehended: but this one thing I do, forgetting those things which are behind, and reaching forth unto those things which are before, I press toward the mark for the prize of the high calling of God in Christ Jesus."

Arrows must be pulled back a bit before they can be launched forward. Yet, they never look back…they are always pointed toward the mark. **We are arrows in the quiver of the Lord.** He points us where He would have us to go, and it is up to us to yield to His direction.

If we allow the winds of this world to sway us, we will miss the mark.
If we try to look back to what is behind us, we will miss the mark.

Dwelling in the past is dangerous.
Jesus warned His disciples against lingering in the past.
Luke 17:31-32
"In that day, he which shall be upon the housetop, and his stuff in the house, let him not come down to take it away: and he that is in the field, let him likewise not return back. Remember Lot's wife."

Those last three words should remind us of how dangerous it is to look back in longing to return to where we once were. She was dissolved into a pillar of salt because of her disobedience.

Paul realized that no matter what has happened in our past, good or bad, we must choose to forget those things.

"…but this one thing I do…"
He made it a priority to focus on what lied ahead, instead of what had happened.

"I press toward…"
What are we eagerly pursuing today?
Who are we seeking?

If we run ahead while looking back,
we are sure to eventually trip and fall.

Sometimes, the only way of forgetting those things is by reaching forth toward the things He has for us.

Bible Reading
1 Chronicles 3-4 | Philippians 2

06.25 | June 25

Trust The Author.

Hebrews 12:2
"Looking unto Jesus the author and finisher of our faith; who for the joy that was set before him endured the cross, despising the shame, and is set down at the right hand of the throne of God."

Before we can reach forth toward those things that He has prepared for us, we must first be aware of where we are looking…
or more importantly, to Who.

Reaching forth with our eyes closed is sure to confuse, and harm, us.
Reaching forth with our eyes on the world will lead us to destruction.
Reaching forth with our eyes on our circumstances will depress us.
Reaching forth with our eyes on other people will certainly distract us.
But if we choose to reach forth with our eyes fixed on Jesus,
He will never lead us astray.

Looking unto Him reminds us of Who we trust.
Isaiah 26:3
"Thou wilt keep him in perfect peace, whose mind is stayed on thee: because he trusteth in thee."

He directs us as we look to Him.
Proverbs 3:5-6
"Trust in the LORD with all thine heart; and lean not unto thine own understanding. In all thy ways acknowledge him, and he shall direct thy paths."

He is the Author, for He originated our faith.
He is the Finisher, for without Him faith would not be possible.

All things begin and end with Him.
Revelation 1:8
"I am Alpha and Omega, the beginning and the ending, saith the Lord, which is, and which was, and which is to come, the Almighty."

Why would we dare to look anywhere
or to anyone else when we can reach forth unto Him?

Reach forth while looking unto Him.
Trust the Author today.

Trust Him to finish what He has started.

Bible Reading
1 Chronicles 5-6 | Philippians 3

June 26 | 06.26

Depend On Him.

Philippians 1:6
"Being confident of this very thing, that he which hath begun a good work in you will perform it until the day of Jesus Christ:"

Many people today are undependable. They may start something, but the odds of them finishing the task before them are not in their favor. This often leads to someone else having to finish the job.

What a reminder of how Jesus Christ is the Author of our salvation! We cannot earn, win, or deserve salvation on our own.
Romans 3:10-12
"As it is written, There is none righteous, no, not one: There is none that understandeth, there is none that seeketh after God. They are all gone out of the way, they are together become unprofitable; there is none that doeth good, no, not one."

We are an undependable people, incapable of meeting the standard of His glory on our own. Because of our sin, we cannot even begin the work of salvation in us. He is the Author.
Romans 3:23
"For all have sinned, and come short of the glory of God;"

He not only began the good work in us, it is up to Him to perform it.
Salvation has nothing to do with our own merit or ability.
We only contribute the sin that makes salvation necessary.
Romans 3:24-25
"Being justified freely by his grace through the redemption that is in Christ Jesus: Whom God hath set forth to be a propitiation through faith in his blood, to declare his righteousness for the remission of sins that are past, through the forbearance of God;"

It is only up to us to believe in what Jesus Christ has done for us and depend on Him for our salvation. **The moment we believe, His work begins in us, and He is the Only One Who is dependable to finish it.**

Are you struggling today? Maybe your salvation is sure, but your walk with Him is not what it should be. He is waiting to walk with you. He wants to direct you. He desires to have fellowship with you.
His Word is waiting with the Answer.
The Author is always present when you open the pages of His Word. Depend on Him today.
Bible Reading
1 Chronicles 7-8 | Philippians 4

06.27 | June 27

Why Can't We?

Matthew 17:19
*"Then came the disciples to Jesus apart, and said,
Why could not we cast him out?"*

We blame toddlers and teenagers for asking the question, "Why can't we…", the most often, but the truth of the matter is that adults ask it just as frequently. Our answer to the younger generation is usually "for your own good" or "just do as I say". Yet so often we neglect our own preaching.

When the disciples asked Jesus, *"Why could not we…"*, it was not for their own good or because they just needed to obey what He said.

It was their unbelief.
Matthew 17:20
"And Jesus said unto them, Because of your unbelief: for verily I say unto you, If ye have faith as a grain of mustard seed, ye shall say unto this mountain, Remove hence to yonder place; and it shall remove; and nothing shall be impossible unto you."

They missed out on seeing miracles take place simply because they did not believe it would happen. Jesus even explained to them that if they just had a little faith nothing would be impossible.

But they doubted; and ultimately, they doubted Him.
They doubted what He could do in and through them
if only they would believe.

**When we believe that with Him anything is possible,
we will begin to see the mountains in our lives begin to move.**

Matthew 17:21
"Howbeit this kind goeth not out but by prayer and fasting."

He wants us to seek Him in faith.
When we doubt that He will do what He said,
we miss out on so much more than just our need.

Unbelief has consequences.

Bible Reading
1 Chronicles 9-10 | Colossians 1

June 28 | 06.28

Our Stay.

2 Samuel 22:19
*"They prevented me in the day of my calamity:
but the LORD was my stay."*

Sometimes, our unbelief keeps us in a place too long,
which can lead to calamity.

Calamity: an event causing great and often sudden damage or distress; a disaster.

Have you ever had a calamity take place in your life?

He knew where to turn in the days of his calamity.
2 Samuel 22:7
"In my distress I called upon the LORD, and cried to my God: and he did hear my voice out of his temple, and my cry did enter into his ears."

The Lord heard him…and He answered.
The Lord was his stay…He supported him.

When you are in distress…call upon Him, and cry unto Him.
He may not answer the way you want or expect, but He will do what He knows is best. His answer to David involved an earthquake, thunder, and lightning because of His wrath defending David.

Perhaps the Lord wants to shake the very ground you walk each day.
**Instead of being fearful,
rejoice that the Lord will fight the battle for you.**

2 Samuel 22:20
*"He brought me forth also into a large place:
he delivered me, because he delighted in me."*

The Lord delivered him, because He delighted in him.
There is such liberty on the other side of the Lord's deliverance.

He supported David in his darkest hour,
as it seemed that everyone else had deserted him.

When oppression overtook him, the Lord was his stay.
He'll do the same for you today.

Bible Reading
1 Chronicles 11-12 | Colossians 2

06.29 | June 29

Sing To The Deliverer.

2 Samuel 22:1
"And David spake unto the LORD the words of this song in the day that the LORD had delivered him out of the hand of all his enemies, and out of the hand of Saul:"

For David, it was his enemies that caused his calamity. He refers to them 17 times within this chapter. But as many times as he focused on them, he chose to look to the Lord many more…at least 85 times.

David chose to focus on his Deliverer instead of his oppressors.
2 Samuel 22:2-3

Who is He to you today?
As your Rock, He gives stability.
As your Fortress, He gives safety.
As your Deliverer, He gives salvation.

Do you trust Him today?
As your Shield, He gives shelter.
As the Horn of Your Salvation, He gives strength.
As your High Tower, He gives security.
As your Refuge, He gives peace.
As your Saviour, He gives deliverance.

Compare 2 Samuel 22 to Psalm 18.
It is almost as if our chapter today is a first draft
before the song is set to music.

David left us such an example that when times get hard,
we can trust the Lord.
2 Samuel 22:31
"As for God, his way is perfect; the word of the LORD is tried: he is a buckler to all them that trust in him."

When we don't understand why or even what is happening, He does.
2 Samuel 22:33
"God is my strength and power: and he maketh my way perfect."

Choose to be thankful in your circumstances today.
2 Samuel 22:50
**Allow your thanksgiving to turn to praise,
even in the midst of those who are against you.**

Bible Reading
1 Chronicles 13-14 | Colossians 3

June 30 | 06.30

The Fruit Of Calamity.

Psalm 18:1
"I will love thee, O LORD, my strength."

Now set to music, David's song begins a little differently. The most recognizable difference between 2 Samuel 22 and Psalm 18 is the addition of this one sentence to begin his song of deliverance.

**The calamity he had faced had led to knowing
and loving his Deliverer more.**

2 Samuel 22:29-31
"For thou art my lamp, O LORD: and the LORD will lighten my darkness. For by thee I have run through a troop: by my God have I leaped over a wall. As for God, his way is perfect; the word of the LORD is tried: he is a buckler to all them that trust in him."

David's love for the Lord grew through the trials he faced.

What if we looked at our trials that way…
**If what we face makes us know and love the Lord more,
is it not worth it?**

It is easier to wait if we spend our time knowing and loving Him.
The pain is less felt when we are focused on Him.

Suffering and affliction are valuable additions to our lives
if while we endure them we choose to turn to Him.

David acknowledged the Lord was the Source of his strength.

Psalm 28:7
"The LORD is my strength and my shield; my heart trusted in him, and I am helped: therefore my heart greatly rejoiceth; and with my song will I praise him."

He lovingly depended upon the Lord for his strength to carry on.
We can choose to do the same in our times of calamity.

In times of waiting, love Him.
In times of discouragement, praise Him.
In times of suffering, seek Him.
In times of doubt, trust Him.

Bible Reading
1 Chronicles 15-16 | Colossians 4

07.01 | July 1

Asking For Wisdom.

1 Kings 3:9
"Give therefore thy servant an understanding heart to judge thy people, that I may discern between good and bad: for who is able to judge this thy so great a people?"

Solomon could have asked for anything he wanted; yet he asked for wisdom. God, in His foreknowledge, knew what Solomon would ask for before He even gave him the opportunity.

Solomon had two specific reasons for asking for wisdom, knowledge and understanding. The anointed king of Israel recognized that his young age provided little experience to perform his duties.

To Fulfill God's Plan

Solomon realized that the task before him was too great to do on his own. He knew that if he tried to accomplish it in his own ability he would surely fail.

2 Chronicles 1:10
"Give me now wisdom and knowledge, that I may go out and come in before this people: for who can judge this thy people, that is so great?"

How many times do we try to complete a task on our own only to fail miserably? If we serve by our own strength and power, little will be done for the cause of Christ. We must acknowledge our need for Him!

To Discern His Problems

If he was to rule over God's chosen people, Solomon knew he had to be able to discern between what was right and wrong.

"…that I may discern between good and bad: for who is able to judge this thy so great a people?"

Discernment is lacking within many professing Christians today.
God is willing and able to give us the ability to discern between good and bad. He only requires that we ask Him to give it to us.

James 1:5
"If any of you lack wisdom, let him ask of God, that giveth to all men liberally, and upbraideth not; and it shall be given him."

We must ask God for wisdom in order to fulfill His plan for our lives and to have discernment while we serve Him.

Bible Reading
1 Chronicles 17-18 | 1 Thessalonians 1

July 2 | 07.02

Entrusted.

1 Kings 3:12
"Behold, I have done according to thy words: lo, I have given thee a wise and an understanding heart; so that there was none like thee before thee, neither after thee shall any arise like unto thee."

Solomon asking for wisdom, knowledge and understanding did not surprise the LORD God one bit.

He knows what we need before we even ask.
Matthew 6:8
"Be not ye therefore like unto them: for your Father knoweth what things ye have need of, before ye ask him."

Solomon's wisdom was displayed in his asking for it in the first place. He was wise enough to ask for more wisdom! God had given him the opportunity, and Solomon had faith that God would provide his request. Because of his faith, God entrusted him with a distinct ability unlike anyone else.

God has a unique plan for each of our lives.
He has entrusted us with the privilege to serve Him, and He knows exactly what we need. We must have enough faith to ask Him to give us the wisdom He knows we need in order to accomplish His will in us.

1 Kings 4:29-30
"And God gave Solomon wisdom and understanding exceeding much, and largeness of heart, even as the sand that is on the sea shore. And Solomon's wisdom excelled the wisdom of all the children of the east country, and all the wisdom of Egypt."

**God allows situations to come into our lives
to allow our faith in Him to grow.**
The more faith we have in Him,
the more He can use us in ways we never dreamed.

1 Kings 4:34
"And there came of all people to hear the wisdom of Solomon, from all kings of the earth, which had heard of his wisdom."

What has God entrusted you with?
Examine your faith in Him today.

Bible Reading
1 Chronicles 19-20 | 1 Thessalonians 2

07.03 | July 3

What Are You Asking For?

1 Kings 3:11
"And God said unto him, Because thou hast asked this thing, and hast not asked for thyself long life; neither hast asked riches for thyself, nor hast asked the life of thine enemies; but hast asked for thyself understanding to discern judgment;"

God must hear requests for long life, riches, honour, or revenge all the time. How much must it grieve His heart for us to ask for any or all of those things rather than asking for wisdom to serve Him?

Solomon could have asked for anything, yet he asked for wisdom. He not only received it, but through God's grace he was also given so much more.

1 Kings 3:12-14
"Behold, I have done according to thy words: lo, I have given thee a wise and an understanding heart; so that there was none like thee before thee, neither after thee shall any arise like unto thee. And I have also given thee that which thou hast not asked, both riches, and honour: so that there shall not be any among the kings like unto thee all thy days. And if thou wilt walk in my ways, to keep my statutes and my commandments, as thy father David did walk, then I will lengthen thy days."

What might the Lord also give us if we will simply ask for the right thing in the first place?

Because he asked for wisdom, God not only granted Solomon's request, but He also bestowed so much more in addition to his plea.

What a picture of the grace of God! He always gives us so much more than we could ever deserve.

If we will simply ask for wisdom, as Solomon did, we too may receive temporal blessings in addition to that which has eternal value.

What have we missed because we simply asked for the wrong thing?

Bible Reading
1 Chronicles 21-22 | 1 Thessalonians 3

July 4 | 07.04

Shine As Lights.

Philippians 2:15
"That ye may be blameless and harmless, the sons of God, without rebuke, in the midst of a crooked and perverse nation, among whom ye shine as lights in the world;"

Our crooked and perverse nation is in distress. **People are looking for hope, seeking answers in all the wrong places.** Darkness seems to be prevailing; yet, we are still here. **That means there is still work for us to do.** There is still time to *"shine as lights"* for others to see.

Proverbs 4:17-19
"For they eat the bread of wickedness, and drink the wine of violence. But the path of the just is as the shining light, that shineth more and more unto the perfect day. The way of the wicked is as darkness: they know not at what they stumble."

In the middle of the darkness, *"the path of the just"* can light the way; because this is not just any shining light.

John 8:12
"Then spake Jesus again unto them, saying, I am the light of the world: he that followeth me shall not walk in darkness, but shall have the light of life."

We have the Light of Christ within us, and it is up to us to shine so that others may see the glorious Light of the Gospel. 2 Corinthians 4:3-4

People all around us are walking in darkness. Their minds are blinded by the devil through disbelief. Only the Light of the Gospel can open their spiritual eyes.

Philippians 2:15-16
"That ye may be blameless and harmless, the sons of God, without rebuke, in the midst of a crooked and perverse nation, among whom ye shine as lights in the world; Holding forth the word of life; that I may rejoice in the day of Christ, that I have not run in vain, neither laboured in vain."

May the Word of Life shine out of our hearts, for it is His Word that makes the difference.

Matthew 5:16
"Let your light so shine before men, that they may see your good works, and glorify your Father which is in heaven."

Shine the Light today. Our nation needs Him more than ever before.

Bible Reading
1 Chronicles 23-24 | 1 Thessalonians 4

07.05 | July 5

Let Thine Heart.

Proverbs 3:1
"My son, forget not my law; but let thine heart keep my commandments:"

We cannot forget what we do not know. **The more we know of God's Word the more of His Word we will want to know.**

The importance of knowing the Word cannot be overstated; however, more than knowing, we must apply the Truth of God's Word to our hearts.

"...but let thine heart..."
What we allow in our hearts determines our words and our actions.

Luke 6:45
"A good man out of the good treasure of his heart bringeth forth that which is good; and an evil man out of the evil treasure of his heart bringeth forth that which is evil: for of the abundance of the heart his mouth speaketh."

What is your heart saying today?

Proverbs 3:3-4
"Let not mercy and truth forsake thee: bind them about thy neck; write them upon the table of thine heart: So shalt thou find favour and good understanding in the sight of God and man."

Engrave the Wisdom of the Word upon your heart and life today.
Read the Word. Recite the Word. Remember the Word.

1 Peter 3:15
"But sanctify the Lord God in your hearts: and be ready always to give an answer to every man that asketh you a reason of the hope that is in you with meekness and fear:"

What answer will you give?
Our hearts speak louder than we realize sometimes.

Bible Reading
1 Chronicles 25-26 | 1 Thessalonians 5

Hate What He Hates.

Proverbs 8:13
"The fear of the LORD is to hate evil: pride, and arrogancy, and the evil way, and the froward mouth, do I hate."

Only when we fear the Lord do we begin to have wisdom.
Psalm 111:10
"The fear of the LORD is the beginning of wisdom: a good understanding have all they that do his commandments: his praise endureth for ever."

Part of the process of truly fearing the Lord is to hate what the Lord hates.
Proverbs 1:7
"The fear of the LORD is the beginning of knowledge: but fools despise wisdom and instruction."

We cannot be friends with the world while also considering ourselves to be friends with Him. God demands that His children disregard what displeases Him. Evil abounds in the world around us, and therefore we must avoid everything that is contrary to the Truth. We must hate evil, pride, arrogance, every evil way, and those who speak not the Truth.

Within the pages of the Word of God we find instructions for how God would have us to live amongst this evil.

Psalm 119:104
"Through thy precepts I get understanding: therefore I hate every false way."

When it seems that there is nowhere to turn due to the increase of evil around us, it is easy to become disheartened and discouraged. Where can we go? What can we do?

Resist the temptation to panic and isolate yourself, and begin to cling to the Word of God to speak peace to your soul.

Psalm 119:128
"Therefore I esteem all thy precepts concerning all things to be right; and I hate every false way."

Strive today to hate what He hates.

Bible Reading
1 Chronicles 27-29 | 2 Thessalonians 1

07.07 | July 7

Wholly Follow.

Joshua 14:8
"Nevertheless my brethren that went up with me made the heart of the people melt: but I wholly followed the LORD my God."

Standing for Truth is rarely easy, but doing right is always the right thing to do. Often there are times in our lives when we must choose whether to follow the crowd or the Lord. This was the case when the spies came back with their report of the land of Canaan. When 10 of the spies chose to let their fearfulness fuel their perception, they brought up an evil report. Rather than a land flowing with milk and honey, they chose to focus on the people. They saw giants of great stature instead of what God had intended for them.

Caleb and Joshua saw the exceeding good land the Lord wanted to give the children of Israel. They knew that the Lord could give them the victory. The majority tried to stone them because of their faith. But the Lord promised to intervene on their behalf and allow them to see the land He had reserved for them. Caleb was 40 years old when Moses sent the spies out, and now he was 85. He waited 45 years.

His testimony throughout those years of waiting is that he wholly followed the Lord. The Lord gave him what was promised.

Joshua 14:13-14
"And Joshua blessed him, and gave unto Caleb the son of Jephunneh Hebron for an inheritance. Hebron therefore became the inheritance of Caleb the son of Jephunneh the Kenezite unto this day, because that he wholly followed the LORD God of Israel."

Throughout the many years of waiting, he was faithful to wholly follow the Lord. **Can the same be said of us?**

While we are now waiting there will be some around us who choose not to follow Him. **Will we follow the majority and miss out on what He has in store? Or will we stay faithful to follow the Lord wherever He leads?**

Victory is found in Him,
but we must be willing to follow Him in order to find it.

**Choose to wholly follow Him today…
no matter how long you have to wait.**

Bible Reading
2 Chronicles 1-2 | 2 Thessalonians 2

As Strong This Day.

Joshua 14:11
"As yet I am as strong this day as I was in the day that Moses sent me: as my strength was then, even so is my strength now, for war, both to go out, and to come in."

Waiting can take a toll on us.
Usually the longer we wait, the more agitated our flesh becomes.

Caleb had waited 45 years to receive what he was promised, yet his strength remained. He was as strong at 85 as he was when he was 40.

"As yet I am as strong this day as I was in the day that Moses sent me…"

His strength never failed because he never trusted in his own strength.

"…as my strength was then, even so is my strength now…"

This was the result of Caleb wholly following the Lord, even through the wilderness. **Perhaps his testimony of relying on the Lord's strength encouraged those who came behind him.**

2 Corinthians 12:8-9
"For this thing I besought the Lord thrice, that it might depart from me. And he said unto me, My grace is sufficient for thee: for my strength is made perfect in weakness. Most gladly therefore will I rather glory in my infirmities, that the power of Christ may rest upon me."

Philippians 4:13
"I can do all things through Christ which strengtheneth me."

Caleb and Paul both realized that it was not their strength that enabled them, it was the Lord. They yielded themselves to His strength.

It is in our times of weakness that the strength of the Lord is shown.
Without Him, we can do nothing;
yet through Him we can do all things.

Allow Him to strengthen you today.

Bible Reading
2 Chronicles 3-4 | 2 Thessalonians 3

07.09 | July 9

Completely.

Proverbs 3:5-6
*"Trust in the LORD with all thine heart;
and lean not unto thine own understanding.
In all thy ways acknowledge him, and he shall direct thy paths."*

One word appears twice in these verses that makes the difference in how we apply them to our walk with the Lord. Just three letters, but so much is found within the word…All. It is often joked that all simply means all. If the whole quantity or extent is not included, it simply is not all. A part is not all. Within these familiar verses, this word is linked to two different aspects of our lives with a possessive pronoun in between which makes them personal to us.

"…with all thine heart…" Partial trust is not really trust at all. Where there is doubt, there is not trust. **Do we trust Him completely?**

"In all thy ways…" Partial recognition will only lead to confusion. We cannot be directed by the Lord if we are doing the navigating. **Are we yielding to Him completely?**

When we seek Him in everything,
we will see Him do more than we could ever imagine.

He may send you on a journey you never planned to go on.
Trust that He orders every situation and every step you take.
Psalm 37:23
*"The steps of a good man are ordered by the LORD:
and he delighteth in his way."*

He may deliver something completely unexpected.
Trust Him to provide what you need.
Psalm 84:11
"For the LORD God is a sun and shield: the LORD will give grace and glory: no good thing will he withhold from them that walk uprightly."

He may cross your paths with someone
just when He knows you both need it.
Trust Him to give you who you need.
Proverbs 17:17
"A friend loveth at all times, and a brother is born for adversity."

With *"all thine heart"* and *"In all thy ways"*…**trust Him completely today.**

Bible Reading
2 Chronicles 5-6 | 1 Timothy 1

July 10 | 07.10

Renewed Mercies.

Lamentations 3:22-23
"It is of the LORD'S mercies that we are not consumed, because his compassions fail not. They are new every morning: great is thy faithfulness."

The Lord corrects us because He loves us that much. The context of this chapter, and much of the Book of Lamentations, deals with the correction of His children. It is through His unending mercy and love that we are not consumed by His wrath.

Many times, this verse is quoted without regard to the reason why we need His mercy. If we did no wrong, mercy would not be needed.

The Lord knows that our sin nature often wins the battle of our behavior, yet He continually gives us mercy. Read Psalm 136 for a reminder of His mercy.

Psalm 136:1
"O give thanks unto the LORD; for he is good: for his mercy endureth for ever."

Mercy does not exempt us from His wrath, for a loving Father faithfully corrects His children; however, His mercy prevents us from being consumed by His wrath.

He renews His love and compassion towards us every morning, simply because He is Faithful.

The sun rises each morning,
because He is Faithful.

The rain comes when it is needed,
because He is Faithful.

When the sun shines through the rain,
He sends us a rainbow to remind us once again that He is Faithful.

Great is His faithfulness!

Psalm 86:15
"But thou, O Lord, art a God full of compassion, and gracious, longsuffering, and plenteous in mercy and truth."

Bible Reading
2 Chronicles 7-8 | 1 Timothy 2

07.11 | July 11

Silent Faith.

Isaiah 53:7
"He was oppressed, and he was afflicted, yet he opened not his mouth: he is brought as a lamb to the slaughter, and as a sheep before her shearers is dumb, so he openeth not his mouth."

Although there can be a cost to silence, there is also times when silence is the best answer. The difference is subtle, yet profound.

Sometimes we are called to speak for our faith, and sometimes our silence shows our faith.

The greatest Example of this is found in the Lord Jesus Christ.

He was oppressed. He was afflicted. He was slaughtered.
He was accused. He was questioned. He was reviled.
He suffered.
Yet through all of this…He remained silent.

Matthew 26:63
"But Jesus held his peace…"

Matthew 27:12-14
"And when he was accused of the chief priests and elders, he answered nothing. Then said Pilate unto him, Hearest thou not how many things they witness against thee? And he answered him to never a word; insomuch that the governor marvelled greatly."

Luke 23:9
"Then he questioned with him in many words; but he answered him nothing."

Throughout the latter chapters of each of the Gospel records there are less and less red letters printed on the pages of our Bibles. **In His darkest hour, Jesus chose to be silent as He trusted in His Father's perfect will.** Despite the pain, the suffering, the betrayal, the agony of what was taking place…
He was silent.
1 Peter 2:21-23
He left us an example that we should follow His steps.

When we experience pain and suffering, remember how He handled Himself. If He chose to be silent through all that He faced would we not be wise to also do the same? **Silence can show Who your faith is in.**

Bible Reading
2 Chronicles 9-10 | 1 Timothy 3

Each Day For A Year.

Numbers 14:34
"After the number of the days in which ye searched the land, even forty days, each day for a year, shall ye bear your iniquities, even forty years, and ye shall know my breach of promise."

We have often heard the phrase "Sin will take you farther than you want to go, and cost you more than you want to pay." How true that is. Perhaps we've seen it in our own personal lives or the lives of our loved ones.

The children of Israel were no different. So much can be learned from the examples that are preserved in the Word of God for us to glean. Their lives were like rollercoasters. Many highs and many lows. Twists and turns that were mostly as a result of their disobedience and disregard for what the Lord said. Their unbelief cost them greatly time and time again. Sound familiar?

They spent 40 years wandering in the wilderness as a result of the 40 days they searched the land. Ten men brought an evil report upon the land and made all the congregation to murmur and slander.

Numbers 14:26-27
"And the LORD spake unto Moses and unto Aaron, saying, How long shall I bear with this evil congregation, which murmur against me? I have heard the murmurings of the children of Israel, which they murmur against me."

What if every day we delay our obedience led to a year of delay of God's blessings?

Many of the children of Israel died in the wilderness.
Many did not get to come into the promised land.

The children of the people that murmured suffered because of their parents' decisions. They bore the repercussions and reproaches. They wandered aimlessly for 40 years bearing their parents' iniquities.

Sin has consequences.
How long will you wander?
Will your children be reproached because of your decisions?
Murmuring hurts not only those whose lips are moving,
but those whose ears hear it.

One day's decision is not worth a year of regret and despair.
Choose to obey today.

Bible Reading
2 Chronicles 11-12 | 1 Timothy 4

07.13 | July 13

Joshua 14:12
"Now therefore give me this mountain, whereof the LORD spake in that day; for thou heardest in that day how the Anakims were there, and that the cities were great and fenced: if so be the LORD will be with me, then I shall be able to drive them out, as the LORD said."

How often do we just depend on ourselves to get something done? The number of times we are successful at that cannot be too high. We fail in our own strength because we are limited creatures. Yet, if we would only look to our Creator for strength, the possibilities are endless.

Caleb realized this. He was 85 years old and declared himself as strong as he was 45 years ago…simply because he knew the Source of his strength.

"…if so be the LORD will be with me …"
His presence makes all the difference.

The three Hebrew boys displayed this same Truth in their hearts before they were thrown into the fiery furnace.

They knew God was able to deliver them.
Daniel 3:17
"If it be so, our God whom we serve is able to deliver us from the burning fiery furnace, and he will deliver us out of thine hand, O king."

We have read and heard what God has done for others.
We can even remember what He has done for us in the past.

"…if so be the LORD will be with me, then I shall be able…"
**When we acknowledge Him in all things,
we are able to see Him do all things through us.**

Romans 8:31
"What shall we then say to these things?
If God be for us, who can be against us?"

Philippians 4:13
"I can do all things through Christ which strengtheneth me."

Bible Reading
2 Chronicles 13-14 | 1 Timothy 5

July 14 | 07.14

True Friendship.

Proverbs 17:17
"A friend loveth at all times, and a brother is born for adversity."

Adversity can build, strengthen or break a friendship. Anyone can be a friend when all is fun and games, but real friends appear or stick around when skies are gray.

Good times and bad times. Sunshine and rain.
Friends are loyal, trustworthy, faithful, and reliable.

"A friend loveth at all times…"
True friendship is a constant.
It withstands a change of circumstance or location,
willing to endure any storm.

"…and a brother is born for adversity."
True friendship is revealed in adversity.
It is in the midst of a trial
that the strength of our relationships is exposed.
No selfishness, but willingness to sacrifice.
Time spent is not a luxury, but a priority.
Nothing is inconvenient, if it is needed.

Friends should sharpen our relationship with the Lord.
Friends should counsel and encourage us with the Word of God.

Jesus Christ is our Ultimate Example of true friendship.
He never changes. He is always available. He will never leave us nor forsake us, and nothing can separate us from His love.

Romans 8:38-39
*"For I am persuaded, that neither death, nor life, nor angels,
nor principalities, nor powers, nor things present, nor things to come,
Nor height, nor depth, nor any other creature,
shall be able to separate us from the love of God,
which is in Christ Jesus our Lord."*

**True friendship is built upon
and strengthened by the Word of God.**

Bible Reading
2 Chronicles 15-16 | 1 Timothy 6

July 15

Genesis 41:51
"And Joseph called the name of the firstborn Manasseh: For God, said he, hath made me forget all my toil, and all my father's house."

Every day we live we endure hardships and situations that make us want to complain. It is in those times that we fail to remember all the good, and instead choose to focus on all that seems to be going wrong.

If anyone had a right to complain, it was Joseph. He expected a birthright from his father. His brothers literally put him in a pit, and then sold him into slavery. He was no stranger to family drama.

Joseph experienced firsthand many toils that we likely will never face. Yet, through it all, he knew God was Faithful. He even chose to name his firstborn Manasseh as a constant reminder of how God had delivered him from all his toil, and made him forget all the sorrow and wearisome trouble that he endured.

Psalm 30:5
"For his anger endureth but a moment; in his favour is life: weeping may endure for a night, but joy cometh in the morning."

Through the Lord's providence, we too can forget it all by choosing to focus on His goodness and grace.

Psalm 103:1-2
"Bless the LORD, O my soul: and all that is within me, bless his holy name. Bless the LORD, O my soul, and forget not all his benefits:"

Joseph allowed the Lord to use any wrong someone tried to do against him for His glory.

Genesis 50:20
"But as for you, ye thought evil against me; but God meant it unto good, to bring to pass, as it is this day, to save much people alive."

We can forget it all when we remind ourselves that He is working it all together for our good and His glory.

Romans 8:28
"And we know that all things work together for good to them that love God, to them who are the called according to his purpose."

Whatever toil you face today, God has allowed it and He has a purpose. Focus on the One Who is Faithful, and He will help you to forget it all.

Bible Reading
2 Chronicles 17-18 | 2 Timothy 1

July 16 | 07.16

Fruitful In Affliction.

Genesis 41:52
*"And the name of the second called he Ephraim:
For God hath caused me to be fruitful in the land of my affliction."*

Throughout most of the life of Joseph, that we have to learn from, he is away from his father. This was the root of his affliction. Later on, in Genesis 49, we see that despite his affliction Joseph was fruitful.

Genesis 49:22
*"Joseph is a fruitful bough, even a fruitful bough by a well;
whose branches run over the wall:"*

Affliction is simply misery, trouble or depression.
Joseph found himself there many times, but he never let it stop him. He could have stayed in that pit. He could have wallowed in the prison. But he knew God had a purpose and greater plan.

**Our affliction can make us miserable or we can choose
to allow the Lord to make us fruitful in the midst of our misery.**

Psalm 119:50
"This is my comfort in my affliction: for thy word hath quickened me."

Allow your affliction to point you to the Word of God.

Psalm 119:71
*"It is good for me that I have been afflicted;
that I might learn thy statutes."*

**Any affliction we endure can be worth it,
if we allow it to make us fruitful.**

2 Corinthians 4:16-18
"For which cause we faint not; but though our outward man perish, yet the inward man is renewed day by day. For our light affliction, which is but for a moment, worketh for us a far more exceeding and eternal weight of glory; While we look not at the things which are seen, but at the things which are not seen: for the things which are seen are temporal; but the things which are not seen are eternal."

Bible Reading
2 Chronicles 19-20 | 2 Timothy 2

07.17 | July 17

Jeremiah 9:23-24
"Thus saith the LORD, Let not the wise man glory in his wisdom, neither let the mighty man glory in his might, let not the rich man glory in his riches: But let him that glorieth glory in this, that he understandeth and knoweth me, that I am the LORD which exercise lovingkindness, judgment, and righteousness, in the earth: for in these things I delight, saith the LORD."

What are you glorying in today? In other words, what do you consider beautiful and meaningful? Each season of life brings our focus on something different; but no matter our experience, we choose where our attention is given.

If we truly examine ourselves in light of what the Word of God has to say about us, we have but only one choice in what to glory in.

2 Corinthians 10:17-18
"But he that glorieth, let him glory in the Lord. For not he that commendeth himself is approved, but whom the Lord commendeth."

Galatians 6:14
"But God forbid that I should glory, save in the cross of our Lord Jesus Christ, by whom the world is crucified unto me, and I unto the world."

Sometimes, the Lord uses pain in our lives to bring Himself glory. When we are wronged, we have to choose how we will react to the affliction. Our choice will determine how much glory we take from or give to Him.

Matthew 5:38-39
"Ye have heard that it hath been said, An eye for an eye, and a tooth for a tooth: But I say unto you, That ye resist not evil: but whosoever shall smite thee on thy right cheek, turn to him the other also."

When we choose to turn the other cheek, it may allow the opportunity for another hit, but more than that it allows Christ to fight the battle for us.

Our wounds cannot compare to what He endured for us or to the glory that will be revealed in us when we suffer willingly for Him.

Romans 8:18
"For I reckon that the sufferings of this present time are not worthy to be compared with the glory which shall be revealed in us."

Bible Reading
2 Chronicles 21-22 | 2 Timothy 3

He Is In Control.

Proverbs 21:1
"The king's heart is in the hand of the LORD, as the rivers of water: he turneth it whithersoever he will."

No matter who holds the highest governmental position in the land, they are still at the footstool of the King of Kings.

Matthew 5:34-35
"But I say unto you, Swear not at all; neither by heaven; for it is God's throne: Nor by the earth; for it is his footstool: neither by Jerusalem; for it is the city of the great King."

No matter how many votes are cast, God in His Wisdom chooses who is elected. They may hold a position, but it is God Who controls what will or will not occur for they are in His hand.

Daniel 2:20-22
"Daniel answered and said, Blessed be the name of God for ever and ever: for wisdom and might are his: And he changeth the times and the seasons: he removeth kings, and setteth up kings: he giveth wisdom unto the wise, and knowledge to them that know understanding: He revealeth the deep and secret things: he knoweth what is in the darkness, and the light dwelleth with him."

God controls everything by His Wisdom, yet offers to give us Wisdom if only we would ask.

James 1:5
"If any of you lack wisdom, let him ask of God, that giveth to all men liberally, and upbraideth not; and it shall be given him."

Proverbs 2:6-7
"For the LORD giveth wisdom: out of his mouth cometh knowledge and understanding. He layeth up sound wisdom for the righteous: he is a buckler to them that walk uprightly."

Thank Him today for all He has given you, and remember that He is in control.

Daniel 2:23
"I thank thee, and praise thee, O thou God of my fathers, who hast given me wisdom and might, and hast made known unto me now what we desired of thee: for thou hast now made known unto us the king's matter."

Bible Reading
2 Chronicles 23-24 | 2 Timothy 4

07.19 | July 19

Bind His Word.

Romans 7:18-20
"For I know that in me (that is, in my flesh,) dwelleth no good thing: for to will is present with me; but how to perform that which is good I find not. For the good that I would I do not: but the evil which I would not, that I do. Now if I do that I would not, it is no more I that do it, but sin that dwelleth in me."

Tying a string on your finger is a way of remembering to do something that you may otherwise forget. We are a forgetful people; often forgetting to do those things we should, and remembering only to do that which we should not.

The Apostle Paul admitted this trait in his letter to the Romans. He confessed that his flesh often got in the way of what his new nature desired.

Acknowledging and depending on the power of the Word of God is the only way to resolve the conflict between our flesh and our spirit.

Three times throughout the Book of Proverbs it is written to *"bind them"* upon ourselves.

Proverbs 3:3-4
"Let not mercy and truth forsake thee: bind them about thy neck; write them upon the table of thine heart: So shalt thou find favour and good understanding in the sight of God and man."

An ornament or locket is often placed around the neck for safekeeping and held close to the heart with special meaning.

What are you keeping in your locket?

Proverbs 6:21
"Bind them continually upon thine heart, and tie them about thy neck."

The heart of the person is displayed in their actions.

What is written on your heart?

Proverbs 7:3
"Bind them upon thy fingers, write them upon the table of thine heart."

We must do whatever is necessary to remember what the Word of God has to say in order to apply the Truth to our lives. Psalm 119:105

What is tied upon your fingers?
Binding His Word upon our lives is imperative to fulfilling our God given purpose.

Bible Reading
2 Chronicles 25-26 | Titus 1

July 20 | 07.20

Proverbs 11:3
*"The integrity of the upright shall guide them:
but the perverseness of transgressors shall destroy them."*

God gives us an example within the Scriptures of how the integrity of the upright shall guide us if only we yield to Him in wisdom.

Job 2:3
"And the LORD said unto Satan, Hast thou considered my servant Job, that there is none like him in the earth, a perfect and an upright man, one that feareth God, and escheweth evil? and still he holdeth fast his integrity, although thou movedst me against him, to destroy him without cause."

Job was such an upright man, full of integrity, that the Lord asked Satan if he had considered him while walking to and fro upon the earth. God had faith in Job that he would remain faithful despite the persecutions upon his life.

Do we have enough integrity for God to recommend us?

Job 2:9
"Then said his wife unto him, Dost thou still retain thine integrity? curse God, and die."

Job even stayed faithful when those closest to him advised him to give up. He refused to give in to Satan's attacks, and remained full of integrity all his days.

Job 27:5
*"God forbid that I should justify you:
till I die I will not remove mine integrity from me."*

Job 31:6
*"Let me be weighed in an even balance,
that God may know mine integrity."*

**Allow the Word of God to teach and guide you today,
for it is only within those Pages that integrity is found.**

Bible Reading
2 Chronicles 27-28 | Titus 2

07.21 | July 21

Wise To Be Fruitful.

Proverbs 11:30-31
"The fruit of the righteous is a tree of life; and he that winneth souls is wise. Behold, the righteous shall be recompensed in the earth: much more the wicked and the sinner."

Many times the Bible refers to fruit as something that is reproduced as a result of something or someone else. In the Garden of Eden and just after the Flood, God spoke the same message to His people.

Genesis 1:28
"And God blessed them, and God said unto them, Be fruitful, and multiply…"

Genesis 9:1
"And God blessed Noah and his sons, and said unto them, Be fruitful, and multiply, and replenish the earth."

The righteous possess Wisdom that can be shared without ever running out. When we give others the Gospel of Jesus Christ, we multiply what He has done within our hearts. When we win souls for Him, we are sharing Wisdom with others.

Christ told of the Source of the fruit.
John 15:4-5
"Abide in me, and I in you. As the branch cannot bear fruit of itself, except it abide in the vine; no more can ye, except ye abide in me. I am the vine, ye are the branches: He that abideth in me, and I in him, the same bringeth forth much fruit: for without me ye can do nothing."

Christ told of our purpose.
John 15:16
"Ye have not chosen me, but I have chosen you, and ordained you, that ye should go and bring forth fruit, and that your fruit should remain: that whatsoever ye shall ask of the Father in my name, he may give it you."

Christ commissioned us to tell the world about Him.
Mark 16:15
"And he said unto them, Go ye into all the world, and preach the gospel to every creature."

A soul winner brings forth fruit for the glory of God… fruit that remains.

Bible Reading
2 Chronicles 29-30 | Titus 3

Vision.

Proverbs 29:18
*"Where there is no vision, the people perish:
but he that keepeth the law, happy is he."*

Helen Keller, who was blind and deaf, is known for having said,
"The only thing worse than being blind is having sight but no vision."

**If we have but little knowledge of the Word of God,
we lack both vision and wisdom.**

Hosea 4:6
*"My people are destroyed for lack of knowledge:
because thou hast rejected knowledge, I will also reject thee, that thou
shalt be no priest to me: seeing thou hast forgotten the law of thy God,
I will also forget thy children."*

Our lack of Biblical knowledge is disastrous to our testimony for the Lord.
We cannot apply what we do not know or understand.

Today, most of the world has the Scriptures available to them, but there will come a day when there will be a famine of the Word of God.

Amos 8:11-12
*"Behold, the days come, saith the Lord GOD,
that I will send a famine in the land, not a famine of bread, nor a thirst for
water, but of hearing the words of the LORD: And they shall wander from
sea to sea, and from the north even to the east, they shall run to and fro
to seek the word of the LORD, and shall not find it."*

**We must seek the Lord through the Word of God
while there is still time for us to do so.**

Psalm 119:2
*"Blessed are they that keep his testimonies,
and that seek him with the whole heart."*

Only when we make the Word a priority in our lives
will we truly be happy.

**For it is then, and only then,
that we will have vision for the days ahead.**

Bible Reading
2 Chronicles 31-32 | Philemon

07.23 | July 23

James 1:22-24
"But be ye doers of the word, and not hearers only, deceiving your own selves. For if any be a hearer of the word, and not a doer, he is like unto a man beholding his natural face in a glass: For he beholdeth himself, and goeth his way, and straightway forgetteth what manner of man he was."

If we choose to only hear the Word, we live under our own wisdom rather than the Wisdom of the Word of God.

We deceive ourselves when we hear but neglect to apply the Truth.

Proverbs 29:19-20
"A servant will not be corrected by words: for though he understand he will not answer. Seest thou a man that is hasty in his words? there is more hope of a fool than of him."

These are those who refuse to be corrected by the Word of God.

Proverbs 26:12
"Seest thou a man wise in his own conceit? there is more hope of a fool than of him."

Applying the Truth of the Scriptures brings blessings upon our lives.

James 1:25
"But whoso looketh into the perfect law of liberty, and continueth therein, he being not a forgetful hearer, but a doer of the work, this man shall be blessed in his deed."

Within the pages of the Word of God there is direction and satisfaction that cannot be found anywhere else.

Why would we choose to look anywhere else?
Hear the Word, and then apply the Word.

Bible Reading
2 Chronicles 33-34 | Hebrews 1

July 24 | 07.24

The Result Of Refusing

Proverbs 15:32
*"He that refuseth instruction despiseth his own soul:
but he that heareth reproof getteth understanding."*

Sin not only hinders our fellowship with God, but it also takes a toll on our perception of our own soul, must less the souls of others.

Matthew 16:26
*"For what is a man profited, if he shall gain the whole world,
and lose his own soul? or what shall a man give in exchange for his soul?"*

The more sin we partake of, the more tolerant of it we become.
Eventually, sin will become so normal
that there is no awareness of it whatsoever.

We must be conscious of sin
in order to be conscious of the souls of others.

**The eternity of those around us may very well depend on
whether or not we personally give them the Gospel of Jesus Christ.**

The drive thru employee's eternity is worth
getting over our fear of them rejecting the tract we hand them.

Someone's soul is worth our inconvenience.

Luke 9:26
*"For whosoever shall be ashamed of me and of my words,
of him shall the Son of man be ashamed, when he shall come in his own
glory, and in his Father's, and of the holy angels."*

What are you doing for the souls of others?

Mark 8:35
*"For whosoever will save his life shall lose it;
but whosoever shall lose his life for my sake and the gospel's,
the same shall save it."*

How much is a soul worth to you?

Bible Reading
2 Chronicles 35-36 | Hebrews 2

07.25 | July 25

Choosing Who To Obey.

Acts 5:29
*"Then Peter and the other apostles answered and said,
We ought to obey God rather than men."*

The three Hebrew boys of the Book of Daniel faced a horrible snare because of their disobedience to King Nebuchadnezzar's demands. Instead, the faith of Shadrach, Meshach, and Abednego, shined brightly through the flames of the fiery furnace because they chose to fear the Lord instead of man.

Daniel 3:16-18
"Shadrach, Meshach, and Abednego, answered and said to the king, O Nebuchadnezzar, we are not careful to answer thee in this matter. If it be so, our God whom we serve is able to deliver us from the burning fiery furnace, and he will deliver us out of thine hand, O king. But if not, be it known unto thee, O king, that we will not serve thy gods, nor worship the golden image which thou hast set up."

Obedience to God instead of men will always result in a higher reward. If the Hebrew boys would have chose to bow, they still would not have burned; however, they would not have seen the glory of the Lord through the flames or been such a pivotal example for us today of what is possible if we would simply obey what God says.

Who do you fear?
Fear of man brings a snare upon us,
which is used here to describe a cause of injury.

Proverbs 29:25
*"The fear of man bringeth a snare:
but whoso putteth his trust in the LORD shall be safe."*

**When we fear God instead of man,
we can be boldly confident that He will help us.**
Hebrews 13:5-6
*"Let your conversation be without covetousness;
and be content with such things as ye have: for he hath said,
I will never leave thee, nor forsake thee. So that we may boldly say,
The Lord is my helper, and I will not fear what man shall do unto me."*

There is no need to fear anyone else, if we have a godly fear of Him.

Bible Reading
Ezra 1-2 | Hebrews 3

July 26 | 07.26

Great Things.

1 Samuel 12:23-24
"Moreover as for me, God forbid that I should sin against the LORD in ceasing to pray for you: but I will teach you the good and the right way: Only fear the LORD, and serve him in truth with all your heart: for consider how great things he hath done for you."

As Samuel rebuked the children of Israel for demanding a king to rule over them, he finished with these two verses about what he would do because of their sin. He not only prayed fervently for them, but he chose to still teach and remind them to consider what the LORD had done for them. Perhaps we also need reminded about the great things He has done for us.

Consider the good and right way.
"Only fear the LORD, and serve him in truth with all your heart"

Consider who taught you about the Truth.
2 Timothy 3:14
"But continue thou in the things which thou hast learned and hast been assured of, knowing of whom thou hast learned them;"

Consider where He has brought you from.
2 Corinthians 5:17
"Therefore if any man be in Christ, he is a new creature: old things are passed away; behold, all things are become new."

Consider how He has provided for you.
Psalm 23:5
"Thou preparest a table before me in the presence of mine enemies: thou anointest my head with oil; my cup runneth over."

Consider how He has enabled you to serve Him.
1 Corinthians 15:10
"But by the grace of God I am what I am: and his grace which was bestowed upon me was not in vain; but I laboured more abundantly than they all: yet not I, but the grace of God which was with me."

He has done so much for us, and we are so undeserving. There are not enough books to contain them. When we stop and consider the great things the Lord has done for us, it should only make us desire to fear Him and serve Him more.

Psalm 126:3
"The LORD hath done great things for us; whereof we are glad."

Bible Reading
Ezra 3-4 | Hebrews 4

07.27 | July 27

Let Him Hear.

Mark 4:9
"And he said unto them, He that hath ears to hear, let him hear."

This same phrase is mentioned a total of seven times throughout the pages of the New Testament. Each one is written in red.

Matthew 11:15
Mark 4:9
Mark 4:23-24
Revelation 2:7
Revelation 2:11
Revelation 2:17
Revelation 2:29

The Creator gave His creation spiritual ears, but He also gives us the choice to hear.

Sometimes the Word falls on deaf ears because someone chooses not to hear Him. If someone does not hear, it is of their own choosing.

We must choose to have faith in Him.
Romans 10:17
"So then faith cometh by hearing, and hearing by the word of God."

Christ said *"let him hear"* seven times within the pages of Scripture, but each and every moment He continues to say the same thing.

He is not willing that any should perish.
2 Peter 3:9
"The Lord is not slack concerning his promise, as some men count slackness; but is longsuffering to us-ward, not willing that any should perish, but that all should come to repentance."

He is willing for all to hear, but it is up to us to tell them.
Romans 10:14
"How then shall they call on him in whom they have not believed? and how shall they believe in him of whom they have not heard? and how shall they hear without a preacher?"

Let them hear of Him today.

Bible Reading
Ezra 5-6 | Hebrews 5

Every Word.

Proverbs 30:5
*"Every word of God is pure:
he is a shield unto them that put their trust in him."*

There is comfort in knowing that not just some of the Words, but every single Word makes a difference. *"Every word of God…"*

When we open our Bibles, we must first consider Who is speaking. Our words are not always true, nor those of our trusted friends and family; but when God speaks, we must remember that He is the Truth.

"Every word of God is pure…"
The Words that we read within the Word of God are pure.
His Words are proven to be without any blemishes, deceit or falsehood.

Psalm 12:6-7
*"The words of the LORD are pure words:
as silver tried in a furnace of earth, purified seven times. Thou shalt keep them, O LORD, thou shalt preserve them from this generation for ever."*

The pureness of His Words enables us to place our trust in Him.
He is our Shield.
Proverbs 30:5
"…he is a shield unto them that put their trust in him."

He is our Buckler.
Psalm 18:30
*"As for God, his way is perfect: the word of the LORD is tried:
he is a buckler to all those that trust in him."*

He is our Refuge.
Psalm 91:2
*"I will say of the LORD, He is my refuge and my fortress:
my God; in him will I trust."*

There is protection, comfort, direction, and provision through Him.
Trust His Every Word.
Whatever you are going through today,
you can trust every Word of His Word.

Bible Reading
Ezra 7-8 | Hebrews 6

07.29 | July 29

His Word Is Sufficient.

Deuteronomy 4:2
"Ye shall not add unto the word which I command you, neither shall ye diminish ought from it, that ye may keep the commandments of the LORD your God which I command you."

Things that are pure have no need for something to be added or taken away from them.

Proverbs 30:5-6
"Every word of God is pure: he is a shield unto them that put their trust in him. Add thou not unto his words, lest he reprove thee, and thou be found a liar."

God has preserved His pure Words for us.

Yet today, there are many people who choose to add, subtract and change the Word of God to suit their own agenda. There are consequences for those who dare try to change the Word of God.

Revelation 22:18-19
"For I testify unto every man that heareth the words of the prophecy of this book, If any man shall add unto these things, God shall add unto him the plagues that are written in this book: And if any man shall take away from the words of the book of this prophecy, God shall take away his part out of the book of life, and out of the holy city, and from the things which are written in this book."

There is no need to add or change His Word, because He does not change.

Malachi 3:6
"For I am the LORD, I change not…"

Hebrews 13:8
"Jesus Christ the same yesterday, and to day, and for ever."

Acknowledging that He is immutable allows us to rest in Him. There is comfort in knowing that we can rely on Him through His Word.

2 Corinthians 12:9
"And he said unto me, My grace is sufficient for thee: for my strength is made perfect in weakness. Most gladly therefore will I rather glory in my infirmities, that the power of Christ may rest upon me."

His grace is sufficient because His Word is Sufficient.

Bible Reading
Ezra 9-10 | Hebrews 7

July 30 | 07.30

His Word Is The Solution.

Psalm 33:10
*"The LORD bringeth the counsel of the heathen to nought:
he maketh the devices of the people of none effect."*

We tend to think that we know what is best for us; and if not, our flesh tends to believe that those closest to us have the answers. What we forget is that, even in the best intentions, the hearts of the people we love and trust are just as deceitful as our own.

Proverbs 19:21
*"There are many devices in a man's heart;
nevertheless the counsel of the LORD, that shall stand."*

God knows our hearts as well as those we seek counsel from and rather than leave us on our own, He provides the Solution.

Psalm 33:11
*"The counsel of the LORD standeth for ever,
the thoughts of his heart to all generations."*

His Word has been proven to be true because He is the Truth.
His Word has been preserved because He was and is and always will be.
His Word has been purified because He is Holy.

Isaiah 40:8
*"The grass withereth, the flower fadeth:
but the word of our God shall stand for ever."*

No other book can even begin to compare to the Truth that the Word of God contains because the Scriptures contain Him. It is within His Word that we learn Who He is, we discover what He has done, what He is doing right now, and what He will do. His promises are true because His grace and mercy confirms those that have already come to pass.

Psalm 119:89
"For ever, O LORD, thy word is settled in heaven."

Rather than seeking the answers in all the wrong places, we can choose to find the Answer to every problem we will ever face within the glorious pages of the Word of God.

His Word is the Solution to any question you have today.

Bible Reading
Nehemiah 1-2 | Hebrews 8

07.31 | July 31

Go Home.

Mark 5:19-20
*"Howbeit Jesus suffered him not, but saith unto him,
Go home to thy friends, and tell them how great things
the Lord hath done for thee, and hath had compassion on thee.
And he departed, and began to publish in Decapolis how great things
Jesus had done for him: and all men did marvel."*

He had just experienced a miracle in his life.
Jesus had intervened when no one else could.

The Maniac of Gadara was once filled with a legion of demons, but when he met Jesus, they were cast into a great herd of swine. This man who was once bound with fetters and chains and cutting himself with stones, was now sitting, and clothed, and in his right mind. Only Jesus could have made such a change.

The man wanted to go with Jesus, but He directed him otherwise.
"…Go home to thy friends, and tell them how great things the Lord hath done for thee, and hath had compassion on thee."

He had to make the decision whether to obey the command of Jesus, or remain silent of the great things that had taken place in his life.

Do we not have the same decision to make?
No, we likely have not had a legion of demons cast out, but the day we repented of our sin and turned to Jesus a miracle took place just the same.

Do we remain silent after all Jesus has done for us?

After we receive His free Gift of salvation,
the great things do not stop there.

Day after day, the Lord continues to do great things within our lives.
Every day He continually shows us compassion.

We too have the choice to remain silent
or *"…Go home to thy friends, and tell them…"*

Bible Reading
Nehemiah 3-4 | Hebrews 9

August 1 | 08.01

Satisfied In The Wilderness.

Mark 8:4
"And his disciples answered him, From whence can a man satisfy these men with bread here in the wilderness?"

Jesus had compassion on the multitude that had nothing to eat after faithfully following Him for three days. He did not want to send them away hungry. His disciples immediately doubted how *"a man"* could feed so many in the middle of the wilderness.

But they forgot that although He was 100% man, He was also 100% God.
A man could not…but God could.

Jesus asked a simple question.
Mark 8:5
"And he asked them, How many loaves have ye? And they said, Seven."

They answered honestly, and then gave Him everything that they had.
Give what you have to the Lord.

Jesus then commanded the people to sit down on the ground.
Sit down, and wait on Him.

Jesus then broke the loaves.
What we give to Him often has to be broken in order to be used for His glory.

Jesus then gave the pieces back to His disciples to be set before the people. After they had eaten, and were filled, there was much left over. Seven baskets full. They began with seven loaves, and left with seven baskets full.

"…can a man satisfy these men with bread here in the wilderness?"
His disciples had that answer to their question.

Sometimes we will find ourselves in the wilderness.
Maybe physically, financially, emotionally, or spiritually.

May we remember that the same God Who fed 4,000 in the wilderness with just seven loaves and a few fishes is the same today. He has not changed.

He is Able to satisfy whatever need we have, whenever and wherever we find ourselves.

Bible Reading
Nehemiah 5-6 | Hebrews 10

08.02 | August 2

He Is Faithful.

1 Corinthians 1:9
*"God is faithful, by whom ye were called
unto the fellowship of his Son Jesus Christ our Lord."*

Many times throughout the Scriptures we find phrases that reiterate the undeniable fact that God is Faithful.

Search the Scriptures to find where a few of these phrases are found:
"God is faithful"
"the faithful God"
"thy counsels of old are faithfulness and truth"
"great is thy faithfulness"
"Faithful is he that calleth you"
"But the Lord is faithful"
"for he is faithful that promised"
"she judged him faithful who had promised"
"was called Faithful and True"

It is a fact that He is Faithful.

Applying that fact to our lives makes it personal…
He is Faithful to us.

It is the application of the facts through belief that makes the difference.
Whether or not we believe the truth does not make it any less true.

What truth are you having trouble believing today?

1 Corinthians 10:13
*"There hath no temptation taken you but such as is common to man:
but God is faithful, who will not suffer you to be tempted above
that ye are able; but will with the temptation also make a way to escape,
that ye may be able to bear it."*

Consider what the Word of God says about your circumstance.

Psalm 100:5
*"For the LORD is good; his mercy is everlasting;
and his truth endureth to all generations."*

**Ponder over how the Truth applies to your life,
then choose to believe that He is Faithful.**

Bible Reading
Nehemiah 7-8 | Hebrews 11

August 3 | 08.03

Let Us Come Boldly.

Hebrews 4:16
*"Let us therefore come boldly unto the throne of grace,
that we may obtain mercy, and find grace to help in time of need."*

There are three types of answers that God gives to our prayers. Sometimes He says "yes"; sometimes He says, "no", and sometimes His answer is "wait".

The Word of God tells us that He will answer.
Matthew 7:7-8
"Ask, and it shall be given you; seek, and ye shall find; knock, and it shall be opened unto you: For every one that asketh receiveth; and he that seeketh findeth; and to him that knocketh it shall be opened."

Imagine what we could be given…imagine what we could find…imagine what could be opened unto us…if only we would ask, seek, and knock.

Great and mighty things await those who call upon Him.
Jeremiah 33:3
*"Call unto me, and I will answer thee,
and shew thee great and mighty things, which thou knowest not."*

God always answers every prayer that we pray.

When we see God's hand in a situation that we have brought to Him, it should encourage us to pray more often.

In Hebrews, we read that not only should we come to God in prayer, but also how we can approach the throne of grace…*"boldly".*

Boldly is to come with confidence…not in ourselves, but in Who He is.

He offers us both mercy and grace, and is waiting to be our Helper just when we need it…which if we are honest, our need for His help is continual.

No wonder every time *"without ceasing"* is mentioned throughout the Scriptures it is directly related to prayer.

Let us come boldly unto Him today.

Bible Reading
Nehemiah 9-11 | Hebrews 12

08.04 | August 4

Let Us Draw Near.

Hebrews 10:22
"Let us draw near with a true heart in full assurance of faith, having our hearts sprinkled from an evil conscience, and our bodies washed with pure water."

We can only *"come boldly"* when we are covered by the Blood of Jesus Christ.
Hebrews 10:19
"Having therefore, brethren, boldness to enter into the holiest by the blood of Jesus,"

It is only through Him that we have the privilege to draw near to God.
But how can we draw near to Him?

A true heart is necessary. *"Let us draw near with a true heart…"*
God is not interested in hypocrisy.
James 4:8
"Draw nigh to God, and he will draw nigh to you. Cleanse your hands, ye sinners; and purify your hearts, ye double minded."

A true confidence is essential.
"Let us draw near with a true heart in full assurance of faith…"
God desires us to come to Him through faith
that rests solely in His works and not our own.
Psalm 73:28
"But it is good for me to draw near to God: I have put my trust in the Lord GOD, that I may declare all thy works."

A true relationship is required.
"Let us draw near with a true heart in full assurance of faith, having our hearts sprinkled from an evil conscience, and our bodies washed with pure water."
Through faith in His blood, our hearts are sprinkled
and our bodies are washed.
1 John 1:6-7
"If we say that we have fellowship with him, and walk in darkness, we lie, and do not the truth: But if we walk in the light, as he is in the light, we have fellowship one with another, and the blood of Jesus Christ his Son cleanseth us from all sin."

Draw near to Him today, and every day.

Bible Reading
Nehemiah 12-13 | Hebrews 13

Let Us Hold Fast.

Hebrews 10:23
"Let us hold fast the profession of our faith without wavering; (for he is faithful that promised;)"

Surface deep, the words *"hold fast"* imply to believe strongly in something; and while we should definitely feel that way in regards to our profession of faith, perhaps there is more meaning here.

To *"hold fast the profession of our faith"* here suggests remaining tightly secure despite any raging waters around us.

Deep within the ocean, root-like aquatic structures that anchor themselves to substrates are called holdfasts. They vary in shapes and forms, but regardless of their size they all have one thing in common… they are secure because of their anchor.

Hebrews 4:14
"Seeing then that we have a great high priest, that is passed into the heavens, Jesus the Son of God, let us hold fast our profession."

There is no reason to waver when our faith is anchored in Him.

Job realized the Source of his righteousness.
Job 27:6
"My righteousness I hold fast, and will not let it go: my heart shall not reproach me so long as I live."

His faith never wavered, simply because he never depended upon himself.

"…without wavering; (for he is faithful that promised;)"

He is Faithful.
He has promised, and He always keeps His promises.

Titus 1:2
"In hope of eternal life, which God, that cannot lie, promised before the world began;"

Embrace the Source of your faith today by holding fast to Him.

Bible Reading
Esther 1-2 | James 1

08.06 | August 6

Let Us Consider.

Hebrews 10:24
*"And let us consider one another
to provoke unto love and to good works:"*

What is your mind attentively fixed upon today?

Many people routinely only consider themselves.
They are only concerned with what is best for them.

**As God's children,
we can set an example for the world
in how we consider one another.**

Philippians 2:3
*"Let nothing be done through strife or vainglory;
but in lowliness of mind
let each esteem other better than themselves."*

Romans 12:10
*"Be kindly affectioned one to another with brotherly love;
in honour preferring one another;"*

Open the door for someone.
Let the other car go first.

In this crazy world we live in, the "little" things
no longer seem so little.

Allow the world to see something,
or rather Someone, different in you.

Hebrews 12:2-3
*"Looking unto Jesus the author and finisher of our faith;
who for the joy that was set before him endured the cross,
despising the shame, and is set down at the right hand of the throne of
God. For consider him that endured such contradiction of sinners against
himself, lest ye be wearied and faint in your minds."*

Above all else, consider Him.

Bible Reading
Esther 3-4 | James 2

August 7 | 08.07

A Better Hope.

Hebrews 7:19
*"For the law made nothing perfect, but the bringing in
of a better hope did; by the which we draw nigh unto God."*

The law could not and cannot bring salvation or justify our guilt. It is simply a schoolmaster to show us that we come short of the glory of God.

Galatians 3:24-25
*"Wherefore the law was our schoolmaster to bring us unto Christ,
that we might be justified by faith. But after that faith is come,
we are no longer under a schoolmaster."*

**It took the precious blood of Jesus Christ
to make justification possible.**
When we have faith in Him, we are no longer under the law.

He is that *"better hope"*,
and the only way we can draw nigh unto God.

Hebrews 7:22
"By so much was Jesus made a surety of a better testament."

He is the Anchor of our salvation.

Hebrews 6:19
*"Which hope we have as an anchor of the soul,
both sure and stedfast, and which entereth into that within the veil;"*

When we are unsure and drifting without hope,
He is stedfast.
He never changes.

Hebrews 7:24-25
*"But this man, because he continueth ever,
hath an unchangeable priesthood. Wherefore he is able also to save
them to the uttermost that come unto God by him,
seeing he ever liveth to make intercession for them."*

He is Able, willing and ready to save anyone who comes to Him.

Do you need a *"better hope"* today?
Look to Him.

Bible Reading
Esther 5-6 | James 3

08.08 | August 8

An Immediate Change.

Mark 10:52
"And Jesus said unto him, Go thy way; thy faith hath made thee whole. And immediately he received his sight, and followed Jesus in the way."

Bartimaeus was a blind beggar. He was desperate both for help and for a drastic change in his life. He could not see, but he could hear. When he heard that Jesus was nearby, he cried out for Jesus to have mercy on him.

Jesus stood still when He heard him cry.
Mark 10:51
"And Jesus answered and said unto him, What wilt thou that I should do unto thee? The blind man said unto him, Lord, that I might receive my sight."

He is still asking today.

What would be your answer to that same question:
"What wilt thou that I should do unto thee?"

What do you desire for Him to do in your life?
He is Able, yet so often we neglect to have the faith that He can and will.

Doubt is the thief of faith.
If Bartimaeus would have doubted the Lord could heal him, he would have never received his sight.

Mark 10:52
"And Jesus said unto him, Go thy way…And immediately he received his sight, and followed Jesus in the way."

Bartimaeus' way became following the Way.

The drastic change he had longed for was more than just an immediate physical healing, his direction was changed when he decided to followed Jesus.

Tell the Lord the answer to the question today, then choose to immediately follow His direction.

Bible Reading
Esther 7-8 | James 4

August 9 | 08.09

Nothing But Leaves.

Mark 11:13
"And seeing a fig tree afar off having leaves, he came, if haply he might find any thing thereon: and when he came to it, he found nothing but leaves; for the time of figs was not yet."

The figs come before the leaves, yet this fig tree stood afar off from Jesus with many leaves…seemly promising fruit, yet leaving Jesus empty handed.

The fig tree gave the appearance that it bore fruit, yet it was fruitless.
Jesus then declared the tree unfruitful forever.

There are many today whose lives bear leaves which portrays themselves as fruit-bearing, yet they are fruitless. Their leaves indicate there is fruit hanging from the branches, yet they are empty.

Imagine yourself as that fig tree which Jesus saw afar off.
Would He find nothing but leaves?
Will you be left empty handed at the Judgment Seat of Christ?

What a solemn and convicting reminder of our need to be fruitful for His glory!

God's first blessing upon Adam and Eve was for them to be fruitful.
Genesis 1:28
"And God blessed them, and God said unto them, Be fruitful, and multiply…"

It is His desire that we be fruitful, not fruitless.
John 15:4-5
"Abide in me, and I in you. As the branch cannot bear fruit of itself, except it abide in the vine; no more can ye, except ye abide in me. I am the vine, ye are the branches: He that abideth in me, and I in him, the same bringeth forth much fruit: for without me ye can do nothing."

There is fruit to bear, if only we will abide in Him.
He has left us here for the purpose of bringing forth fruit for His glory.
John 15:16
"Ye have not chosen me, but I have chosen you, and ordained you, that ye should go and bring forth fruit, and that your fruit should remain: that whatsoever ye shall ask of the Father in my name, he may give it you."
Ask Him to enable you to be fruitful for His glory.

Bible Reading
Esther 9-10 | James 5

08.10 | August 10

Called To Mind.

Mark 14:72
"And the second time the cock crew. And Peter called to mind the word that Jesus said unto him, Before the cock crow twice, thou shalt deny me thrice. And when he thought thereon, he wept."

Peter had heard Christ Himself tell him what would happen that evening. Even though he vehemently denied that he would ever deny Jesus.

Mark 14:30
"And Jesus saith unto him, Verily I say unto thee, That this day, even in this night, before the cock crow twice, thou shalt deny me thrice."

The cock crew immediately after Peter had denied Him the third time. **Just as Jesus had said.** As soon as Peter heard the cock crow the second time, he remembered.

Matthew 26:75
"And Peter remembered the word of Jesus, which said unto him, Before the cock crow, thou shalt deny me thrice. And he went out, and wept bitterly."

The Word of the Lord was called to his mind.

How many times in our lives do we find ourselves in the middle of something we should not be doing and suddenly a verse of Scripture comes to mind?

Psalm 119:11
"Thy word have I hid in mine heart, that I might not sin against thee."

Hide His Word within your heart, then ask the Lord to call His Word to your mind.

For every situation that we face…every trial we endure…every temptation we experience…every thought…every word…every action… every inaction…there is a verse.

Hebrews 4:12
"For the word of God is quick, and powerful, and sharper than any twoedged sword, piercing even to the dividing asunder of soul and spirit, and of the joints and marrow, and is a discerner of the thoughts and intents of the heart."

Allow His Word to pierce through today, so that you can recall the Scriptures to your mind just when you need to be reminded of the Truth.

Bible Reading
Job 1-2 | 1 Peter 1

August 11 | 08.11

Willing To Content.

Mark 15:15
"And so Pilate, willing to content the people, released Barabbas unto them, and delivered Jesus, when he had scourged him, to be crucified."

In politics there is always an ulterior motive. We have learned from experience that there are very few people you can trust to do what they say they will do.

Pilate marvelled over the silence of Jesus as He was accused of many things by the chief priests. Pilate himself even asked Him why He was silent.

He knew there was something different about Jesus.
Luke 23:14
"Said unto them, Ye have brought this man unto me, as one that perverteth the people: and, behold, I, having examined him before you, have found no fault in this man touching those things whereof ye accuse him:"

So, Pilate devised a plan to save his career by giving the people a choice of who he should release at the feast. He found Barabbas, who was guilty of insurrection and murder. Surely the people would choose to free Jesus instead of such a wicked man. **Yet, his plan backfired.** The chief priests moved the people to choose to release Barabbas.

Mark 15:12-14
*"And Pilate answered and said again unto them,
What will ye then that I shall do unto him whom ye call
the King of the Jews? And they cried out again, Crucify him.
Then Pilate said unto them, Why, what evil hath he done?
And they cried out the more exceedingly, Crucify him.""*

Pilate was dumbfounded. **He had to choose.** The ball was in his court. It was up to him to decide the fate of Jesus. **He was willing to content the people, so he compromised what he knew in his heart was right.** He chose popularity and politics over the Truth.

How many times in our lives have we been presented with the same decision? **Choosing to stand for the Truth is never popular or easy.** Choosing right over wrong seems to be a rarity today. Are we willing to content the people around us rather than stand on the Lord's side?

Oftentimes, we are no better than Pilate.
Day after day we are left with the same choice… Him or people.
Choose Jesus.

Bible Reading
Job 3-4 | 1 Peter 2

08.12 | August 12

Thorns.

Judges 2:3
"Wherefore I also said, I will not drive them out from before you; but they shall be as thorns in your sides, and their gods shall be a snare unto you."

We have all experienced someone being "a thorn in our side". It's likely there is a face, or perhaps many faces, showing up in your mind.

Have we ever stopped to consider the purpose of that thorn? Often, we do not give it much thought, other than the annoyance the person causes us.

At this point within the children of Israel's journey, these thorns were sent by the Lord Himself. Yes, you read that right.

The people had directly disobeyed what the Lord told them to do.
Judges 2:2
"…but ye have not obeyed my voice: why have ye done this?"

How many times has the Lord said
and asked the same thing about us?

When God sends us thorns, He is trying to teach us a lesson.
Sometimes, that even involves allowing our adversary to have his way.

1 Peter 5:8
*"Be sober, be vigilant; because your adversary the devil,
as a roaring lion, walketh about, seeking whom he may devour:"*

Thorns can lead us to repentance.
They can cause us to admit our sin
and allow us to weep and worship the Lord.

Judges 2:4-5
"And it came to pass, when the angel of the LORD spake these words unto all the children of Israel, that the people lifted up their voice, and wept. And they called the name of that place Bochim: and they sacrificed there unto the LORD."

**Whatever or whoever your thorn is today,
choose to allow it to bring you closer to Him.**

Bible Reading
Job 5-6 | 1 Peter 3

August 13 | 08.13

A Thorn In The Flesh.

2 Corinthians 12:7
"And lest I should be exalted above measure through the abundance of the revelations, there was given to me a thorn in the flesh, the messenger of Satan to buffet me, lest I should be exalted above measure."

Paul was perhaps the greatest disciple to walk the face of the earth. He never forgot what the Lord had delivered him from. He had a pedigree of accolades, yet he remained humble.

2 Corinthians 12:6
"For though I would desire to glory, I shall not be a fool; for I will say the truth: but now I forbear, lest any man should think of me above that which he seeth me to be, or that he heareth of me."

God allowed a thorn of the flesh to remind Paul of his need for Him.
Although he besought the Lord to remove it,
he chose to allow his infirmity to make his faith stronger.

2 Corinthians 12:9
"And he said unto me, My grace is sufficient for thee: for my strength is made perfect in weakness. Most gladly therefore will I rather glory in my infirmities, that the power of Christ may rest upon me."

**Paul gladly chose the pain of his thorn in the flesh
so that the Lord's strength could be shown through his weakness.**

We are faced with the same choice today.

Will we allow a thorn of the flesh to hinder our service to Him?
May we admit our weaknesses
and allow the Lord to show His strength in us.

2 Corinthians 12:10
*"Therefore I take pleasure in infirmities, in reproaches,
in necessities, in persecutions, in distresses for Christ's sake:
for when I am weak, then am I strong."*

Bible Reading
Job 7-8 | 1 Peter 4

08.14 | August 14

Lying Words.

Jeremiah 7:8
"Behold, ye trust in lying words, that cannot profit."

Jeremiah was standing in the gate of the Lord's house.
Jeremiah 7:2
"Stand in the gate of the LORD'S house, and proclaim there this word, and say, Hear the word of the LORD, all ye of Judah, that enter in at these gates to worship the LORD."

He was proclaiming the Word of the Lord, begging for people to enter into house of the Lord. But there was a problem.
Jeremiah 7:3
"Thus saith the LORD of hosts, the God of Israel, Amend your ways and your doings, and I will cause you to dwell in this place."

They must first amend their ways. They had made the Word of the Lord a reproach unto themselves. They had no delight in the Word. They had chosen not to stand in the old paths. They had chosen not to walk in the good way. They had rejected the Words of the Lord.

So, the Lord sent stumblingblocks.
Jeremiah 6:21
"Therefore thus saith the LORD, Behold, I will lay stumblingblock before this people, and the fathers and the sons together shall fall upon them; the neighbour and his friend shall perish."

Stumblingblocks can cause us to trust in things that are untruthful.
Jeremiah 7:4
"Trust ye not in lying words, saying, The temple of the LORD, The temple of the LORD, The temple of the LORD, are these."

Even people who portray themselves to be spiritual Christians, can become stumblingblocks to our walk with the Lord.
Proverbs 6:16-19
The Lord hates these things, yet so often we find ourselves trusting those who are consumed by them.
James 1:8
"A double minded man is unstable in all his ways."
There is no profit is putting our trust in lying words.
Instead, may we choose to only trust the Lord.
Psalm 2:11-12

Bible Reading
Job 9-10 | 1 Peter 5

August 15 | 08.15

Most Surely Believed.

Luke 1:1
"Forasmuch as many have taken in hand to set forth in order a declaration of those things which are most surely believed among us,"

Lies should remind us of the necessity of declaring the Truth.
What do you most surely believe today?
What are you certain of?

If any answers to those questions are not based upon the Truth found in the pages of the Word of God, we are asking for trouble.

Luke mentions that there are *"many"* who have *"taken in hand…those things which are most surely believed".*

They were confident in what they believed because they saw the evidence for themselves.
They were eyewitnesses of the Truth.
They walked with Him. They spoke with Him.
They learned from Him.

And now, they knew that it was up to them to declare the Truth.
If they didn't, who would?

Luke believed the things that were *"most surely believed"* ought to be taught to others.

He was burdened to speak the Truth so that others could also believe.

Luke 1:4
"That thou mightest know the certainty of those things, wherein thou hast been instructed."

What do you believe today?
What are you certain of?

Do you believe the Gospel?
Do you believe God can do the impossible?

Are you certain about your belief in Him?
Then declare it to others.

Bible Reading
Job 11-12 | 2 Peter 1

08.16 | August 16

Sincerity & Truth.

Joshua 24:14
"Now therefore fear the LORD, and serve him in sincerity and in truth: and put away the gods which your fathers served on the other side of the flood, and in Egypt; and serve ye the LORD."

Joshua had given the people reason after reason to keep their eyes on the Lord.

Joshua 23:3
"And ye have seen all that the LORD your God hath done unto all these nations because of you; for the LORD your God is he that hath fought for you."

He pleaded with them to have courage to continue in the Truth.
Joshua 23:6
"Be ye therefore very courageous to keep and to do all that is written in the book of the law of Moses, that ye turn not aside therefrom to the right hand or to the left;"

He reminded them to love Him above all else.
Joshua 23:11
"Take good heed therefore unto yourselves, that ye love the LORD your God."

Now it was up to the people to make their choice.
"Now therefore…"
We have the same choice to make.

Are we serving Him?
If so, are we doing it out of obligation or sincerity?

The only way to serve the Lord in sincerity and in truth is to remove anything that hinders our walk with Him. With all that He has done for us, the least we can do is serve Him in sincerity and truth.

1 Samuel 12:24
"Only fear the LORD, and serve him in truth with all your heart: for consider how great things he hath done for you."

Bible Reading
Job 13-14 | 2 Peter 2

August 17 | 08.17

2 Corinthians 9:8
"And God is able to make all grace abound toward you; that ye, always having all sufficiency in all things, may abound to every good work:"

The phrase *"God is able"* is found five times throughout the pages of Scripture. **Each time it is directly related to something that only God can do.**

Matthew 3:9
Luke 3:8
Romans 11:23
2 Corinthians 9:8

The Jews rejected Christ, which made way for the Gospel to be sent to the Gentiles. Yet, the Lord still has open arms for anyone who chooses to dismiss their unbelief and by faith trust Him. **God is Able to save anyone who comes to Him.** He is not willing that any should perish, but that all would come to repentance.

Romans 14:4
*"Who art thou that judgest another man's servant?
to his own master he standeth or falleth. Yea, he shall be holden up:
for God is able to make him stand."*

God is Able to cause you to stand. He can enable you to have the strength to stand, even when you feel like giving up. He can enable you to have the courage to stand, even when no one else does. We do not stand or fall because of the judgment of someone else, for it is only the Lord's judgment that truly matters. **Allow Him to hold you up today.**

The context of this passage in 2 Corinthians 9 is all about giving back to God. The more we sow, the more we will reap. He loveth a cheerful giver. **God is able to make all grace abound toward us, when we give to Him.** What a promise that entails! Think for a moment of how powerful the grace of God is. It is His grace that bringeth salvation. It is by His grace that we are saved. And yet, He reminds us that He is Able to give us all grace if we will simply give what we have to Him. He gave us everything we have, the least we can do is give it back for Him to use for His glory.

Whatever your need is today, God is Able.
What seems impossible to you, is possible with Him.
He is Able.

Bible Reading
Job 15-16 | 2 Peter 3

08.18 | August 18

If Thou Wouldest Believe.

John 11:40
*"Jesus saith unto her, Said I not unto thee, that,
if thou wouldest believe, thou shouldest see the glory of God?"*

God is Able, but He often asks for something from us in order to see Him do the impossible.

"…if thou wouldest believe…"
Jesus had already asked Martha if she believed in Him.
John 11:25-26
"Jesus said unto her, I am the resurrection, and the life: he that believeth in me, though he were dead, yet shall he live: And whosoever liveth and believeth in me shall never die. Believest thou this?"

She said she believed…and then went her way.
Now, here they stood at the grave of Lazarus, the brother of her and Mary. Jesus said for the stone to be taken away from the grave, and Martha immediately had something negative to say.

"…if thou wouldest believe…"
She was about to see the glory of God with her own eyes, and yet she still doubted.
John 11:41-43
"Then they took away the stone from the place where the dead was laid. And Jesus lifted up his eyes, and said, Father, I thank thee that thou hast heard me. And I knew that thou hearest me always: but because of the people which stand by I said it, that they may believe that thou hast sent me. And when he thus had spoken, he cried with a loud voice, Lazarus, come forth."

Lazarus was alive, and Martha is not mentioned again in the chapter. The next time we find her she is once again serving, setting the table where Lazarus sat to eat supper with Jesus. The glory of God sat before her at the table she was serving.

The Lord desires to do the impossible in our lives.
He only asks that we simply believe that He is Able.

What do you need Him to do in your life today?
"…if thou wouldest believe…"

Bible Reading
Job 17-18 | 1 John 1

August 19 | 08.19

Filtered By Him.

Jeremiah 10:23
*"O LORD, I know that the way of man is not in himself:
it is not in man that walketh to direct his steps."*

Jeremiah prayerfully acknowledged a Truth that is so often the difference in living in victory or defeat.

We are conditioned to believe that we create our own purpose, decide our own way, determine our own future. The culture around us continually preaches that we should follow our hearts and do whatever makes us feel good at the time. This is not the Biblical way to live. In fact, it is completely contrary to what God intends for us.

Our freewill to choose does not negate His sovereignty.

Divine providence. Divine direction. Divine deliverance.
Divine persecution. Divine correction. Divine wrath.

All are directly from Him.
Everything is filtered by Him.

Jeremiah 10:24
*"O LORD, correct me, but with judgment; not in thine anger,
lest thou bring me to nothing."*

We are incapable of directing our own steps.
The creation must be directed by the Creator.

He simply desires that we submit ourselves to Him.
He delights to order our steps according to His will.

Psalm 37:23
*"The steps of a good man are ordered by the LORD:
and he delighteth in his way."*

**When we choose His way,
we find true delight as we delight in Him.**

Bible Reading
Job 19-20 | 1 John 2

08.20 | August 20

Heavy Hands.

Exodus 17:12
"But Moses' hands were heavy; and they took a stone, and put it under him, and he sat thereon; and Aaron and Hur stayed up his hands, the one on the one side, and the other on the other side; and his hands were steady until the going down of the sun."

Moses stood on top of the hill and held the rod of God in his hand. That rod is a picture of the Word of God.

Exodus 17:11
"And it came to pass, when Moses held up his hand, that Israel prevailed: and when he let down his hand, Amalek prevailed."

When we put down the Word, the flesh will prevail. **Oftentimes, when we are serving the Lord our hands will get heavy.** Especially when we are so busy in service that we neglect to spend time within the Word to strengthen our hearts. **We cannot pour from an empty cup.** Thankfully, the Lord often places people within our lives to help us carry the burdens that come with living a life faithful to Him.

The Lord had Moses take Aaron and Hur with him up on that hill because the Lord knew that he would need them. When Moses' hands were heavy, Aaron and Hur took a stone for Moses to sit and rest. He was able to sit upon the stone to regain his strength. What a picture of the Rock of Ages that we have to rest upon! While Moses was sitting upon the stone, Aaron and Hur stayed up his hands so that they could remain steady in the fight. Each of these men were placed there by the Lord for a specific purpose. Moses was to hold the rod of God up. Aaron and Hur were to help him carry out the purpose the Lord had for him.

Sometimes our hands get heavy, and we need an Aaron and a Hur to hold us up. Sometimes, we need to recognize a Moses in our lives and be willing to guide them to the Rock of Ages. Then, do all we can to help them keep their hands up in the battle. Romans 15:1

Whether you find yourself as a Moses or an Aaron/Hur today…ask the Lord to strengthen your heart and your hands in order to fulfill whatever purpose the Lord has in store. Colossians 1:9-11

**Heavy hands can be strengthened
when we faithfully and purposefully pray for them.**

Bible Reading
Job 21-22 | 1 John 3

Search The Heart.

Jeremiah 17:10
"I the LORD search the heart, I try the reins, even to give every man according to his ways, and according to the fruit of his doings."

When investigating to find the truth of a matter, most detectives start with the visual evidence before them. They evaluate each and every piece of material left behind. They can only search out what they see.

The Lord works in a completely different way.
While men look on the outward appearance of things to determine the truth, He looks upon our hearts. He sees what you and I cannot see.

1 Samuel 16:7
"But the LORD said unto Samuel, Look not on his countenance, or on the height of his stature; because I have refused him: for the LORD seeth not as man seeth; for man looketh on the outward appearance, but the LORD looketh on the heart."

He looks beyond the façade that we create and portray to those around us. He looks straight into the heart of our souls. On their own, the state of our hearts is quite depressing.

Jeremiah 17:9
"The heart is deceitful above all things, and desperately wicked: who can know it?"

We are desperately wicked on our own. Yet, we have the option of trading our deceitfulness for His righteousness. After salvation, He searches our hearts according to our fruit.

Who our hearts trust in determines the fruit of our lives.
We have only two choices...
Trust in People - Jeremiah 17:5-6
or
Trust in the Lord - Jeremiah 17:7-8

What a clear difference there is in these outcomes, and it all depends on Who we choose to trust. **Search your heart today.** Evaluate who you are trusting. The best way to truly know this is to simply examine the fruit of your life. Psalm 139:23-24

**Use the mirror of the Word of God
to show the intentions of your heart today.**
Hebrews 4:12

Bible Reading
Job 23-24 | 1 John 4

08.22 | August 22

John 15:5
"I am the vine, ye are the branches: He that abideth in me, and I in him, the same bringeth forth much fruit: for without me ye can do nothing."

He is the Vine. We are the branches. There can be no fruit but that which is given and supplied through Him as we yield ourselves to Him, for Him to work through us. In this chapter we see four categories of fruit bearing spoken of by the Lord Jesus Christ.

No Fruit
"Every branch in me that beareth not fruit he taketh away…"
If we neglect to allow Him to work through us,
we will have no fruit and be left empty handed.

Fruit
"…and every branch that beareth fruit, he purgeth it…"
As we bear fruit, we can expect Him to cleanse us
in order for us to be able to be more fruitful.

More Fruit
"…that it may bring forth more fruit."
The result of us being purged is always worth it,
for He knows what is best.

Much Fruit
*"… He that abideth in me, and I in him,
the same bringeth forth much fruit…"*
The ultimate goal of our walk with Him
is to bring forth much fruit for His glory.

Fruit That Remains - John 15:16
"Ye have not chosen me, but I have chosen you, and ordained you, that ye should go and bring forth fruit, and that your fruit should remain: that whatsoever ye shall ask of the Father in my name, he may give it you."

Which category are you in?
Seek to be fruitful today and every day.

Colossians 1:10
"That ye might walk worthy of the Lord unto all pleasing, being fruitful in every good work, and increasing in the knowledge of God;"

Bible Reading
Job 25-26 | 1 John 5

August 23 | 08.23

Stedfastly Minded.

Ruth 1:18
"When she saw that she was stedfastly minded to go with her, then she left speaking unto her."

Have you ever met someone who was so fixated on something that they refused to give in or change their mind? Some may call it stubborn, and yes, sometimes that term can most definitely apply. The Bible uses a unique phrase to describe someone who is strong, alert, courageous, brave, bold and determined.

"…she was stedfastly minded…"
What are we stedfastly minded about?

Naomi pleaded with her daughter-in-law to return to her own people, but Ruth refused.

Ruth 1:16-17
"And Ruth said, Intreat me not to leave thee, or to return from following after thee: for whither thou goest, I will go; and where thou lodgest, I will lodge: thy people shall be my people, and thy God my God: Where thou diest, will I die, and there will I be buried: the LORD do so to me, and more also, if ought but death part thee and me."

She was stedfastly minded.
God had a purpose and a plan.
If Ruth had given in to Naomi's request, she may have never met Boaz.

**If we give in to the pressure of others,
we may miss God's will for our lives.**

Deuteronomy 31:6
"Be strong and of a good courage, fear not, nor be afraid of them: for the LORD thy God, he it is that doth go with thee; he will not fail thee, nor forsake thee."

Isaiah 41:10
"Fear thou not; for I am with thee: be not dismayed; for I am thy God: I will strengthen thee; yea, I will help thee; yea, I will uphold thee with the right hand of my righteousness."

**May we too be stedfastly minded
in pursuit of all He has prepared for us.**

Bible Reading
Job 27-28 | 2 John

08.24 | August 24

Happenstance.

Ruth 2:3
"And she went, and came, and gleaned in the field after the reapers: and her hap was to light on a part of the field belonging unto Boaz, who was of the kindred of Elimelech."

Some believe in fortune or fate. Serendipity means a fortunate accident… a happenstance. **There are no accidents or coincidences with God.** He orders our steps even when we do not realize it at the time.

It was not by chance that Ruth ended up in the part of the field that belonged to Boaz. He was the kinsman redeemer that she and Naomi needed.

"And she went…"
God gave her the faith to go.

"And she went, and came…"
God directed her steps of where she should go.

"And she went, and came, and gleaned…"
God provided exactly what she needed, when and where she needed it.

Ruth found grace in the eyes of Boaz. He knew who she was, and had heard of how she had left her people in order to stay with Naomi.

Ruth 2:12
"The LORD recompense thy work, and a full reward be given thee of the LORD God of Israel, under whose wings thou art come to trust."

Boaz commanded his servants to leave behind just what Ruth needed.

Ruth 2:16
"And let fall also some of the handfuls of purpose for her, and leave them, that she may glean them, and rebuke her not."

It was those handfuls of purpose that revealed to Naomi that the Lord had led Ruth to their kinsman redeemer. There was no happenstance in Ruth's life. God ordered her steps, and He is willing and able to order yours.

Whatever your situation is today, God can direct you to where you need to be in order for Him to meet your need.

He has handfuls of purpose waiting for you to glean from His Word.

Bible Reading
Job 29-30 | 3 John

August 25 | 08.25

Ruth 3:18
"Then said she, Sit still, my daughter, until thou know how the matter will fall: for the man will not be in rest, until he have finished the thing this day."

Ruth had told Boaz he was a near kinsman, and he graciously comforted her that he would do what needed to be done, one way or another.

Ruth 3:11
"And now, my daughter, fear not; I will do to thee all that thou requirest: for all the city of my people doth know that thou art a virtuous woman."

There was a nearer kinsman, and Boaz must go to him first to see if he would redeem them. Ruth returned to Naomi and explained what had occured.

Naomi then spoke words of wisdom to Ruth.

Ruth 3:18
"Then said she, Sit still, my daughter, until thou know how the matter will fall…"

They had done what they could.
Now all they could do was wait.
Ever been there? Waiting is not fun.

Instead of pacing the floors in worry or fear, Naomi told Ruth not just to sit, but to sit still. Such wise advice that we could all glean from!

The best way we can sit still is to allow the Word of God to still the waters of our flesh.

Psalm 37:5
"Commit thy way unto the LORD; trust also in him; and he shall bring it to pass."

Isaiah 26:3-4
"Thou wilt keep him in perfect peace, whose mind is stayed on thee: because he trusteth in thee. Trust ye in the LORD for ever: for in the LORD JEHOVAH is everlasting strength:"

Psalm 46:10
"Be still, and know that I am God…"

Choose to sit still today.

Bible Reading
Job 31-32 | Jude

08.26 | August 26

Redemption.

Ruth 4:8
*"Therefore the kinsman said unto Boaz, Buy it for thee.
So he drew off his shoe."*

This Jewish custom may sound strange to us, but it was used as a symbol of redemption.

Ruth 4:7
"Now this was the manner in former time in Israel concerning redeeming and concerning changing, for to confirm all things; a man plucked off his shoe, and gave it to his neighbour: and this was a testimony in Israel."

The transaction had been made, and Boaz was now able to redeem Naomi and make Ruth his wife. **This is a beautiful picture of how Christ has redeemed us.**

Colossians 1:14, 20
"In whom we have redemption through his blood, even the forgiveness of sins… And, having made peace through the blood of his cross, by him to reconcile all things unto himself; by him, I say, whether they be things in earth, or things in heaven."

Romans 3:23-25
"For all have sinned, and come short of the glory of God; Being justified freely by his grace through the redemption that is in Christ Jesus: Whom God hath set forth to be a propitiation through faith in his blood, to declare his righteousness for the remission of sins that are past, through the forbearance of God;"

If you have been redeemed by His blood, take time to thank Him today.

Redemption gave Naomi and Ruth a new life.
The baby that Boaz and Ruth had was Obed,
the grandfather of King David…directly in the lineage of Jesus Christ.
Read Matthew 1:5-17
That Baby was born for one purpose.
Matthew 1:21
"And she shall bring forth a son, and thou shalt call his name JESUS: for he shall save his people from their sins."

Redemption required the life of Jesus Christ.
Redemption made salvation possible.
Redemption changes everything.

Bible Reading
Job 33-34 | Revelation 1

August 27 | 08.27

It Shall Not Return Void.

Isaiah 55:11
"So shall my word be that goeth forth out of my mouth: it shall not return unto me void, but it shall accomplish that which I please, and it shall prosper in the thing whereto I sent it."

Have you ever walked outside during a summer rain and instead of rushing to seek cover, you took a moment to admire the droplets falling from the sky? Or when that perfect snow globe effect happens during the winter and the beauty of a snow-covered field just stops you in your tracks? Each of these can be majestic reminders of a wonderful Truth about the Word of God.

Isaiah 55:10-11
"For as the rain cometh down, and the snow from heaven, and returneth not thither, but watereth the earth, and maketh it bring forth and bud, that it may give seed to the sower, and bread to the eater: So shall my word be that goeth forth out of my mouth: it shall not return unto me void, but it shall accomplish that which I please, and it shall prosper in the thing whereto I sent it."

We have this promise that His Word will not return void.
The amazing thing is that not only will the Word never return void, but He also promises that His Word will accomplish what He pleases and will prosper in what He has planned.

God gave His only begotten Son because He loves us that much.
Jesus gave His life for our sins because only He could pay the debt we owe. He is not willing that any should perish, but that all should come to repentance. The only condition to this promise is up to us.

His Word must be spoken. His Word must be given. His Word must be sent.

If our Bibles remain closed, His Word is not going in us. If we keep His Word to ourselves, His Word is not going out to others. If we stay silent, His Word will not be heard by someone else. If we refuse to plant the Seed, what harvest are we missing?

Rain and snow water the earth where Seeds are planted. The Lord gives the increase and allows for the Seed to come forth and bud as He pleases.

Our only responsibility is to plant the Seed of the Word.
Allow the Lord to take care of the rest.

Bible Reading
Job 35-36 | Revelation 2

08.28 | August 28

Jeremiah 18:1-2
"The word which came to Jeremiah from the LORD, saying, Arise, and go down to the potter's house, and there I will cause thee to hear my words."

Jeremiah had an invitation to hear the Word of the Lord at the potter's house. He just simply had to do one thing…*"Arise, and go…"*

How many times in our lives has God had something prepared just for us, and He asked us to do one simple thing in order to receive it? So often this exact situation happens to us all, and we neglect to do what He says.

"Arise, and go…"
Sometimes it's just a matter of sitting down and opening your Bible…
…or opening the door with a smile for a stranger.
…or walking across the street to invite your neighbor to church.
…or giving a tract to a cashier.
…or calling that friend who you know is lonely.
…or getting up out of bed and go to church,
like you know you're supposed to do.
…or choosing to have faith instead of being consumed with fear.
…or _____.

Whatever it is for you right now, the Lord has something that fits in that blank space. There is no question that He has something in mind for each of us to do at this moment…otherwise He would have already called us home to be with Him. **What a glorious day that will truly be, however we still have work to do.** That is why we are here…to glorify Him in all we say and do until that day when we will see Him face-to-face.

Jeremiah 18:2
"Arise, and go…and there I will…"

Jeremiah went to where God had told him to go, and he heard from the Lord in a special way. God did exactly what He told him He would do. Jeremiah only had to obey what the Lord said in order to receive it.

What is your *"Arise, and go…"* today?

Please don't let the devil talk you out of it.
Whatever it is, God had a plan and a purpose for it.

Bible Reading
Job 37-38 | Revelation 3

August 29 | 08.29

He Wrought A Work.

Jeremiah 18:3
*"Then I went down to the potter's house,
and, behold, he wrought a work on the wheels."*

If you have ever seen a potter at work, you know that it is not an easy task to make something beautiful out of what begins as a glob of mud. It is often a messy job as the potter molds the clay with his hands. The potter places the clay in the center of a wheel that spins around so that each side can be molded in the same way.

Notice the verse does not say there is only one wheel, but rather *"a work on the wheels."* **God always has multiple things in motion in order to bring His will to pass.**

Jeremiah 18:4
"And the vessel that he made of clay was marred in the hand of the potter: so he made it again another vessel, as seemed good to the potter to make it."

The clay was marred, it had blemishes and bruises from all that it had been through, but it was now in the hand of the potter. **Now there was potential for something new to come out of the blemished clay.**

It was then that Jeremiah began to see what the Lord had for him, and us, to learn from this picture.

Jeremiah 18:6
"O house of Israel, cannot I do with you as this potter? saith the LORD. Behold, as the clay is in the potter's hand, so are ye in mine hand, O house of Israel."

God is willing and able to mold us into what He has in store.
We are the clay; He is the Potter.

Isaiah 64:8
"But now, O LORD, thou art our father; we are the clay, and thou our potter; and we all are the work of thy hand."

We need only yield ourselves into His hands as a moldable vessel and allow Him to do a work in and through us.

Bible Reading
Job 39-40 | Revelation 4

08.30 | August 30

Faith Without Works.

James 2:20
"But wilt thou know, O vain man, that faith without works is dead?"

The best way to get to know someone is to pay attention to what is important to them. A mother will talk much about her children, their day to day activities and moments. A baseball fan will likely attend or watch many baseball games, and occasionally wear apparel from their favorite team while speaking of their latest game. A mechanic will make references to cars and their parts and can often be found tinkering with tools in a garage.

Would you know that someone was a mother if you never saw her with a child? In order to be known as something, we must be found or known for actively taking part in various activities that correspond with that description.

How would someone know you are a child of God?
We are justified in His eyes by our faith in Him.
Romans 5:1
"Therefore being justified by faith, we have peace with God through our Lord Jesus Christ:"

Faith is invisible.
Only the Lord can see our faith in Him.
Hebrews 11:1
"Now faith is the substance of things hoped for, the evidence of things not seen."

The only way others can see our faith in Christ is by the works we do.
In the eyes of man, we are justified by our works.
James 2:17
"Even so faith, if it hath not works, is dead, being alone."

Have you ever taken a moment to consider what evidence there is that you are a Christian?
James 2:18
"Yea, a man may say, Thou hast faith, and I have works: shew me thy faith without thy works, and I will shew thee my faith by my works."

Do something today.
Create some evidence so that others may see your faith in Him.

Bible Reading
Job 41-42 | Revelation 5

August 31 | 08.31

Stablish Your Hearts.

James 5:8
*"Be ye also patient; stablish your hearts:
for the coming of the Lord draweth nigh."*

No one likes to wait.
Especially when what you are waiting on means so much to you.

Times of waiting are opportunities to strengthen our faith.

Psalm 31:24
*"Be of good courage, and he shall strengthen your heart,
all ye that hope in the LORD."*

James connects this Truth to the coming of our Lord and Saviour. To *"stablish your hearts"* refers to strengthening, or making firm, your faith. **What could strengthen our faith more than the comfort of knowing that He is coming soon?**

1 Peter 4:7
*"But the end of all things is at hand: be ye therefore sober,
and watch unto prayer."*

The fact that He is coming should encourage us to pray more.
Pray for souls that still do not know Him.
Pray for fruit that may abound to your account.
Pray for whatever the Lord lays on your heart.

Ephesians 6:18
*"Praying always with all prayer and supplication in the Spirit,
and watching thereunto with all perseverance
and supplication for all saints;"*

In uncertain days…we can be certain.
In unpeaceful days…we can have peace.
In dark days…we can rest in the Light.

Psalm 27:14
*"Wait on the LORD: be of good courage,
and he shall strengthen thine heart: wait, I say, on the LORD."*

Bible Reading
Ecclesiastes 1-2 | Revelation 6

09.01 | September 1

Cause Me To Know.

Psalm 143:8
*"Cause me to hear thy lovingkindness in the morning;
for in thee do I trust: cause me to know the way wherein I should walk;
for I lift up my soul unto thee."*

Before the days of GPS, paper maps and directions guided our way as we made a trip from point A to point B. Whether traveling for business or family vacation, when we are in unfamiliar territory, we need something to guide us to our destination.

"…cause me to know the way wherein I should walk…"
**Many times we desire the Lord's direction,
yet we fail to consult the right Source.**

We are quick to pick up the phone to call or text a trusted friend, especially if we know they will give us Biblical advice. However, the answer we need may be something that God wants to teach us Himself instead of through someone else.

Printed in black and white, and sometimes red, the Solution to our problem can be found…but only if our Bibles are open and our hearts ready to hear His Words.

Psalm 5:8
*"Lead me, O LORD, in thy righteousness because of mine enemies;
make thy way straight before my face."*

Oftentimes, if we will earnestly ask the Lord to guide us through His Word, He will show us the Answer was right before our eyes all along, we just had never seen it that way before.

Psalm 143:10
*"Teach me to do thy will; for thou art my God: thy spirit is good;
lead me into the land of uprightness."*

He desires to teach us and lead us,
and cause us to know.
We simply must first acknowledge Him.

Proverbs 3:6
"In all thy ways acknowledge him, and he shall direct thy paths."

Bible Reading
Ecclesiastes 3-4 | Revelation 7

September 2 | 09.02

The Root Of Deception.

Luke 4:7
"If thou therefore wilt worship me, all shall be thine."

At first glance, the sentence found within our verse today appears to be a promise that we should desire. If read alone, one could assume that if we choose to worship God we shall have anything we want. Yet the context of this verse is the exact opposite from that assumption. What an example of how context is key to the interpretation of Scripture.

It is not the Lord speaking in this verse, but rather Satan himself. **The devil promises us a lot of things, but never discloses what the attempt to possess those things will cost us.**

The root of deception is pride.
It was his pride that caused Lucifer to fall in the first place, why would he not continue to use it in his attempt to cause others to fall? Pride is found in the desire to be worshipped, but it is also found in the fleshly desire to possess things.

Satan thought that he could tempt Jesus into wanting things. The truth of the matter is that they were already His to begin with, for He created all that they saw from that high mountain.

Luke 4:8
"And Jesus answered and said unto him, Get thee behind me, Satan: for it is written, Thou shalt worship the Lord thy God, and him only shalt thou serve."

Jesus used the Word of God to rebuke Satan.
We have the same Weapon available to us today, and the only Weapon we will ever need in order to defeat our enemy.

Proverbs 16:18
"Pride goeth before destruction, and an haughty spirit before a fall."

1 John 2:16
"For all that is in the world, the lust of the flesh, and the lust of the eyes, and the pride of life, is not of the Father, but is of the world."

When the root of deception creeps in, defeat it with the Word of God.

Bible Reading
Ecclesiastes 5-6 | Revelation 8

09.03 | September 3

Weighed By Him.

1 Samuel 2:2-3
"There is none holy as the LORD: for there is none beside thee: neither is there any rock like our God. Talk no more so exceeding proudly; let not arrogancy come out of your mouth: for the LORD is a God of knowledge, and by him actions are weighed."

Oftentimes, we only compare ourselves horizontally.
"Oh, compared to her…I'm a great Christian."
"Have you seen her lately? She needs our prayers."

We want the opportunity to puff ourselves up by finding people we deem to be less than us. It makes us feel holy and honest when we pick and choose to whom we compare ourselves. The truth is, that type of comparison is always biased in hopes of fulfilling an agenda.

**Boasting may lift us for a moment,
only to deflate us later when the truth comes out.**

Hannah's prayer of rejoicing is a reminder of how we should judge ourselves. We must use a vertical scale of comparison.

1 Samuel 2:3
*"Talk no more so exceeding proudly;
let not arrogancy come out of your mouth:
for the LORD is a God of knowledge, and by him actions are weighed."*

There is only One by Whom we are to weigh our actions.
There is no one like Him.

Put whatever you want or desire on the scales,
and He will win every time.
There can be no balance when we weigh our actions to Him.

**When we compare ourselves only to Him,
we have no reason to talk proudly.**

If we truly want to be lifted,
we must first bow before Him.

James 4:10
*"Humble yourselves in the sight of the Lord,
and he shall lift you up."*

Bible Reading
Ecclesiastes 7-8 | Revelation 9

Take Your Journey.

Deuteronomy 1:40
"But as for you, turn you, and take your journey into the wilderness by the way of the Red sea."

Along the paths of our lives, we will have many turns which we may not understand at the time. But we can choose to have joy in the midst of our circumstances when we remind ourselves that God has a plan.

Every turn He takes us on is part of the journey He has prepared for us.
Deuteronomy 1:7
"Turn you, and take your journey, and go to the mount of the Amorites, and unto all the places nigh thereunto, in the plain, in the hills, and in the vale, and in the south, and by the sea side, to the land of the Canaanites, and unto Lebanon, unto the great river, the river Euphrates."

He gives us strength to walk through the plains and valleys, then climb the mountains and hills. Scenic views await us, but sometimes it is a struggle to get there and see them. Some days, it seems we will never reach the top, but rest assured that He knows just where you are on your journey.

Deuteronomy 1:40
"But as for you, turn you, and take your journey into the wilderness by the way of the Red sea."

He gives us strength to endure the wilderness that sometimes our choices have created. The children of Israel wandered for 40 years in the wilderness instead of what could have been an eleven-day journey. They took the ultimate scenic route.

Your wilderness may look different than someone else's. Sometimes it's a barren place. Sometimes it's confusing. Sometimes it's a discouraging place. The wilderness is never an enjoyable part of our journey, but the Lord places us there for a purpose.

Deuteronomy 2:24
"Rise ye up, take your journey, and pass over the river..."

Sometimes instead of another turn, the Lord desires for us to rise up and pass over what lies in front of us. Eventually, regardless of how long it takes or what we endure, there is victory ahead if we allow Him to enable us to contend for the faith along the way. **Continue to take your journey today with Him as your guide.**

Bible Reading
Ecclesiastes 9-10 | Revelation 10

September 5

Rehearse It.

1 Samuel 8:21
"And Samuel heard all the words of the people, and he rehearsed them in the ears of the LORD."

It appeared that the people had rejected Samuel, but the Lord showed him what was really going on.

1 Samuel 8:7
"And the LORD said unto Samuel, Hearken unto the voice of the people in all that they say unto thee: for they have not rejected thee, but they have rejected me, that I should not reign over them."

The people wanted a king, simply because everyone else had one.

1 Samuel 8:20
"That we also may be like all the nations; and that our king may judge us, and go out before us, and fight our battles."

They were deceived into thinking that a king would be the solution to their problems.

How many times in our lives do we fixate our minds on something or someone and convince ourselves that they have or are the answer? Sounds like our world today. Politicians claim they can fix everything the current person has done wrong in their eyes, yet their agenda is often rooted in their pride and desire for power.

1 Samuel 8:19
"Nevertheless the people refused to obey the voice of Samuel; and they said, Nay; but we will have a king over us;"

Samuel heard all the words of the people and chose to do the only thing he knew would be beneficial to the situation. He took it to the Lord in prayer. The Scripture says he rehearsed it in the ears of the Lord. He took it to the Lord privately. Not where everyone could see, but in that secret place where it was just him and God. **He sought the Lord's direction over the matter.**

In times of doubt, despair, discontent or distress we need only to rehearse it to the Lord. When we are tempted to mull over and over a situation, may we instead take it to the Lord in prayer. See Psalm 18:6.

Rehearse it before Him today.

Bible Reading
Ecclesiastes 11-12 | Revelation 11

September 6 | 09.06

Reminded By His Word.

Jeremiah 32:17
*"Ah Lord GOD! behold, thou hast made the heaven and the earth
by thy great power and stretched out arm,
and there is nothing too hard for thee:"*

What a way to begin a prayer! Jeremiah acknowledged Who he was praying to in a powerful way, that perhaps was also a reminder to himself of Who the Lord is.

Luke 1:37
"For with God nothing shall be impossible."

Sometimes we go to God in prayer and declare something we know to be True, yet by the end of our prayer doubt has crept in. One minute we can believe that with all our heart, and then we take our eyes of faith off of Him, and our mustard seed disappears. **It is in these moments that we must resort to the Word of God and remind ourselves of Who He truly is.**

Have you ever opened the pages of your Bible searching for an answer to whatever is on your mind, and a verse seems to jump off the page?

The Lord's answer to Jeremiah began with Him reminding him of what he had just prayed.

Jeremiah 32:27
*"Behold, I am the LORD, the God of all flesh:
is there any thing too hard for me?"*

The Lord knows when we need to be reminded of Who He is.

Isaiah 46:9-10
*"Remember the former things of old: for I am God,
and there is none else; I am God, and there is none like me, Declaring the end from the beginning, and from ancient times the things that are not yet done, saying, My counsel shall stand, and I will do all my pleasure:"*

Our flesh wants us to forget His power.
The world wants us to disregard the Truth.
Our enemy wants us to neglect His Word, so that we ignore His direction.
What do you need to be reminded of today?
Open your Bible and allow Him to speak just what your heart needs.

Matthew 19:26
*"But Jesus beheld them, and said unto them,
With men this is impossible; but with God all things are possible."*

Bible Reading
Song Of Solomon 1-2 | Revelation 12

09.07 | September 7

That We Might Have Hope.

Romans 15:4
"For whatsoever things were written aforetime were written for our learning, that we through patience and comfort of the scriptures might have hope."

In these dark days we are living in, there is one thing that everyone can agree on that we all need…hope. Chaos and turmoil are all around us; yet no matter how dark and confusing it may be, a glimmer of hope can shine bright.

There is a constant Source of Hope available to us at all times.
Hope we can learn from.
Hope to help us as we wait.
Hope that comforts our hearts.
Hope in the darkness.

This Hope is found written on the pages of the Word of God.

2 Timothy 3:16-17
"All scripture is given by inspiration of God, and is profitable for doctrine, for reproof, for correction, for instruction in righteousness: That the man of God may be perfect, throughly furnished unto all good works."

The very Words breathed from God have been preserved for us down through the ages, so that we may learn and apply them to our lives.

2 Peter 1:21
"For the prophecy came not in old time by the will of man: but holy men of God spake as they were moved by the Holy Ghost."

The Lord orchestrated this
so that we might know Him…so that we might have Hope.

Those who do not know Him, have no hope today.
They are condemned already;
but the Lord has made a Way for them to find Hope.

**Find Him in the pages of Scripture,
and share that Hope with someone today.**

Bible Reading
Song Of Solomon 3-4 | Revelation 13

September 8 | 09.08

Strange Things.

Luke 5:26
*"And they were all amazed, and they glorified God,
and were filled with fear, saying, We have seen strange things to day."*

Those services where no one can explain it. Those miracles for which doctors have no answers. Like when a bill needs paid, and the exact amount shows up unexpectedly just in time. We have all seen strange things like this happen that have no other explanation, except that it was the Lord.

Strange things will cause us to be amazed at Who He Is.
Mark 2:12
"And immediately he arose, took up the bed, and went forth before them all; insomuch that they were all amazed, and glorified God, saying, We never saw it on this fashion."

Strange things enable us to glorify Him.
Acts 4:21
"So when they had further threatened them, they let them go, finding nothing how they might punish them, because of the people: for all men glorified God for that which was done."

Strange things should fill us with a holy fear of Him.
1 Samuel 12:24
"Only fear the LORD, and serve him in truth with all your heart: for consider how great things he hath done for you."

**Remind yourself today of some strange things
that the Lord has done for you.**

Often times we are awestruck in the moment; but when we look back, the hindsight ought to implore us to thanksgiving and supplication.

Ephesians 3:20-21
"Now unto him that is able to do exceeding abundantly above all that we ask or think, according to the power that worketh in us, Unto him be glory in the church by Christ Jesus throughout all ages, world without end. Amen."

Strange things should only leave us craving for more.

Bible Reading
Song Of Solomon 5-6 | Revelation 14

09.09 | September 9

If It Had Not Been.

Psalm 124:1-2
*"If it had not been the LORD who was on our side, now may Israel say;
If it had not been the LORD who was on our side,
when men rose up against us:"*

Take a moment and earnestly consider this…
If it had not been for the Lord, where would you be?

What if He had not come as a baby?
What if He had not died on the cross?
What if He had not loved us that much?

What if He had not risen?
What if He had not given salvation?
What if He had not set you free?

What if He had not shown you mercy?
What if He had not given His grace?

What if your life had never been changed?

How many times has He forgiven?
How many times has He delivered?
How many times has He provided?
How many times has He directed?
How many times has He blessed?

Psalm 54:4
*"Behold, God is mine helper:
the Lord is with them that uphold my soul."*

Psalm 118:6
*"The LORD is on my side; I will not fear:
what can man do unto me?"*

Hebrews 13:5-6
*"…for he hath said, I will never leave thee, nor forsake thee.
So that we may boldly say, The Lord is my helper,
and I will not fear what man shall do unto me."*

How many times?
If it had not been for Him…

Bible Reading
Song Of Solomon 7-8 | Revelation 15

The Lord Is My Helper.

Hebrews 13:6
*"So that we may boldly say, The Lord is my helper,
and I will not fear what man shall do unto me."*

Years ago, there was a fad amongst churches of license plates and hats that said, "Jesus is my Co-Pilot". While the motive of most was likely pure, really consider that statement…do you really desire for Him to be in the passenger seat? Passengers do not decide where the vehicle is going.

We have been given the privilege to declare *"The Lord is my helper"*. This simply acknowledges that He enables us, for we cannot do anything without Him.

John 15:5
"I am the vine, ye are the branches: He that abideth in me, and I in him, the same bringeth forth much fruit: for without me ye can do nothing."

How can we even know that He is our Helper, much less boldly proclaim it? The *"So that…"* leads us back to the previous verse.

Hebrews 13:5
*"Let your conversation be without covetousness;
and be content with such things as ye have: for he hath said,
I will never leave thee, nor forsake thee."*

When the Lord says something once, it is True.
Yet this principle is found all throughout the pages of His Word.

He will never leave us, nor forsake us.
It is that Truth that allows us to boldly say *"The Lord is my helper"*.

Psalm 30:10
*"Hear, O LORD, and have mercy upon me:
LORD, be thou my helper."*

Allow the Lord to enable you today.
He desires to help us in every aspect of our lives,
how sad it is that most of the time
we attempt to do most things on our own.

Bible Reading
Isaiah 1-2 | Revelation 16

09.11 | September 11

Fear To Follow.

1 Samuel 12:14
"If ye will fear the LORD, and serve him, and obey his voice, and not rebel against the commandment of the LORD, then shall both ye and also the king that reigneth over you continue following the LORD your God:"

All throughout the Scriptures there are conditional blessings from the Lord. We can find many of them by looking for an if that is followed by a then. *"If...then..."*

1 Samuel 12:14
"If ye will fear the LORD, and serve him, and obey his voice, and not rebel against the commandment of the LORD, then..."

The Lord used Samuel to speak unto the people of Israel and continue to teach them of the repercussions of their demanding a king. Would the Lord use King Saul in the lives of His children? Absolutely, but it was not what the Lord had intended for them. In order to continue following the Lord, the people had to first fear Him. This is a fear of reverence and respect for Who He is, a holy fear.

If we do not first fear Him, we cannot make wise decisions.
Proverbs 9:10
"The fear of the LORD is the beginning of wisdom: and the knowledge of the holy is understanding."

Fearing the Lord leads to serving and obeying Him.
Joshua 24:14
"Now therefore fear the LORD, and serve him in sincerity and in truth: and put away the gods which your fathers served on the other side of the flood, and in Egypt; and serve ye the LORD."

Some are fearful to follow Him simply because they are unwilling to give up what their flesh craves; yet, they still desire to follow.
Job 28:28
"And unto man he said, Behold, the fear of the Lord, that is wisdom; and to depart from evil is understanding."

If we want to follow the Lord, we must first have a holy fear Him.

Bible Reading
Isaiah 3-4 | Revelation 17

Idol Works & Idleness.

Jeremiah 44:8
"In that ye provoke me unto wrath with the works of your hands, burning incense unto other gods in the land of Egypt, whither ye be gone to dwell, that ye might cut yourselves off, and that ye might be a curse and a reproach among all the nations of the earth?"

They had provoked the Lord to wrath by making idols of other gods in the land of Egypt. The Lord called this a great evil against their souls.

The works of their hands led to their downfall.
Isaiah 3:8
"For Jerusalem is ruined, and Judah is fallen: because their tongue and their doings are against the LORD, to provoke the eyes of his glory."

Idolatry is the quickest way to face the wrath of God.
Deuteronomy 32:16
"They provoked him to jealousy with strange gods, with abominations provoked they him to anger."

He tells us over and over that He is a Jealous God, and that we should have no other gods before Him. Yet, so often we put so many other things before Him.

1 Timothy 6:10
"For the love of money is the root of all evil: which while some coveted after, they have erred from the faith, and pierced themselves through with many sorrows."

**If He is not our priority,
the idols in our lives can quickly cause idleness in our service.**

If our hands are idle,
there is no work being done, no souls being won.

Proverbs 11:30
"The fruit of the righteous is a tree of life; and he that winneth souls is wise."

The works of our hands determine the fruit we possess.

Bible Reading
Isaiah 5-6 | Revelation 18

09.13 | September 13

Upheld By Him.

Isaiah 41:10
"Fear thou not; for I am with thee: be not dismayed; for I am thy God: I will strengthen thee; yea, I will help thee; yea, I will uphold thee with the right hand of my righteousness."

Some days feel like a whirlwind. Some feel like they will never end. Some are enjoyed from the mountaintop, while some are endured in the valley. Some days are a rollercoaster of emotions. Some leave you wondering what could possibly be next.

Regardless of what your day looks like, there is something in today's verse that can apply.
Fearful? He is with you.
Dismayed or confused? He is still on the throne.
Weak or tired? He wants to be your Strength.
Overwhelmed with your to-do list? He desires to help.
Feeling good? He still is there to hold you up on that mountain.
Feeling low? He can lift you up.

Maybe no one understands, maybe no one even knows about it… but God does.

Psalm 63:8
"My soul followeth hard after thee: thy right hand upholdeth me."

Who sits at the right hand of God?
His only begotten Son, Jesus Christ.
Hebrews 12:2
"Looking unto Jesus the author and finisher of our faith; who for the joy that was set before him endured the cross, despising the shame, and is set down at the right hand of the throne of God."

The Lord upholds His children through His Son.
Even in the worst of times…He is always by our side. He is Sufficient for our every need. He gives us strength to face another day. He sustains us.

Isaiah 41:13
"For I the LORD thy God will hold thy right hand, saying unto thee, Fear not; I will help thee."

We have no reason to fear with Him holding our hand.

Bible Reading
Isaiah 7-8 | Revelation 19

September 14 | 09.14

Unless I Had Believed.

Psalm 27:13
"I had fainted, unless I had believed to see the goodness of the LORD in the land of the living."

David clearly says that he would have fainted if he had not believed. He had enemies and false witnesses rising up around him that were cruel. He knew that his belief…his faith…had made the difference.

Consider for a moment placing yourself in David's shoes in this verse. We surely would have also fainted.
"…unless I had believed…"

Who would we be?
What would we be doing?
Where would we be?
Why would we do anything?
How would we be?
"…unless I had believed…"

The changes that take place the moment we place our faith in Him should encourage us to continue to do so. Believing in Him does not stop with salvation…it should be shown in our lives every day.

Psalm 31:19
"Oh how great is thy goodness, which thou hast laid up for them that fear thee; which thou hast wrought for them that trust in thee before the sons of men!"

Our walk with Him is a process of continually believing in His goodness which changes our perspective.

2 Corinthians 4:8-9
"We are troubled on every side, yet not distressed; we are perplexed, but not in despair; Persecuted, but not forsaken; cast down, but not destroyed;"

2 Corinthians 4:16
"For which cause we faint not; but though our outward man perish, yet the inward man is renewed day by day."

Renewing our faith takes place when we spend time in His Word and in prayer. Take your burden to Him today, knowing that your faith in His goodness can carry you through anything you are facing.

Bible Reading
Isaiah 9-10 | Revelation 20

09.15 | September 15

Watched.

Luke 6:7
"And the scribes and Pharisees watched him, whether he would heal on the sabbath day; that they might find an accusation against him."

Have you ever noticed birds circling over the same wooded area for an extended period of time? They are carefully watching over their intended target, waiting for just the right moment to pounce on their victim.

The scribes and Pharisees watched Jesus like hawks watch their prey. They desired to find something, anything, that they could hold against Him.

Luke 11:54
"Laying wait for him, and seeking to catch something out of his mouth, that they might accuse him."

Have you ever felt that way? Or even noticed someone eyeballing your every move? Critiquing your every word?

Be encouraged that such things make us more like Jesus.

John 15:18-19
"If the world hate you, ye know that it hated me before it hated you. If ye were of the world, the world would love his own: but because ye are not of the world, but I have chosen you out of the world, therefore the world hateth you."

There will be people who watch us with an agenda in mind. Commit them to the Lord and allow Him to deal with their hearts.

2 Samuel 22:18
"He delivered me from my strong enemy, and from them that hated me: for they were too strong for me."

But may this also remind us that there are also some who watch us for the example we are setting for them.

1 Timothy 4:12
2 Timothy 3:14

Everyone needs a Paul, a mentor, to learn from, but everyone also needs a Timothy to teach.

Instead of focusing on those who seek to do you harm, concern yourself more with those who seek to follow you as you follow the Lord.

Bible Reading
Isaiah 11-12 | Revelation 21

September 16 | 09.16

Luke 6:22
"Blessed are ye, when men shall hate you, and when they shall separate you from their company, and shall reproach you, and cast out your name as evil, for the Son of man's sake."

No one likes to be left out and uninvited, but what if the Lord is protecting us from being included into something? No one likes to be excluded from the company of those you considered family. But what if the Lord removed you in order to prevent a greater disappointment later?

Our human flesh hates dissatisfaction and displeasure.
Both of them often lead to being discontent.

Jesus understands our pain, and He is Able to comfort us like no one else can. He faced the same disappointments, yet it never caused Him to sin.

Hebrews 2:18
"For in that he himself hath suffered being tempted, he is able to succour them that are tempted."

Hebrews 4:15
"For we have not an high priest which cannot be touched with the feeling of our infirmities; but was in all points tempted like as we are, yet without sin."

**Instead of focusing on what was lost,
we can choose to rejoice in what we have been given.**

Luke 6:23
"Rejoice ye in that day, and leap for joy: for, behold, your reward is great in heaven: for in the like manner did their fathers unto the prophets."

Our reward is so much greater than anything we think we have lost.
Anything we are willing to lose for Him is always replaced with something better.

**When we are excluded from something,
it is an opportunity to be set apart unto Him.**

2 Timothy 2:21
"If a man therefore purge himself from these, he shall be a vessel unto honour, sanctified, and meet for the master's use, and prepared unto every good work."

Bible Reading
Isaiah 13-14 | Revelation 22

09.17 | September 17

Distracted.

Deuteronomy 5:32
"Ye shall observe to do therefore as the LORD your God hath commanded you: ye shall not turn aside to the right hand or to the left."

The devil will allow distraction after distraction to try and keep you from spending time with the Lord in His Word. You place your Bible on the table…and you get a text message. Open your Bible, and there is a knock at the door. Sit back down, and realize your coffee is now cold…so you have to go warm it up. While waiting, a child has woken up and needs your attention. All the while your open Bible is still there on the table…waiting.

The list could go on and on of how our enemy attacks when we try to make the Lord our priority. Unless we are intentional, those distractions will soon no longer be needed when we get in the habit of doing anything and everything else first.

1 Samuel 12:20
"And Samuel said unto the people, Fear not:
ye have done all this wickedness: yet turn not aside from following the LORD, but serve the LORD with all your heart;"

**Serving the Lord with all your heart begins
by putting Him above anyone or anything else.**
Talk to Him first.
Spend time in His Word first.

When faced with a choice, choose Him.

Deuteronomy 5:33
"Ye shall walk in all the ways
which the LORD your God hath commanded you, that ye may live, and that it may be well with you, and that ye may prolong your days in the land which ye shall possess."

Blessings abound when we avoid the distractions
and simply walk in His ways.

Bible Reading
Isaiah 15-16 | Proverbs 1

September 18 | 09.18

Confused.

James 3:16
"For where envying and strife is, there is confusion and every evil work."

In the maze of life, we sometimes wander aimlessly, unsure which way to go and often forgetting which way we came.

It is so easy to be confused about our surroundings.
Sometimes it's the place that feels unfamiliar and sometimes it's the people. One turn of events can cause us to stumble through our days out of habit instead of steps of faith.

**When we are confused,
we need to remember that it did not come from God.**

1 Corinthians 14:33
*"For God is not the author of confusion, but of peace,
as in all churches of the saints."*

**Our confusion can be replaced by His peace
when we take every thing to Him in prayer.**

Philippians 4:6-7
*"Be careful for nothing; but in every thing by prayer and supplication
with thanksgiving let your requests be made known unto God.
And the peace of God, which passeth all understanding,
shall keep your hearts and minds through Christ Jesus."*

Pour out your confusion to Him.
Ask for that miracle.
Cry to Him for deliverance.
Beg for His forgiveness.
Plead for His guidance.
Seek His face through His Word.

Psalm 71:1
*"In thee, O LORD, do I put my trust:
let me never be put to confusion."*

**We can wipe away our confusion today
simply by trusting in Him.**

Bible Reading
Isaiah 17-18 | Proverbs 2

09.19 | September 19

Frustrated.

Galatians 2:21
"I do not frustrate the grace of God: for if righteousness come by the law, then Christ is dead in vain."

Some people want to do everything themselves.
Maybe you are even one of them.

Though we all struggle with this characteristic from time to time, there is one thing we must come to realize that we ourselves simply cannot contribute any part… our salvation.

Other than our sin to make it necessary and our faith to believe in Jesus, any attempt to contribute to our salvation nullifies our justification.

Ephesians 2:8-9
"For by grace are ye saved through faith; and that not of yourselves: it is the gift of God: Not of works, lest any man should boast."

Grace is getting something we do not deserve, a Gift.

Romans 3:24
"Being justified freely by his grace through the redemption that is in Christ Jesus:"

Romans 6:23
"For the wages of sin is death; but the gift of God is eternal life through Jesus Christ our Lord."

If you have to work or pay for something is it still a gift?
Works negate grace.
Romans 11:6
"And if by grace, then is it no more of works: otherwise grace is no more grace. But if it be of works, then is it no more grace: otherwise work is no more work."

If we try to mix in our works, we disregard His plan of salvation. There is nothing we can do to earn our way to Heaven, other than receive His grace through faith in the finished work of Jesus Christ. Any attempt to work our way to Heaven will only leave us frustrated and exhausted.

Romans 4:5
"But to him that worketh not, but believeth on him that justifieth the ungodly, his faith is counted for righteousness."

Jesus paid it all. Rest in His grace today.

Bible Reading
Isaiah 19-20 | Proverbs 3

Say In A Word.

Luke 7:7
*"Wherefore neither thought I myself worthy to come unto thee:
but say in a word, and my servant shall be healed."*

The meekness of this certain centurion should humble us. Though he was a man of great authority, power and pride had not overcome him. He knew he was not worthy to approach Jesus on his own; yet he believed that if Jesus just said a Word his servant would be healed.

"…say in a word…"
His great faith in just one Word caused even Jesus to marvel.
This man knew that one word from the Word changes everything.

Who else can speak things into existence?
Psalm 33:8-9
*"Let all the earth fear the LORD: let all the inhabitants of the world stand in awe of him. For he spake, and it was done;
he commanded, and it stood fast."*

Who else can speak peace to a raging storm?
Matthew 8:26
"And he saith unto them, Why are ye fearful, O ye of little faith? Then he arose, and rebuked the winds and the sea; and there was a great calm."

Who else can speak and cast out demons?
Luke 4:36
*"And they were all amazed, and spake among themselves, saying, What a word is this! for with authority and power
he commandeth the unclean spirits, and they come out."*

Who else can speak eternal life?
John 5:24
*"Verily, verily, I say unto you, He that heareth my word,
and believeth on him that sent me, hath everlasting life, and shall not come into condemnation; but is passed from death unto life."*

In times of doubt, uncertainty, chaos, confusion, or fear, look to Him.
Just a word from the Word is all we need today.

Bible Reading
Isaiah 21-22 | Proverbs 4

09.21 | September 21

Motivation.

2 Corinthians 5:14
"For the love of Christ constraineth us; because we thus judge, that if one died for all, then were all dead:"

From time to time, it is good to stop and reflect on what motivates us.
What motives, if any, do we have?
Why do we do what we do?

The Apostle Paul in his second letter to the church at Corinth, writes of the urgency that he felt because of the love of Christ.

He was motivated by His love.

When we evaluate ourselves with the questions above, is the love of Christ even considered?

His love for us.
2 Corinthians 5:15
"And that he died for all, that they which live should not henceforth live unto themselves, but unto him which died for them, and rose again."

Our love for Him.
1 John 4:19
"We love him, because he first loved us."

If we are not motivated by both directions of the love of Christ, there is something or someone that has taken His place.

Romans 8:35
*"Who shall separate us from the love of Christ?
shall tribulation, or distress, or persecution,
or famine, or nakedness, or peril, or sword?"*

Are you motivated to serve Him?
Tell someone about what He has done for you.

Encourage a friend you know is struggling
by pointing them to Him.

Remind yourself and those around you of the love of Christ today.

Bible Reading
Isaiah 23-24 | Proverbs 5

September 22 | 09.22

Determination.

Isaiah 26:3
"Thou wilt keep him in perfect peace, whose mind is stayed on thee because he trusteth in thee."

Everyone desires peace. God promises *"perfect peace"* to those *"whose mind is stayed"* on Him.

There is no perfect peace to be found, outside of the Lord. **This perfect peace is only found when we completely rest in Him.**

We must acknowledge that we are sustained and supported only by Him. We must admit there is nothing we can do on our own, and entirely depend upon Him. We must fully trust in Him alone. That is when *"perfect peace"* can be found.

Though storms may rage...
Mark 4:39
"And he arose, and rebuked the wind, and said unto the sea, Peace, be still. And the wind ceased, and there was a great calm."

Though enemies may try to break through a garrison...
Philippians 4:7
"And the peace of God, which passeth all understanding, shall keep your hearts and minds through Christ Jesus."

Though we are fearful…
John 16:33
"These things I have spoken unto you, that in me ye might have peace. In the world ye shall have tribulation: but be of good cheer; I have overcome the world."

Regardless of the situation we find ourselves in, we can choose and determine to trust in Him. Each trial is another opportunity to display our faith in Him. **Perfect peace only comes when we trust in Him at all times.**
Isaiah 26:4
*"Trust ye in the LORD for ever:
for in the LORD JEHOVAH is everlasting strength:"*
When we trust in Him,
He gives us everlasting strength to continue to trust Him.
Psalm 62:8
**Determine to keep your mind stayed upon Him,
today and every day.**

Bible Reading
Isaiah 25-26 | Proverbs 6

09.23 | September 23

Procrastination.

Isaiah 40:31
*"But they that wait upon the LORD shall renew their strength;
they shall mount up with wings as eagles; they shall run,
and not be weary; and they shall walk, and not faint."*

Some pay their bill the day it arrives, others wait until the day it's due. To some, 10 o'clock is past their bedtime, others see a few more productive hours. Some plan months in advance, while others wait until the last minute. Some need to schedule out their strategy, others work best under pressure.

Regardless of whether or not you consider yourself a procrastinator, there is one matter where it always pays to procrastinate…

Psalm 27:14
*"Wait on the LORD: be of good courage,
and he shall strengthen thine heart: wait, I say, on the LORD."*

No one likes to wait.
We want things now.

Our timing is rarely, if ever, His.
Isaiah 55:8-9
"For my thoughts are not your thoughts, neither are your ways my ways, saith the LORD. For as the heavens are higher than the earth, so are my ways higher than your ways, and my thoughts than your thoughts."

Until He leads…
Until He directs…
Until He guides…
Until He provides…
Until you have peace…
Wait on Him.

Lamentations 3:25-26
*"The LORD is good unto them that wait for him,
to the soul that seeketh him. It is good that a man should both hope
and quietly wait for the salvation of the LORD."*

The best form of procrastination is always waiting on Him.

Bible Reading
Isaiah 27-28 | Proverbs 7

September 24 | 09.24

Expectation.

Isaiah 30:18
"And therefore will the LORD wait, that he may be gracious unto you, and therefore will he be exalted, that he may have mercy upon you: for the LORD is a God of judgment: blessed are all they that wait for him."

Have you ever rushed around trying to get wherever you were scheduled to be and found people waiting for you? Maybe they waited patiently, maybe they needed to extend more grace. Regardless, they were expecting you.

Oftentimes when we are late for something the reasons turn into excuses and sometimes, we even shift the blame to someone else in order to subtly plead for the mercy of those who had to wait on us.

Read today's verse again.
Has the Lord ever waited on you?
It is a convicting thought when we realize
just how much it applies to our lives.

He waits to extend His grace upon us.
He waits to be exalted, so that He can show us mercy.
All through His grace and mercy,
He waits for us to wait for Him.

Psalm 86:15
"But thou, O Lord, art a God full of compassion, and gracious, ongsuffering, and plenteous in mercy and truth."

Through His longsuffering, He patiently waits for us…
…to believe on Him.
…to confess to Him.
…to call upon Him.
…to hear Him.
…to trust Him.
…to choose Him.
…to follow Him.
…to serve Him.
…to praise Him.

Instead of making excuses, seek His forgiveness.
Rather than running in the opposite direction, fall at His feet.

Is He waiting on you today?

Bible Reading
Isaiah 29-30 | Proverbs 8

09.25 | September 25

Direction.

Psalm 32:8
*"I will instruct thee and teach thee in the way which thou shalt go:
I will guide thee with mine eye."*

Eyes do not speak so that we can hear.
An eye does not point like a finger to tell us which way to go.
Yet…
"I will guide thee with mine eye."

How can we be guided by His eye, if we are not looking at Him?

Hebrews 12:2
*"Looking unto Jesus the author and finisher of our faith;
who for the joy that was set before him endured the cross, despising the shame, and is set down at the right hand of the throne of God."*

While we may feel we know which way to go or what is the best solution to our problem, if we only consult ourselves, we are doomed to fail.

Remember what happened when Peter took his eyes off Jesus as he was walking on the water? He began to sink.

The same thing happens to us when we take our eyes off of Him.

Proverbs 16:9
"A man's heart deviseth his way: but the LORD directeth his steps."

Our eyes must be upon the eye of the Word of God.

Where are you looking today?
Why make a move without His direction?
Why take a step of faith without Him guiding the way?

**True direction only comes
when we are completely yielded to Him.**

Proverbs 3:6
"In all thy ways acknowledge him, and he shall direct thy paths."

Bible Reading
Isaiah 31-32 | Proverbs 9

September 26 | 09.26

Pray For Them.

1 Samuel 12:23
"Moreover as for me, God forbid that I should sin against the LORD in ceasing to pray for you: but I will teach you the good and the right way:"

When Samuel was reminded that the Lord will not forsake His people, it reminded him of his responsibility to others.

"Moreover as for me…"

He knew he was to teach the people *"the good and the right way"*, yet he calls neglecting to pray for the people a sin against the Lord. He took his responsibility to intercede for the people that seriously.

None of us are a prophet like Samuel was, yet we all still have a responsibility to carry out the purpose God intends for the life that He has given us. From the very breath in our lungs to every single thing we have or possess, it is all because of Him.

Should we not also evaluate and remind ourselves from time to time what we should be doing?

"Moreover as for me…"

Pray for others.

"God forbid that I should sin against the LORD in ceasing to pray for you"
When was the last time you purposefully prayed for the needs of others? Maybe there was not a specific problem or situation, but have you ever intentionally prayed for the day-to-day aspects of those you claim to love and care about?

Take a day or a week and pray specifically for someone else.
Pray for their marriage. Pray for their children. Pray for their ministry. Pray for their health. Pray for their needs. Pray for their job. Pray for them to reach souls. Pray for them to have a child. Pray for them to be a blessing to someone. Pray for them to receive a blessing. Pray for them to be encouraged. Pray for them to have courage. Pray for them to have wisdom. Pray for them to _____.

Whatever the situation…pray for them. As you pray, watch and see how God answers. When you see Him at work, it will encourage you to continue to pray for others.

Jesus Christ prayed for others much more than He prayed for Himself.
John 17:9 - *"I pray for them…"*
May we follow His example and pray for others today, and every day.

Bible Reading
Isaiah 33-34 | Proverbs 10

09.27 | September 27

Shut The Door.

2 Kings 4:5
"So she went from him, and shut the door upon her and upon her sons, who brought the vessels to her; and she poured out."

There can be many reasons to shut the door behind you once you have entered into a particular place. Safety. Privacy. Security. To rest. To hide. To avoid. To focus.

Shutting the door places a barrier between the inside and the outside. It also creates a boundary that must be crossed in order to enter or exit.

In the Scriptures, we see several instances where a door is shut. God shut Noah and his family inside the ark. Elisha instructed a widow to shut the door and pour out her oil into borrowed empty vessels. Elisha later shut the door of the Shunammite's house to pray unto the Lord. In the Sermon on the Mount, Jesus preached to the multitudes that they should shut the door before they prayed to the Father.

Matthew 6:6
"But thou, when thou prayest, enter into thy closet, and when thou hast shut thy door, pray to thy Father which is in secret; and thy Father which seeth in secret shall reward thee openly."

There is one thing in common with these examples of shutting the door. His presence.

When was the last time you shut the door so that you could spend time with only Him?

The secret to being with Him in secret is that many things can only be found when we shut the door to everything else around us, and focus solely on Him.

Psalm 91:1
"He that dwelleth in the secret place of the most High shall abide under the shadow of the Almighty."

Intentionally shut the door and abide with Him in secret today, and every day.

Bible Reading
Isaiah 35-36 | Proverbs 11

September 28 | 09.28

Under His Wings.

Psalm 91:3-4
"Surely he shall deliver thee from the snare of the fowler, and from the noisome pestilence. He shall cover thee with his feathers, and under his wings shalt thou trust: his truth shall be thy shield and buckler."

The secret place is where we find things that cannot be found anywhere else. When we spend time alone with the Lord, we find He is just what we need.

Abiding under His shadow causes our perspective to change.

Psalm 91:1-2
"He that dwelleth in the secret place of the most High shall abide under the shadow of the Almighty. I will say of the LORD, He is my refuge and my fortress: my God; in him will I trust."

Acknowledging Who He is encourages us to trust in Him instead of depending on our own abilities.

He is Able to deliver us from any situation.
No matter how bleak.
No matter how chaotic.
No matter how confusing.
No matter how discouraging.
No matter what.

Run under His wings today.
His wings can cover you with comfort and peace.

We have no need to fear when we are under His wings.

Psalm 91:5-6
"Thou shalt not be afraid for the terror by night; nor for the arrow that flieth by day; Nor for the pestilence that walketh in darkness; nor for the destruction that wasteth at noonday."

Sometimes He stirs up our nest so that we are reminded of the shelter and safety that is found under His wings. As our Buckler, He literally surrounds us with His presence as the Truth of His Word supplies the Answer to every problem.

Whatever your need today, you can find it under His wings.

Bible Reading
Isaiah 37-38 | Proverbs 12

09.29 | September 29

In The Time Of Trouble.

Psalm 27:5
"For in the time of trouble he shall hide me in his pavilion: in the secret of his tabernacle shall he hide me; he shall set me up upon a rock."

When trouble arises, our flesh responds in one of two ways.
Fight or flight.
This is a psychological reaction, an acute stress response, that prepares us to either stay and deal with the situation or run and hide.

What we often fail to realize is that we choose from the same two responses on how we deal with things spiritually.
Do we attempt to fight the battle on our own?
Do we run and hide?

The difference is the psychological and the spiritual "run and hide" have two very different meanings. One is avoidance. The other is dependence.

Do we run and hide to avoid the situation?
Or do we run and hide *"in the secret of his tabernacle"*?

One is fleshly. The other is wise.

Psalm 119:114
"Thou art my hiding place and my shield: I hope in thy word."

Choose to run and hide in Him today.
Seek safety in His pavilion.
Proverbs 18:10
"The name of the LORD is a strong tower: the righteous runneth into it, and is safe."

There you will find a Rock.
"...he shall set me up upon a rock."

That Rock is Jesus.
Psalm 61:2
"From the end of the earth will I cry unto thee, when my heart is overwhelmed: lead me to the rock that is higher than I."

In the time of trouble, run and hide in Him.

Bible Reading
Isaiah 39-40 | Proverbs 13

September 30 | 09.30

In The Midst Of Trouble.

Psalm 138:7
*"Though I walk in the midst of trouble, thou wilt revive me:
thou shalt stretch forth thine hand against the wrath of mine enemies,
and thy right hand shall save me."*

While we hide ourselves in Him, the Lord does so much more than just protect us from harm.

He revives. He sustains.
He restores. He encourages.
He fights. He gives.
He heals. He preserves.
He strengthens. He cares.
He comforts. He delivers.

David, a man after God's own heart, expected to walk through his troubles simply because he knew the Lord was by his side.

We know that we will face days of persecution, turmoil, regret, and dismay. It is not a matter of if, but rather when those days will happen. Though we cannot prevent or avoid these days, we can choose how we endure them.

James 1:2-3
*"My brethren, count it all joy when ye fall into divers temptations;
Knowing this, that the trying of your faith worketh patience."*

Job 13:15
*"Though he slay me, yet will I trust in him:
but I will maintain mine own ways before him."*

Nahum 1:7
*"The LORD is good, a strong hold in the day of trouble;
and he knoweth them that trust in him."*

David repeatedly chose to encourage himself in the Lord in the midst of his trouble.

1 Samuel 30:6
"And David was greatly distressed; for the people spake of stoning him, because the soul of all the people was grieved, every man for his sons and for his daughters: but David encouraged himself in the LORD his God."

Encourage yourself through His Word today, and every day.

Bible Reading
Isaiah 41-42 | Proverbs 14

10.01 | October 1

Yet.

Habakkuk 3:18
"Yet I will rejoice in the LORD, I will joy in the God of my salvation."

In the midst of trouble, we have a choice to make.
Sometimes the effects of our troubles are clearly seen. Sometimes the results are invisible to most people. Regardless, troublesome times either take away what was once there, or add something that was never intended.

Habakkuk 3:16-17
"When I heard, my belly trembled; my lips quivered at the voice: rottenness entered into my bones, and I trembled in myself, that I might rest in the day of trouble: when he cometh up unto the people, he will invade them with his troops. Although the fig tree shall not blossom, neither shall fruit be in the vines; the labour of the olive shall fail, and the fields shall yield no meat; the flock shall be cut off from the fold, and there shall be no herd in the stalls:"

One word…the next word…is the turning point.
Habakkuk 3:18
"Yet…"
Despite what was gone,
notwithstanding what did not happen as it should…
"Yet…"

How often do things happen just as we had planned or hoped?
Rarely, if ever.

**Even when things do not go our way,
we can choose to rejoice.**
Habakkuk 3:18
"Yet I will rejoice in the LORD…"

Rejoice in Who you know.
Rejoice in the Truth.
Rejoice in His Word.

Philippians 4:4
"Rejoice in the Lord alway: and again I say, Rejoice."

Choose to rejoice in Him regardless of your circumstances.
Habakkuk 3:18
"Yet I will rejoice in the LORD, I will joy in the God of my salvation."

Bible Reading
Isaiah 43-44 | Proverbs 15

October 2 | 10.02

He Knows What Is Best.

Proverbs 16:8-9
"Better is a little with righteousness than great revenues without right. A man's heart deviseth his way: but the LORD directeth his steps."

We may desire to be rich in revenue, but the Lord knows what is best. **He provides every need when we choose to seek Him first.**
Matthew 6:33
"But seek ye first the kingdom of God, and his righteousness; and all these things shall be added unto you."

When we begin to realize the amount of blessings we have in Him, we find we are much richer than we could ever be without Him.
Ephesians 1:17-19
"That the God of our Lord Jesus Christ, the Father of glory, may give unto you the spirit of wisdom and revelation in the knowledge of him: The eyes of your understanding being enlightened; that ye may know what is the hope of his calling, and what the riches of the glory of his inheritance in the saints, And what is the exceeding greatness of his power to us-ward who believe, according to the working of his mighty power,"

Our wealth on earth fades away quickly, for it is only temporal. **The riches that are found in Christ are eternal, and will never fade away.**
Romans 11:33
"O the depth of the riches both of the wisdom and knowledge of God! how unsearchable are his judgments, and his ways past finding out!"

His direction is worth more than anything money can buy. Sometimes we do not even realize that the Lord has directed us to exactly where we need to be, but He does just that, each and every single day.

He orders our steps away from sin.
Psalm 119:133
"Order my steps in thy word: and let not any iniquity have dominion over me."

He orders our steps to lead us to the right people and places.
Psalm 32:8
"I will instruct thee and teach thee in the way which thou shalt go: I will guide thee with mine eye."
When we allow Him to direct us, we can never go wrong; for He knows what is best.

Bible Reading
Isaiah 45-46 | Proverbs 16

10.03 | October 3

The Gift Of Wisdom.

Proverbs 2:6
"For the LORD giveth wisdom: out of his mouth cometh knowledge and understanding."

God gives us wisdom, but we have to find it within a specific Place by His specific methods. **The importance of God's Word can never be overstated or exaggerated.**

Proverbs 2:1-5
"My son, if thou wilt receive my words, and hide my commandments with thee; So that thou incline thine ear unto wisdom, and apply thine heart to understanding; Yea, if thou criest after knowledge, and liftest up thy voice for understanding; If thou seekest her as silver, and searchest for her as for hid treasures; Then shalt thou understand the fear of the LORD, and find the knowledge of God."

Wisdom is a Gift, that is found within the pages of the Word of God.
"...out of his mouth cometh knowledge and understanding."

If we are to receive knowledge and understanding, we must see and hear what the Lord has to say. His Word is vital to our whole existence, our walk with Him, our testimony to others, our life, our well-being, our service for Him, and our worship to Him.

We cannot be wise without His Word!

Many conditional blessings are found throughout the Book of Proverbs. These are promises that the Lord wishes to bestow upon His children, if we will simply do as He says. The Creator of the Universe, the Almighty God, offers us these opportunities, and it would be foolish for us to ignore them.

We must take God at His Word,
believing with childlike faith that His promises are true.

James 1:5
"If any of you lack wisdom, let him ask of God, that giveth to all men liberally, and upbraideth not; and it shall be given him."

God wants to give us wisdom.
Are we willing to ask Him?

Bible Reading
Isaiah 47-48 | Proverbs 17

October 4 | 10.04

Come & Buy.

Isaiah 55:1
*"Ho, every one that thirsteth, come ye to the waters,
and he that hath no money; come ye, buy, and eat; yea, come,
buy wine and milk without money and without price."*

How can we buy without money or price? Only by His mercy and grace.

Titus 3:5-7
*"Not by works of righteousness which we have done, but according
to his mercy he saved us, by the washing of regeneration,
and renewing of the Holy Ghost; Which he shed on us abundantly
through Jesus Christ our Saviour; That being justified by his grace,
we should be made heirs according to the hope of eternal life."*

What a picture of the free Gift of Salvation that is available to all who believe on Him! All we must do is come to Him believing in Who He is and what He has done for us. But this invitation does not stop with us. **Once we have came to Him, it is now our responsibility to invite others to come to Him as well.** People today are thirsty, yet most of them do not even realize for what they are thirsting.

"come ye to the waters"

Invite them to come and drink from the Well of Everlasting Life.

John 4:13-14
*"Jesus answered and said unto her, Whosoever drinketh of this water
shall thirst again: But whosoever drinketh of the water that I shall give him
shall never thirst; but the water that I shall give him shall be in him
a well of water springing up into everlasting life."*

The woman at the well drank of this Water, and she immediately began inviting others to do the same.

John 4:29
*"Come, see a man, which told me all things that ever I did:
is not this the Christ?"*

In the final chapter of the Scriptures, the Message is still the same.

Revelation 22:17
*"And the Spirit and the bride say, Come. And let him that heareth say,
Come. And let him that is athirst come. And whosoever will, let him take
the water of life freely."*

Invite someone to come to Him today.

Bible Reading
Isaiah 49-50 | Proverbs 18

10.05 | October 5

Think On These Things.

Philippians 4:8
*"Finally, brethren, whatsoever things are true,
whatsoever things are honest, whatsoever things are just,
whatsoever things are pure, whatsoever things are lovely,
whatsoever things are of good report; if there be any virtue,
and if there be any praise, think on these things."*

Our minds are powerful. They control what we think, what we feel, how we act, what we do, etc. More often than not they are racing at ninety nine miles an hour, constantly processing countless things simultaneously, all the while leaving us feeling worried, rushed, and ultimately exhausted.

While in prison, Paul writes to the church at Philippi exhorting them to be joyful despite their circumstances. If anyone's mind should have been filled with gloom and despair, it should have been him as he was detained. Yet, he chose to set his mind on the joy within him instead of the turmoil around him.

What are you thinking about today?
Think: To consider, to take account of, to weigh,
to meditate on, to have continual regard.

Paul brings out eight qualities by which everything we think about should be qualified.
True – It is truthful? – Ephesians 4:25
Honest – It is honorable? – 2 Corinthians 8:21
Just – Is it right? – Deuteronomy 16:20
Pure – Is it faultless? – James 3:17
Lovely – Is it acceptable and pleasing? – 1 Corinthians 13
Of Good Report – Is it reputable? – Acts 6:3
Virtue – Is it virtuous? – 2 Peter 1:3-4
Praise – Is it commendable? – Proverbs 31:31

Simply put…If it is, continue to think about it.
If it is not, disregard it entirely.

We are to *"think on these things"* if we desire *"the peace of God, which passeth all understanding"*. The devil wants to steal away our joy and peace that is only found in Christ Jesus. When we allow our minds to think on other things, we take our spiritual eyes off of Him. **Decide today to** *"think on these things"*.

Bible Reading
Isaiah 51-52 | Proverbs 19

October 6 | 10.06

The Sword.

1 Kings 3:24-25
*"And the king said, Bring me a sword.
And they brought a sword before the king. And the king said, Divide the living child in two, and give half to the one, and half to the other"*

Two women. One child. Both ladies claimed that the living child was theirs, while pointing to the other woman as the mother of the dead child. There were no witnesses, so how could a verdict be given as to whom the living child belonged to? Enter Solomon.

He used a sword to discern the hearts of the two women before him. When he gave the command for the living child to be divided in two, only one woman spoke up before her child was slain.

The Wisdom of Solomon brought out the truth of the matter, all because he chose to use a sword. All of Israel then saw the godly wisdom that Solomon possessed, and God used the event as evidence that His hand was in him.

1 Kings 3:28
*"And all Israel heard of the judgment which the king had judged;
and they feared the king:
for they saw that the wisdom of God was in him, to do judgment."*

**We also have a Sword at our disposal
to enable us to discern the Truth.**

Hebrews 4:12
"For the word of God is quick, and powerful, and sharper than any twoedged sword, piercing even to the dividing asunder of soul and spirit, and of the joints and marrow, and is a discerner of the thoughts and intents of the heart."

**Each day we have an opportunity to allow the Word of God
to display the Wisdom of the Word of God in our lives.**

Ephesians 6:17
*"And take the helmet of salvation, and the sword of the Spirit,
which is the word of God:"*

Bible Reading
Isaiah 53 | Proverbs 20

10.07 | October 7

Iron Friends.

Proverbs 27:17
*"Iron sharpeneth iron;
so a man sharpeneth the countenance of his friend."*

The blade of a sword is only sharpened by another blade. When the blade is used against anything else it begins to become dull.

Ephesians 6:17
*"And take the helmet of salvation,
and the sword of the Spirit, which is the word of God:"*

Hebrews 4:12
*"For the word of God is quick, and powerful, and sharper
than any twoedged sword, piercing even to the dividing asunder
of soul and spirit, and of the joints and marrow, and is a discerner
of the thoughts and intents of the heart."*

The Sword of the Spirit is our only means of offense against the wiles of the devil and the world around us. There are only two ways to sharpen our spirits: by spending time in the Word of God ourselves, and with other believers who point us to the Scriptures.

1 Samuel 23:16
*"And Jonathan Saul's son arose, and went to David into the wood,
and strengthened his hand in God."*

If we attempt to remain sharp on our own, we will surely fail.
God has given us people to sharpen our spirits by pointing us to Him.

Proverbs 27:9
*"Ointment and perfume rejoice the heart:
so doth the sweetness of a man's friend by hearty counsel."*

If our friends are not pointing us to Christ through His Word,
our friendships and our spirits are sure to become dull
in our walk with Him.
Who are you sharpened by?

Ephesians 3:16-17
*"That he would grant you, according to the riches of his glory,
to be strengthened with might by his Spirit in the inner man;
That Christ may dwell in your hearts by faith;
that ye, being rooted and grounded in love,"*

Bible Reading
Isaiah 54-55 | Proverbs 21

October 8 | 10.08

Thank God For Them.

Philippians 1:3-5
*"I thank my God upon every remembrance of you,
Always in every prayer of mine for you all making request with joy,
For your fellowship in the gospel from the first day until now;"*

God crosses our paths with different people every day. Some for a season. Some for a lesson. Some for a trial. Some for a blessing. Some for a lifetime.

"I thank my God upon every remembrance of you"
Who is it that every time they come to your mind you should thank God for them? Your parents. Your spouse. Your children. Your siblings. Your family. Your best friend. Your friends. Your pastor. Your pastor's wife. Your church family. Your _____.

"Always in every prayer of mine for you all making request with joy"
Are they a part of every prayer?
Whether we thank the Lord for them, or joyfully ask Him to work in their lives, we should be praying consistently for those most important to us.

Colossians 1:3,9-12
*"We give thanks to God and the Father of our Lord Jesus Christ, praying always for you…For this cause we also, since the day we heard it, do not cease to pray for you, and to desire that ye might be filled with the knowledge of his will in all wisdom and spiritual understanding;
That ye might walk worthy of the Lord unto all pleasing, being fruitful in every good work, and increasing in the knowledge of God;
Strengthened with all might, according to his glorious power, unto all patience and longsuffering with joyfulness;
Giving thanks unto the Father, which hath made us meet to be partakers of the inheritance of the saints in light:"*

He gave them to us.
Why would we not faithfully speak to Him on their behalf?

"For your fellowship in the gospel from the first day until now;"
The Lord crosses our paths with just the right people, just when He knows we need them. Their fellowship in the Gospel has made a difference in our lives since the first day until now.

Thank God for them today. Reach out and remind them that you love them and are thankful for them.

Bible Reading
Isaiah 56-57 | Proverbs 22

10.09 | October 9

What He Has Done.

Psalm 118:23
"This is the LORD'S doing; it is marvellous in our eyes."

There are many things that can only be described that it was the Lord. Sometimes we cannot trace His hand, but we still can choose to trust Him. Sometimes we can look back and trace His hand through every detail.

Ephesians 3:20-21
"Now unto him that is able to do exceeding abundantly above all that we ask or think, according to the power that worketh in us, Unto him be glory in the church by Christ Jesus throughout all ages, world without end. Amen."

Recognize the things that only He could have done.
Nothing in ourselves could have made it happen, for there is simply nothing good that we can do without Him.

John 15:5
"I am the vine, ye are the branches: He that abideth in me, and I in him, the same bringeth forth much fruit: for without me ye can do nothing."

The Lord Jesus Himself quoted this verse:
Matthew 21:42
"Jesus saith unto them, Did ye never read in the scriptures, The stone which the builders rejected, the same is become the head of the corner: this is the Lord's doing, and it is marvellous in our eyes?"

Why would we want to try and build something on anything but Him?
He is that Rock the wise man built his house upon.

When the rain descends, and the floods come, we can be sure that we are safe and secure in Him.

Every day, every moment, He is working in our lives.

Psalm 118:24
"This is the day which the LORD hath made; we will rejoice and be glad in it."

The greatest thing we can do is exalt Him, and thank Him for what He has done.

Bible Reading
Isaiah 58-59 | Proverbs 23

October 10 | 10.10

Luke 22:32
*"But I have prayed for thee, that thy faith fail not:
and when thou art converted, strengthen thy brethren."*

Praying for others is so important.
It is always encouraging to hear someone is praying for us.

But no matter how much time a person spends praying for us,
there is Someone Who is praying more.

He prayed for Peter before he denied Him three times.
He prayed for us in the Garden.

John 17:9
*"I pray for them: I pray not for the world,
but for them which thou hast given me; for they are thine."*

John 17:14,17
*"I have given them thy word…Sanctify them through thy truth:
thy word is truth."*

He is still praying for us.

Romans 8:27
*"And he that searcheth the hearts knoweth
what is the mind of the Spirit, because he maketh intercession
for the saints according to the will of God."*

He is constantly praying for us.

Hebrews 7:25
*"Wherefore he is able also to save them to the uttermost that come unto
God by him, seeing he ever liveth to make intercession for them."*

What a comfort it is to know, that our Lord and Saviour,
Jesus Christ, continually prays for us
while He waits to come back for us.

**Whatever you are facing today,
rest in the fact that He is praying for you.**

Bible Reading
Isaiah 60-61 | Proverbs 24

10.11 | October 11

This Man.

Matthew 13:54
"And when he was come into his own country, he taught them in their synagogue, insomuch that they were astonished, and said, Whence hath this man this wisdom, and these mighty works?"

They were amazed at what He said.
But they were confused…because they only saw His humanity.
Matthew 13:55-56
"Is not this the carpenter's son? is not his mother called Mary? and his brethren, James, and Joses, and Simon, and Judas? And his sisters, are they not all with us? Whence then hath this man all these things?"

**This Man was the carpenter's Son,
but He was also the Son of God.**

Their amazement changed to confusion,
and then ultimately to envy and strife.
Matthew 13:57
"And they were offended in him. But Jesus said unto them, A prophet is not without honour, save in his own country, and in his own house."

Their choices cost them
from seeing Him do many mighty works among them.
Matthew 13:58
"And he did not many mighty works there because of their unbelief."

What have we missed out on simply because we refused to believe He could work in the situation? We read what He has said within His Word, and yet so often we make the same mistake they did…we choose to think of Him as just a man because of our unbelief in Who He really Is.

This Man still wants to do many mighty works among us.
He can do the impossible, if only we would ask and believe.
This Man never changes.
He is still the Son of God. He is still holy. He is still sinless.
This Man shed His precious blood and died on the cross for our sins.
He rose again. He is now sitting on the right hand of God
making intercession for us.
Read His Word today.
You too will be astonished at what this Man says,
then choose to believe while you trust and obey.

Bible Reading
Isaiah 62-63 | Proverbs 25

October 12 | 10.12

He Will Speak Peace.

Psalm 85:8
"I will hear what God the LORD will speak: for he will speak peace unto his people, and to his saints: but let them not turn again to folly."

We all desire peace, yet so often look for it in all the wrong places. Amazon cannot deliver peace…for no amount of material goods will speak peace to our hearts. A drink or drug may deceive us into a temporary fix, only leaving the desire for more to fill the void again. Our favorite destination spot may help us avoid our problems for a few days, but eventually it is back to reality.

True peace is only found in God, who is the Author.
1 Corinthians 14:33
"For God is not the author of confusion, but of peace, as in all churches of the saints."

For us to find peace, we must first listen to what He has to say.
Psalm 85:8
"I will hear what God the LORD will speak…"

He has promised to speak peace to our weary souls.
Psalm 85:8
"…for he will speak peace unto his people, and to his saints…"

**No matter what you are going through today,
He will speak peace to your heart
if you will simply hear what His Word says.**

Philippians 4:7
"And the peace of God, which passeth all understanding, shall keep your hearts and minds through Christ Jesus."

John 14:27
"Peace I leave with you, my peace I give unto you: not as the world giveth, give I unto you. Let not your heart be troubled, neither let it be afraid."

You will never find peace if your Bible is closed.
Open the Word today.

Bible Reading
Isaiah 64-65 | Proverbs 26

10.13 | October 13

The Other Side.

Mark 4:35
*"And the same day, when the even was come, he saith unto them,
Let us pass over unto the other side."*

Jesus promised that they would reach the other side before they even got in the ship. He knew they would arrive safely. He also knew that they would have to go through a storm in order to get there. The disciples did not know either of these truths, only Jesus did.

Isn't that just like our lives sometimes?
We set out in faith, not knowing what will transpire before we get there.

Is Jesus in your ship?
His presence makes all the difference.
Mark 4:37
"And there arose a great storm of wind, and the waves beat into the ship, so that it was now full."

Are you in a great storm today?
Are the waves beating against your ship?

Even with Jesus onboard, we are not immune to facing storms along the way. He may have been sleeping in the hinder part of their ship, but He was there. They knew exactly Who to go to even when fear made their faith disappear.

Fear had overtaken them so much that they questioned if Jesus even cared. May we never allow any storm or circumstance to make us even consider such an ignorant thought.

1 Peter 5:7
"Casting all your care upon him; for he careth for you."

**Whatever storm you find yourself in the middle of today,
you can run to the Master of the wind.**

Mark 4:39
*"And he arose, and rebuked the wind, and said unto the sea,
Peace, be still. And the wind ceased, and there was a great calm."*

He has promised that you will reach the other side.
While you weather the storm,
allow Him to work in and through you for His glory.

Bible Reading
Isaiah 66 | Proverbs 27

October 14 | 10.14

The Bridge.

1 Timothy 2:5
"For there is one God, and one mediator between God and men, the man Christ Jesus;"

In Bible times, a ship or boat was the form of transportation to get from one side to the other of a body of water. Today, instead of a boat most of the time we use a bridge.

Bridges make a way for us to go somewhere we could not otherwise. Much like lakes or rivers that impede us from getting from one place to the other, our sin stands between us and the One True God.

We have a way of crossing the great divide by the Bridge of Salvation, our Lord and Saviour, Jesus Christ.

He is The Bridge.
He is the one Mediator between us and God.

Without Him,
we are heading down the road to destruction
that will lead to our eternal death.

With Him,
and only because of Him can we come to God at all.

When we cannot get from one side to the other, there is a Way.

John 14:6
"Jesus saith unto him, I am the way, the truth, and the life: no man cometh unto the Father, but by me."

The Bridge is the Way, the Truth, and the Life.
By Him, we are passed from death unto life.

John 5:24
"Verily, verily, I say unto you, He that heareth my word, and believeth on him that sent me, hath everlasting life, and shall not come into condemnation; but is passed from death unto life."

Next time you see a bridge or go across one,
remember…He is The Bridge.

Bible Reading
Jeremiah 1-2 | Proverbs 28

10.15 | October 15

A Controlled Life.

Ephesians 5:18
"And be not drunk with wine, wherein is excess; but be filled with the Spirit;"

Any substance that lowers our inhibitions causes us to lose control. Alcohol and drugs rob us of our sobriety and awareness.

Proverbs 20:1
"Wine is a mocker, strong drink is raging: and whosoever is deceived thereby is not wise."

The Apostle Paul, under the inspiration of the Holy Spirit, used the contrast of being drunk with wine and filled with the Spirit.

In order to be filled with Him, we must first be empty.
Empty of ourselves.
Empty of our pride.
Empty of our strength.
Empty of anything, but Him.

It is then, and only then, we can have a controlled life. Not one where we are in control, but where He controls our every move as we submit to Him.

A controlled life is simply a Spirit filled life.

Galatians 5:25
"If we live in the Spirit, let us also walk in the Spirit."

Without Him, we are out of control.
Without Him, we have no direction.
Without Him, we are prone to wander.

Galatians 5:16
"This I say then, Walk in the Spirit, and ye shall not fulfil the lust of the flesh."

The key to being filled, is to simply yield.
Yield to Him today.

Bible Reading
Jeremiah 3-4 | Proverbs 29

October 16 | 10.16

Full Of His Fruit.

Galatians 5:22-23
"But the fruit of the Spirit is love, joy, peace, longsuffering, gentleness, goodness, faith, Meekness, temperance: against such there is no law."

When we are filled with Him, we will see fruit. His fruit.
"But the fruit of the Spirit…"

It is His fruit for it is Him that works in and through us. Without Him, we have no fruit that will remain. The fruit of the Spirit has nine parts, to make one whole proof that He is at work.

Love.
Love for God. Love for thy neighbor.

Joy.
Regardless of the circumstances, we can count it all joy through Him.

Peace.
That passes all of our understanding. That only comes from Him.

Longsuffering.
Patient in trouble, deferring anger and willing to endure.

Gentleness.
Sweet, kind, and forgiving.

Goodness.
Ready to do good always when given the opportunity.

Faith.
Belief and conviction in the Truth.

Meekness.
Not easily provoked.

Temperance.
Able to remain in control, without excess.

Is *"the fruit of the Spirit"* evident within our testimony?
Or are we full of ourselves?

Seek to be full of His fruit today. Colossians 1:10-11
"That ye might walk worthy of the Lord unto all pleasing, being fruitful in every good work, and increasing in the knowledge of God; Strengthened with all might, according to his glorious power, unto all patience and longsuffering with joyfulness;"

Bible Reading
Jeremiah 5-6 | Proverbs 30

10.17 | October 17

He Will Guide.

John 16:13
"Howbeit when he, the Spirit of truth, is come, he will guide you into all truth: for he shall not speak of himself; but whatsoever he shall hear, that shall he speak: and he will shew you things to come."

It has often been said that the Bible is too hard to understand. If we try to comprehend the Word through our own abilities, we will surely be confused. This is why we are not meant to read and study the Truth by ourselves.

The Bible is the only Book where the Author is always present. God the Father gave the Word. Jesus is the Word. The Holy Spirit guides us through the Word. Jesus spoke these Words of our verse today as part of His answer to Judas not Iscariot's question.

John 14:22
"Judas saith unto him, not Iscariot, Lord, how is it that thou wilt manifest thyself unto us, and not unto the world?"

Several verses later, we learn that the Holy Spirit is a Person, and He will guide us into not just some truth, but all Truth.

John 14:26
"But the Comforter, which is the Holy Ghost, whom the Father will send in my name, he shall teach you all things, and bring all things to your remembrance, whatsoever I have said unto you."

When we read the Word, the Holy Spirit helps us to discern what the Word means.
1 Corinthians 2:10
"But God hath revealed them unto us by his Spirit: for the Spirit searcheth all things, yea, the deep things of God."

There is so much in His Word that He has prepared for us. **But these things cannot be learned on our own, He must guide us.**
1 Corinthians 2:13-14
"Which things also we speak, not in the words which man's wisdom teacheth, but which the Holy Ghost teacheth; comparing spiritual things with spiritual. But the natural man receiveth not the things of the Spirit of God: for they are foolishness unto him: neither can he know them, because they are spiritually discerned."
Ask the Lord to guide you in His Word today.

Bible Reading
Jeremiah 7-8 | Proverbs 31

October 18 | 10.18

A True Servant.

Philippians 2:5-8
"Let this mind be in you, which was also in Christ Jesus: Who, being in the form of God, thought it not robbery to be equal with God: But made himself of no reputation, and took upon him the form of a servant, and was made in the likeness of men: And being found in fashion as a man, he humbled himself, and became obedient unto death, even the death of the cross."

Jesus Christ, the only begotten Son of God willingly chose to humble Himself and become a Servant. In the context of this passage, the Apostle Paul was exhorting the church of Philippi to be like Christ. The same applies to us today…*"Let this mind be in you, which was also in Christ Jesus".*

He was not worried about what others thought of Him. He was willing to make Himself the Servant of Servants. He was robed in human flesh just like us. He was tempted just like us, yet He did not sin. He humbled Himself far beneath Who He truly was and is. He was obedient, even unto death. He suffered and willingly died on the cross for us. The Servant of Servants is the Ultimate Example of what it means to serve. **The only way we can strive to have *"this mind"* is to strive to become more like Him.**

We need no reputation, so that others may see Him.
Are we serving others or serving ourselves?
Pride and humility cannot coexist.
Are we obedient? Even if it costs us our lives?

Mark 8:35
"For whosoever will save his life shall lose it; but whosoever shall lose his life for my sake and the gospel's, the same shall save it."

Dying to ourselves daily is part of walking with the Lord; but someday, we may be forced to decide whether or not we are willing to die for our faith.

If we will choose to let the mind of Christ be in us, we too can become a true servant for His glory.

Acts 20:24
"But none of these things move me, neither count I my life dear unto myself, so that I might finish my course with joy, and the ministry, which I have received of the Lord Jesus, to testify the gospel of the grace of God."

Bible Reading
Jeremiah 9-10 | Psalm 1-3

10.19 | October 19

Isaiah 43:2
"When thou passest through the waters, I will be with thee; and through the rivers, they shall not overflow thee: when thou walkest through the fire, thou shalt not be burned; neither shall the flame kindle upon thee."

Many times in our lives it feels like the situation we are in will never end. We are convinced that the storm will never cease, the waves will always crash, and the wind will always rage.

The truth is, in those moments, we have forgotten Whose we are.
Isaiah 43:1
"But now thus saith the LORD that created thee, O Jacob, and he that formed thee, O Israel, Fear not: for I have redeemed thee, I have called thee by thy name; thou art mine."

Because we are His, we can look at our storms and trials differently.

"When thou passest through the waters, I will be with thee…"
When we are in deep waters, we can past through them because He promises that He will be with us.

"…and through the rivers, they shall not overflow thee…"
Remember the Lord parting the Red Sea? He can hold back the waters of the rivers in front of us so that we can pass through without them overflowing upon us.

"…when thou walkest through the fire, thou shalt not be burned; neither shall the flame kindle upon thee."
The three Hebrew boys experienced this and found this very promise to be true. We too can walk through the fires of our lives without being burned or even smelling like smoke.

**Whatever you are facing today,
He can lead you through.**

Psalm 23:4
"Yea, though I walk through the valley of the shadow of death, I will fear no evil: for thou art with me; thy rod and thy staff they comfort me."

Bible Reading
Jeremiah 11-12 | Psalm 4-6

October 20 | 10.20

For A Season.

1 Peter 1:6
*"Wherein ye greatly rejoice, though now for a season,
if need be, ye are in heaviness through manifold temptations:"*

What is your favorite season? Fall, Winter, Spring, Summer. Baseball, football, basketball, soccer. Waiting, trusting, rejoicing, mourning, growing, moving, standing still.

"for a season"
A promise that our circumstance today will not last forever.

Seasons come and seasons go.
Sometimes we rejoice for a season, and sometimes we mourn.
Sometimes we wait, sometimes we move forward.

Ecclesiastes 3:1
*"To every thing there is a season,
and a time to every purpose under the heaven:"*

A new season comes to bring about a needed change.
"if need be"
Sometimes the Lord allows a season, for which only He knows the reason. Rest assured that if He sees fit to allow it, He knows we need something that will come out of it.

He has a reason, and He has a purpose.
1 Peter 1:7
"That the trial of your faith, being much more precious than of gold that perisheth, though it be tried with fire, might be found unto praise and honour and glory at the appearing of Jesus Christ:"

The trials we face all have one thing in common...His purpose.
No matter the trial, His purpose remains the same...
that it might bring Him praise, honour and glory.

"though it be tried with fire"
How we handle ourselves in the fire, the choices me make,
will determine whether people see us or if they see Him.

**Whatever season you are facing today,
allow Him to get the glory through it.**

Bible Reading
Jeremiah 13-14 | Psalm 7-9

10.21 | October 21

As For Me.

Psalm 69:13
"But as for me, my prayer is unto thee, O LORD, in an acceptable time: O God, in the multitude of thy mercy hear me, in the truth of thy salvation."

There comes a turning point in every battle, every storm, every trial, where one must choose how they, as an individual, will respond and give account for their actions. There are times when teamwork takes precedent, but in the end, the team does not give account to the Lord as a whole. **Each of us will stand before the Lord someday and give an account for us alone.**

For the first twelve verses of Psalm 69, David lays out his situation. How the deep waters are overtaking his soul, and he feels as if he is sinking in the mire. He is weary from crying because of those who hate him without a cause. He pleads to God for deliverance. But in verse 13, we see four words that are the turning point of David's mindset. *"But as for me…"*

What a reminder for us to have a checkpoint within ourselves of how we are handling the situation around us! **When was the last time you stopped and considered how you were conducting yourself in the midst of your circumstances?** Here are some examples of some questions we can ask ourselves in reference to *"as for me"*:

What did I choose? - Joshua 24:15
"…but as for me and my house, we will serve the LORD."

How did I respond? - Psalm 55:16
"As for me, I will call upon God; and the LORD shall save me."

How did I react? - Psalm 26:11
"But as for me, I will walk in mine integrity: redeem me, and be merciful unto me."

How did I handle myself in the middle of my storm? - Daniel 7:28
"Hitherto is the end of the matter. As for me Daniel, my cogitations much troubled me, and my countenance changed in me: but I kept the matter in my heart."

How often did I pray for others? - 1 Samuel 12:23
"Moreover as for me, God forbid that I should sin against the LORD in ceasing to pray for you: but I will teach you the good and the right way:"

When all is said and done, each of us only have to answer for *"as for me"*.

Bible Reading
Jeremiah 15-16 | Psalm 10-12

October 22 | 10.22

Faint Not.

2 Corinthians 4:1
*"Therefore seeing we have this ministry,
as we have received mercy, we faint not;"*

Have you ever physically fainted? Maybe you hadn't eaten all day and your body was desperate for nourishment, or you had just expended all your energy. Fainting refers to being weary to the point of exhaustion which renders us utterly spiritless.

Now consider if you have ever fainted spiritually.
When we find references to fainting in the Scriptures, it is often connected to yielding to the Holy Spirit of God.

Before the *"Therefore…"* we find these two verses at the end of chapter 3.
2 Corinthians 3:17-18
*"Now the Lord is that Spirit: and where the Spirit of the Lord is,
there is liberty. But we all, with open face beholding as in a glass
the glory of the Lord, are changed into the same image from glory to
glory, even as by the Spirit of the Lord."*

When we are filled with the Spirit,
we find liberty to be able to give God the glory He deserves.

"Therefore seeing we have this ministry…"
Giving Him glory is the ultimate purpose of any ministry He gives us.
2 Corinthians 4:15-16
*"For all things are for your sakes, that the abundant grace might through
the thanksgiving of many redound to the glory of God.
For which cause we faint not; but though our outward man perish,
yet the inward man is renewed day by day."*

**It is a daily decision to yield to Him
in order to keep from fainting spiritually.**

Open up His Word and allow
the Truth of the Scriptures to renew you today.

Galatians 6:9
*"And let us not be weary in well doing:
for in due season we shall reap, if we faint not."*

Bible Reading
Jeremiah 17-18 | Psalm 13-15

10.23 | October 23

Galatians 6:8
*"For he that soweth to his flesh shall of the flesh reap corruption;
but he that soweth to the Spirit shall of the Spirit reap life everlasting."*

Every day, every moment, of our lives we are sowing something. Every decision, every thought, every move, every action is sown to either our flesh or the Spirit of God.

We are promised to reap whatsoever we sow.
Galatians 6:7
*"Be not deceived; God is not mocked:
for whatsoever a man soweth, that shall he also reap."*

Sowing to our flesh refers to fulfilling our own desires.
"For he that soweth to his flesh…"

It is personal, but more than that, if it selfish to sow to our flesh.
Doing so only leads to corruption or destruction.
"For he that soweth to his flesh shall of the flesh reap corruption"

Selfish sowing results in only temporary satisfaction.
James 4:14
"Whereas ye know not what shall be on the morrow. For what is your life? It is even a vapour, that appeareth for a little time, and then vanisheth away."

Sowing to the Spirit is not about us.
"…but he that soweth to the Spirit…"
It is selfless, because it is not directed to us,
it is only directed to Him for His glory.

Sowing to the Spirit brings everlasting life.
"…but he that soweth to the Spirit shall of the Spirit reap life everlasting."

Who are we sowing for?
How much sowing do we do for Him in comparison for ourselves?
How devoted are we to sowing purposefully?

Evaluate where you are sowing your time,
your effort, and your faith today.
There will soon be a harvest of whatever we have sown.

Bible Reading
Jeremiah 19-20 | Psalm 16-18

October 24 | 10.24

The Sower.

Mark 4:3
"Hearken; Behold, there went out a sower to sow:"

Imagine the Sea of Galilee on a bright and perfect day, the breeze gently blowing, across the surface of the water. There is a great multitude of people from every city gathered together, standing on the shore.

Jesus had been sitting by the sea side.
When people heard, they gathered around Him.

Seeing the opportunity, He entered into a ship that sat in the sea, and began to teach many things by parables. The first of which being about the sower.

Matthew 13:3-4
"And he spake many things unto them in parables, saying, Behold, a sower went forth to sow; And when he sowed, some seeds…"

The sower first had to go out from where he was.
What if the sower had kept the seeds to himself, and never planted them?

Mark 4:14
"The sower soweth the word."

Luke 8:11
"Now the parable is this: The seed is the word of God."

**Each of us are sowers
that have the Seed of the Word of God in our possession.**
Will we stay where we are, refusing to go forth to sow?

Jesus spoke this parable so that the people may see the need.
Soil is all around us.
The outcome of the Seed being planted is not up to us.
**Our responsibility is only to sow the Seed of the Word of God
and allow the Lord to do the rest.**

Isaiah 55:10-11
*"For as the rain cometh down, and the snow from heaven,
and returneth not thither, but watereth the earth, and maketh it bring forth
and bud, that it may give seed to the sower, and bread to the eater:
So shall my word be that goeth forth out of my mouth: it shall not return
unto me void, but it shall accomplish that which I please,
and it shall prosper in the thing whereto I sent it."*

Bible Reading
Jeremiah 21-22 | Psalm 19-21

10.25 | October 25

Luke 8:5-8
"A sower went out to sow his seed: and as he sowed, some fell by the way side; and it was trodden down, and the fowls of the air devoured it. And some fell upon a rock; and as soon as it was sprung up, it withered away, because it lacked moisture. And some fell among thorns; and the thorns sprang up with it, and choked it. And other fell on good ground, and sprang up, and bare fruit an hundredfold. And when he had said these things, he cried, He that hath ears to hear, let him hear."

God gives the Seed of the Word of God that we are to go out and sow.
The Seed must be planted in soil.

Every person has a heart of soil within them that is in need of hearing the Gospel of Jesus Christ. How the soil receives the Word is not up to us, but we must still plant the Seed. Three times within these verses we see the word *"some"* repeated. Some Seeds will fall by the way side. Some upon a rock. Some among thorns.

The Way Side. - Luke 8:12
Sometimes when we sow, the devil will take the Word out of the hearts of those that received the Seed.

The Rock. - Luke 8:13
Sometimes the Seed springs up quickly, yet because it never took root, it withers away when temptation comes.

The Thorns. - Luke 8:14
Sometimes the thorns of the cares and pleasures of this life get in the way of the Seed, causing it to become unfruitful.

But sometimes...there are other Seeds which fall on good ground.

Luke 8:15
"But that on the good ground are they, which in an honest and good heart, having heard the word, keep it, and bring forth fruit with patience."

Pray for the soil around you.
Pray that some Seeds you plant fall upon good ground.

And as you pray, remember...
Every person has a heart of soil in need of the Seed.

Bible Reading
Jeremiah 23-24 | Psalm 22-24

October 26 | 10.26

The Seed.

Luke 8:11
"Now the parable is this: The seed is the word of God."

Jesus explained the parable to His disciples, emphasizing the importance of the Seed. **Without the Seed, everything we do is in vain.** The Seed of the Word of God is what makes the difference.

Luke 8:5
"A sower went out to sow his seed..."

In order for the Seed to be sown,
there must be a sower that is willing to give whatever is needed.

Mark 4:14
"The sower soweth the word."

How willing are we to sow the Seed?

How faithful are we at sowing?

Many different things can happen to a Seed when it is sown.

**It is only our responsibility to sow the Seed,
and leave the rest up to Him.**

Sometimes, we plant a Seed.
Sometimes, we water a Seed that has already been planted.
And sometimes, as we water,
we are able to see a soul trust Jesus Christ through faith
and by His grace as their Saviour.

**It is up to us to sow and water the Seed of the Word of God,
then allow God to give the increase.**

1 Corinthians 3:6-8
"I have planted, Apollos watered; but God gave the increase. So then neither is he that planteth any thing, neither he that watereth; but God that giveth the increase. Now he that planteth and he that watereth are one: and every man shall receive his own reward according to his own labour."

Plant the Seed today, and every day.

Bible Reading
Jeremiah 25-26 | Psalm 25-27

10.27 | October 27

All Or Nothing.

Philippians 4:13
"I can do all things through Christ which strengtheneth me."

It is so easy to hear a familiar verse and overlook some of the Truth found within. This verse may only contain 10 words, but there is so much life changing Truth that we can apply to our lives.

We can parallel this verse with one found in John 15.
John 15:5
"I am the vine, ye are the branches: He that abideth in me, and I in him, the same bringeth forth much fruit: for without me ye can do nothing."

Through Him, we can do all things.
Without Him, we can do nothing.

The difference is our dependence upon Him,
allowing His sufficient grace to strengthen and enable us.

2 Corinthians 12:9
*"And he said unto me, My grace is sufficient for thee:
for my strength is made perfect in weakness.
Most gladly therefore will I rather glory in my infirmities,
that the power of Christ may rest upon me."*

How can we do all things through Him?
Because our strength and sufficiency must come from Him.

2 Corinthians 3:5
*"Not that we are sufficient of ourselves
to think any thing as of ourselves; but our sufficiency is of God;"*

**Trying to accomplish anything on our own
will only result in temporal results.**

Rest in Him today.
Allow His strength to be made perfect in your weakness.

**The choice between all things or nothing
is a result of the Source of our strength.**

Bible Reading
Jeremiah 27-28 | Psalm 28-30

October 28 | 10.28

Choose The Fear.

Proverbs 1:29
*"For that they hated knowledge,
and did not choose the fear of the LORD:"*

Wisdom begins with a choice.
Proverbs 1:5-7
*"A wise man will hear, and will increase learning;
and a man of understanding shall attain unto wise counsels:
To understand a proverb, and the interpretation; the words of the wise,
and their dark sayings. The fear of the LORD is the beginning
of knowledge: but fools despise wisdom and instruction."*

At the root of many of the problems we face today is a lack of the fear of the Lord – a holy reverence, respect and awe of Him. When we truly fear the Lord we submit to His authority, deity and sovereignty.

"…but fools despise wisdom and instruction."

We are warned that where there is no fear of Him, there is no wisdom or instruction. You cannot begin to understand without first starting as you were instructed.

Those that despise wisdom and instruction
are referred to as fools.

Psalm 14:1
"The fool hath said in his heart, There is no God. They are corrupt, they have done abominable works, there is none that doeth good."

The fear of the Lord is only the beginning.
When we fear Him,
we begin to experience all that He is,
and all that He wants us to have through Him.

We must choose to fear Him
so that He can begin to work in and through us.

Bible Reading
Jeremiah 29-30 | Psalm 31-33

10.29 | October 29

Psalm 42:1-2
"As the hart panteth after the water brooks, so panteth my soul after thee,
O God. My soul thirsteth for God, for the living God:
when shall I come and appear before God?"

When we receive Christ, we have Wisdom.
Our faith in Him determines the course of every decision we make.
Philippians 3:8-10
"Yea doubtless, and I count all things but loss for the excellency
of the knowledge of Christ Jesus my Lord: for whom I have suffered
the loss of all things, and do count them but dung, that I may win Christ,
And be found in him, not having mine own righteousness,
which is of the law, but that which is through the faith of Christ,
the righteousness which is of God by faith: That I may know him,
and the power of his resurrection, and the fellowship of his sufferings,
being made conformable unto his death;"

**Each day we must choose Him
by faithfully spending time within His Word.**
Proverbs 4:5
"Get wisdom, get understanding: forget it not;
neither decline from the words of my mouth."

The longer we go without a drink, the more we need the refreshment. When our body is dehydrated, there is craving for water that is instilled in us by our Creator.
He gave us the ability to be thirsty.
When our time with Him declines, our soul begins to thirst for Him.

Just as our physical body needs nourishment,
God placed within us the desire for Him.

**The longer we go without the Word,
the more our soul desires Him.**
Psalm 63:1
"O God, thou art my God; early will I seek thee: my soul thirsteth for thee,
my flesh longeth for thee in a dry and thirsty land, where no water is;"

Are you thirsty?
Refresh your soul today with the Wisdom of the Word of God.

Bible Reading
Jeremiah 31-32 | Psalm 34-36

Delight In Him.

Psalm 37:4
*"Delight thyself also in the LORD;
and he shall give thee the desires of thine heart."*

Some read this verse and assume that if we focus on the Lord, He will give us exactly what we want. While that may encourage us to move our attention toward Him, it gives us the wrong motive and only sets us up to be disappointed.

**Delighting in the Lord enables our desires
to be molded into what He has in store.**

"God always gives His best to those who leave the choice with Him."
Jim Elliot

**The process of delighting in Him
is found within the pages of Scripture.**
Isaiah 58:13-14
*"If thou…shalt honour him, not doing thine own ways,
nor finding thine own pleasure, nor speaking thine own words:
Then shalt thou delight thyself in the LORD; and I will cause thee to ride upon the high places of the earth, and feed thee with the heritage of Jacob thy father: for the mouth of the LORD hath spoken it."*

The ifs and thens of the Word of God teach countless principles that need applied to our walk with Him. If we will honor Him…If we will do things His way, and not ours…If we will not seek our own pleasure…If we will not speak our own words…Then…and only then…can we truly delight ourselves in Him.

**He has promised, that if we will simply delight in Him,
His desires will become our desires…
we will want what He wants for us.**

Wanting what we think is best will only give us temporary results.
His Way lasts for eternity.

Psalm 37:23
*"The steps of a good man are ordered by the LORD:
and he delighteth in his way."*

Bible Reading
Jeremiah 33-34 | Psalm 37

10.31 | October 31

The Results Of Delighting.

Isaiah 58:14
"Then shalt thou delight thyself in the LORD;
and I will cause thee to ride upon the high places of the earth,
and feed thee with the heritage of Jacob thy father:
for the mouth of the LORD hath spoken it."

When we delight ourselves in Him, He not only promises to make His will become our desires, but He has so much more in store.

"Then shalt thou delight thyself in the LORD…"
He promises there are results of delighting in Him.
"…and I will cause thee to ride upon the high places of the earth, and feed thee…"

**Delighting in Him causes us to be strengthened
to reach places we never could on our own.**
Habakkuk 3:19
"The LORD God is my strength,
and he will make my feet like hinds' feet,
and he will make me to walk upon mine high places.
To the chief singer on my stringed instruments."

When He speaks, He promises.
"…for the mouth of the LORD hath spoken it."

Anything and everything He has said is true.
If it has not happened yet, it will.
His Word is powerful.

If you are struggling today, delight in Him.
If you are filled with doubt, choose instead to delight in Him.
If fear has stolen your joy, decide to delight in Him.

**The results of delighting in Him
cannot be expressed in any other words but His.**
Psalm 37:4-5
"Delight thyself also in the LORD;
and he shall give thee the desires of thine heart.
Commit thy way unto the LORD; trust also in him;
and he shall bring it to pass."

Bible Reading
Jeremiah 35-36 | Psalm 38-40

November 1 | 11.01

Therefore I Will Give Thanks.

2 Samuel 22:50
*"Therefore I will give thanks unto thee, O LORD,
among the heathen, and I will sing praises unto thy name."*

**The more we delight ourselves in the Lord,
the more thankful we will be unto Him.**
"Therefore…"
David realized there were many reasons
for him to give thanks unto the Lord.
How many reasons do you have today?
If you began to count them,
it likely would not be too long before you lost count.

The first day of November should cause us
to dwell on all the Lord has blessed us with.

What are you thankful for today?
To Whom are you giving thanks for what you have?
Though we should be thankful to those who have contributed, we must always remember that everything really comes from the same Source.

"Therefore I will give thanks unto thee, O LORD…"
He is the Source for all that we have.
Psalm 145:1-2
*"I will extol thee, my God, O king;
and I will bless thy name for ever and ever. Every day will I bless thee;
and I will praise thy name for ever and ever."*

Even when he was surrounded by the heathen, he still chose to praise the One Who had delivered him from the hand of his enemies.

2 Samuel 22:48-49
*"It is God that avengeth me, and that bringeth down
the people under me, And that bringeth me forth from mine enemies:
thou also hast lifted me up on high above them that rose up against me:
thou hast delivered me from the violent man."*

**Regardless of your situation today,
there is still a Reason to be thankful.**

Give Him the thanks and praise that He alone deserves
today, and every day.

Bible Reading
Jeremiah 37-38 | Psalm 41-43

11.02 | November 2

Thanks In Prayer & Praise.

Psalm 105:1
*"O give thanks unto the LORD; call upon his name:
make known his deeds among the people."*

How can we give thanks unto Him?
In this one verse we see the recipe for true thanksgiving unto the Lord.
"O give thanks unto the LORD; call upon his name…"

Calling upon the Name of the Lord in prayer is a simple, yet amazing, way to give thanks unto Him.

Psalm 116:1-2
*"I love the LORD, because he hath heard my voice
and my supplications. Because he hath inclined his ear unto me,
therefore will I call upon him as long as I live."*

How often do you call upon His Name?
If we only wait to call upon Him when we are in need, we will have missed out on one of the greatest privileges of prayer…to thank Him.

"…make known his deeds among the people."
Making known His deeds and mighty works is the simplest form of praise to Him.

Psalm 145:11-12
*"They shall speak of the glory of thy kingdom, and talk of thy power;
To make known to the sons of men his mighty acts,
and the glorious majesty of his kingdom."*

What mighty acts has He done in your life?
Tell someone what He has done for you.

Time after time He has come through.
Day after day He has provided.

If we are willing to share with others what He has done for us,
we can also encourage them that He is Able to do the same for them.

**Lift up your thanks to Him
through prayer and praise today and every day.**

Bible Reading
Jeremiah 39-40 | Psalm 44-46

November 3 | 11.03

A Thankful Voice.

Psalm 26:7
*"That I may publish with the voice of thanksgiving,
and tell of all thy wondrous works."*

A man after God's own heart, David walked in his integrity.
He trusted in the Lord completely.

Psalm 26:3
*"For thy lovingkindness is before mine eyes:
and I have walked in thy truth."*

He had purposefully prepared his heart through His Word.

"I have walked in thy truth." Psalm 26:3
"I have not sat with vain persons" Psalm 26:4
"I have hated the congregation of evil doers" Psalm 26:5
"I will wash mine hands in innocency" Psalm 26:6

He did all of this with the intent of having a thankful voice
to declare what the Lord had done.

Psalm 26:7
*"That I may publish with the voice of thanksgiving,
and tell of all thy wondrous works."*

How thankful is your voice?
How faithful are you to speak of what the Lord has done for you?

Consider today what you can do to purposefully give Him thanks.
It all begins with saturating ourselves with the Truth of His Word.

Psalm 119:27
*"Make me to understand the way of thy precepts:
so shall I talk of thy wondrous works."*

Regardless of what happened yesterday…
Regardless of what is happening today…
Regardless of what happens tomorrow…
How thankful is your voice?

Bible Reading
Jeremiah 41-42 | Psalm 47-49

11.04 | November 4

In Every Thing.

1 Thessalonians 5:18
*"In every thing give thanks:
for this is the will of God in Christ Jesus concerning you."*

When things do not go our way…give thanks.
When the victory is won…give thanks.

If the earth moves from under your feet…give thanks.
If you have reached the top of the mountain…give thanks.

Though fear grips your heart…give thanks.
Though the raging waves are now calm…give thanks.

When enemies surround you…give thanks.
When friends support and encourage you…give thanks.

If you cannot find the words to pray…give thanks.
If your prayer has been answered…give thanks.

Though trouble is all around you…give thanks.
Though the battle seems to be over…give thanks.

It is the will of God for us to be thankful in every thing.
This should also encourage us that even when things do not work out like we had hoped, or even prayed, it is still the will of God.

Psalm 34:1
*"I will bless the LORD at all times:
his praise shall continually be in my mouth."*

He is still in control,
and He is still concerned about us.

So much so He gave His only begotten Son
so that His will could be accomplished.

Ephesians 5:20
*"Giving thanks always for all things unto God
and the Father in the name of our Lord Jesus Christ;"*

**Even though we may not be thankful for everything that happens,
we can choose to be thankful in every thing.**

Bible Reading
Jeremiah 43-44 | Psalm 50-52

November 5 | 11.05

Peaceful & Thankful.

Colossians 3:15
*"And let the peace of God rule in your hearts,
to the which also ye are called in one body; and be ye thankful."*

As children of God we are set to a higher standard; not because of who we are, but rather Whose we are. We are bought with a price. God gave His only begotten Son to shed His precious blood for our sins.

Paul wrote to the people of Colosse under the inspiration of the Holy Spirit and admonished them how to live as unto the Lord.

Colossians 3:12-14
*"Put on therefore, as the elect of God, holy and beloved,
bowels of mercies, kindness, humbleness of mind, meekness,
longsuffering; Forbearing one another, and forgiving one another,
if any man have a quarrel against any: even as Christ forgave you,
so also do ye. And above all these things put on charity,
which is the bond of perfectness."*

These same attributes should be seen in our lives as the His children. Merciful. Kind. Humble. Meek. Longsuffering. Patient. Forgiving. Loving. Peaceful. Thankful.

Philippians 4:6-7
*"Be careful for nothing; but in every thing by prayer and supplication
with thanksgiving let your requests be made known unto God.
And the peace of God, which passeth all understanding,
shall keep your hearts and minds through Christ Jesus."*

When we come to God in prayer for our needs with thankful hearts as we ask for His help, we are promised to have peace which passeth all understanding.

Isaiah 26:3
*"Thou wilt keep him in perfect peace, whose mind is stayed on thee:
because he trusteth in thee."*

Let His peace rule within your heart today.
Chaos and confusion abound all around us, but through it all
we can endure it peacefully because of Him.

Colossians 2:7
*"Rooted and built up in him, and stablished in the faith,
as ye have been taught, abounding therein with thanksgiving."*

Bible Reading
Jeremiah 45-46 | Psalm 53-55

11.06 | November 6

Songs Of Thanks.

Colossians 3:16-17
"Let the word of Christ dwell in you richly in all wisdom; teaching and admonishing one another in psalms and hymns and spiritual songs, singing with grace in your hearts to the Lord. And whatsoever ye do in word or deed, do all in the name of the Lord Jesus, giving thanks to God and the Father by him."

Peace and thankfulness are found within the pages of the Word.
Jesus Christ is the Word that was made flesh and dwelt among us.
John 1:1,14
"In the beginning was the Word, and the Word was with God, and the Word was God… And the Word was made flesh, and dwelt among us, (and we beheld his glory, the glory as of the only begotten of the Father,) full of grace and truth."

Have you ever been so full of the Word of God
that songs of praise just overflowed from your heart?
A thankful heart always has a song to sing unto Him.
Psalm 28:7
"The LORD is my strength and my shield; my heart trusted in him, and I am helped: therefore my heart greatly rejoiceth; and with my song will I praise him."

The songs in our hearts should change the way we do things.
Every word we say. Every deed that we do.
Every thought. Every move. Every step.
Every opportunity comes with a choice to give thanks
and praise to Him or to ourselves.
Matthew 6:2
"Therefore when thou doest thine alms, do not sound a trumpet before thee, as the hypocrites do in the synagogues and in the streets, that they may have glory of men. Verily I say unto you, They have their reward."

For whom are you doing things today?
1 Corinthians 10:31
"Whether therefore ye eat, or drink, or whatsoever ye do, do all to the glory of God."
Who are you intending to get the thanks?
Colossians 3:23
"And whatsoever ye do, do it heartily, as to the Lord, and not unto men;"
Bible Reading
Jeremiah 47-48 | Psalm 56-58

A Testimony Of Thanks.

Romans 1:8
*"First, I thank my God through Jesus Christ for you all,
that your faith is spoken of throughout the whole world."*

The Apostle Paul was thanking God for the people of Rome, and their testimony that he had heard as he traveled. Imagine someone traveling to a place where the people there knew of you. **What testimony would they give of your faith?** A convicting thought.

Would they have anything to say at all?
Matthew 5:14-16
*"Ye are the light of the world. A city that is set on an hill cannot be hid.
Neither do men light a candle, and put it under a bushel,
but on a candlestick; and it giveth light unto all that are in the house.
Let your light so shine before men, that they may see your good works,
and glorify your Father which is in heaven."*

Would it be positive or negative?
Titus 2:7-8
"In all things shewing thyself a pattern of good works: in doctrine shewing uncorruptness, gravity, sincerity, Sound speech, that cannot be condemned; that he that is of the contrary part may be ashamed, having no evil thing to say of you."

Whether we realize it or not, we are influencing people.
What type of example are you leaving for those around you?
1 Timothy 4:12
*"Let no man despise thy youth; but be thou an example of the believers,
in word, in conversation, in charity, in spirit, in faith, in purity."*

**Sometimes people misinterpret our motives or example,
but the Lord knows our hearts.**
1 Peter 3:15
*"But sanctify the Lord God in your hearts: and be ready always to give
an answer to every man that asketh you a reason of the hope
that is in you with meekness and fear: Having a good conscience;
that, whereas they speak evil of you, as of evildoers, they may
be ashamed that falsely accuse your good conversation in Christ."*

**May we all have a testimony that causes others to give thanks
and praise God through our Lord Jesus Christ.**

Bible Reading
Jeremiah 49-50 | Psalm 59-61

11.08 | November 8

Sacrifice The Thanks.

Hebrews 13:15
"By him therefore let us offer the sacrifice of praise to God continually, that is, the fruit of our lips giving thanks to his name."

It is only through the Lord Jesus Christ
that we are able to point others to God instead of ourselves.
Without Him, we can do nothing.
John 15:5
"I am the vine, ye are the branches: He that abideth in me, and I in him, the same bringeth forth much fruit: for without me ye can do nothing."

But through Him, we can do all things.
Philippians 4:13
"I can do all things through Christ which strengtheneth me."

Anything that we do which causes others to want to praise us should only be directed to Him. We must sacrifice the praise of ourselves so that He alone gets the glory.
Psalm 107:21-22
"Oh that men would praise the LORD for his goodness, and for his wonderful works to the children of men! And let them sacrifice the sacrifices of thanksgiving, and declare his works with rejoicing."

There will never be a time when we will ever be worthy of the praise that He deserves.
"…let us offer the sacrifice of praise to God continually…"

1 Peter 4:11
"If any man speak, let him speak as the oracles of God; if any man minister, let him do it as of the ability which God giveth: that God in all things may be glorified through Jesus Christ, to whom be praise and dominion for ever and ever. Amen."

Sacrifice the praise.
Sacrifice the thanks.
Instead, point them to Him.

Every commendation we receive is only because of Him.
The fruit of our lips should always be giving thanks to Him.

Bible Reading
Jeremiah 51-52 | Psalm 62-64

Rooted With Thanksgiving

Colossians 2:7
*"Rooted and built up in him, and stablished in the faith,
as ye have been taught, abounding therein with thanksgiving."*

Remember the parable that Jesus told about the men who built their houses upon different foundations? One man chose to build his upon the rock, the other upon the sand. Each faced the same storm, but only one was left standing after the rain descended.

Matthew 7:24-25
*"Therefore whosoever heareth these sayings of mine, and doeth them,
I will liken him unto a wise man, which built his house upon a rock:
And the rain descended, and the floods came, and the winds blew,
and beat upon that house; and it fell not: for it was founded upon a rock."*

What they were built upon determined their outcome.
Christ spoke of the difference in the men; one was wise and the other foolish. The house built foolishly upon the sand suffered a great fall.

What we build ourselves upon determines whether or not we will be able to withstand the storms of life. Thankfully, God does not leave us to build alone, He has provided the Foundation.

1 Corinthians 3:9
"For we are labourers together with God: ye are God's husbandry, ye are God's building. According to the grace of God which is given unto me, as a wise masterbuilder, I have laid the foundation, and another buildeth thereon. But let every man take heed how he buildeth thereupon. For other foundation can no man lay than that is laid, which is Jesus Christ."

Jesus Christ must be our only Foundation.
He is the Word;
and it is through Him that we find wisdom,
understanding, and knowledge.

Our lives must be built upon Him, and Him alone.
Every decision we make and every desire we have,
must be rooted and built up in His Word.

Bible Reading
Lamentations 1-3 | Psalm 65-67

11.10 | November 10

Thankful He Is In Control.

Daniel 2:23
"I thank thee, and praise thee, O thou God of my fathers, who hast given me wisdom and might, and hast made known unto me now what we desired of thee: for thou hast now made known unto us the king's matter."

No matter who holds the highest governmental position in the land, they are still at the footstool of the King of Kings.

Matthew 5:34-35
"But I say unto you, Swear not at all; neither by heaven; for it is God's throne: Nor by the earth; for it is his footstool: neither by Jerusalem; for it is the city of the great King."

**No matter how many votes are cast,
God in His Wisdom chooses who is elected.**

Proverbs 21:1
"The king's heart is in the hand of the LORD, as the rivers of water: he turneth it whithersoever he will."

They may hold a position, but it is God Who controls what will or will not occur for they are in His hand.

Daniel 2:20-22
"Daniel answered and said, Blessed be the name of God for ever and ever: for wisdom and might are his: And he changeth the times and the seasons: he removeth kings, and setteth up kings: he giveth wisdom unto the wise, and knowledge to them that know understanding: He revealeth the deep and secret things: he knoweth what is in the darkness, and the light dwelleth with him."

**God controls everything by His Wisdom,
yet offers to give us Wisdom if only we would ask.**

James 1:5
"If any of you lack wisdom, let him ask of God, that giveth to all men liberally, and upbraideth not; and it shall be given him."

Proverbs 2:6-7
"For the LORD giveth wisdom: out of his mouth cometh knowledge and understanding. He layeth up sound wisdom for the righteous: he is a buckler to them that walk uprightly."

**Thank Him today for all He has given you,
and remember that He is in control.**

Bible Reading
Lamentations 4-5 | Psalm 68-70

November 11 | 11.11

Thankful To Serve.

2 Timothy 1:3
"I thank God, whom I serve from my forefathers with pure conscience, that without ceasing I have remembrance of thee in my prayers night and day;"

Veteran's Day is a day set aside each year to remember those who have served in the Armed Forces of the United States of America. It occurs on this day in honor of the end of World War 1 in 1918 on "the eleventh hour of the eleventh day of the eleventh month". We remember and are thankful for those who have served, as well as those who have given the ultimate sacrifice so that we can have the freedoms we still have today.

This day ought to also cause us to remember the Ultimate Soldier,
Matthew 20:28
"Even as the Son of man came not to be ministered unto, but to minister, and to give his life a ransom for many."

John 15:13
"Greater love hath no man than this, that a man lay down his life for his friends."

Jesus Christ gave His life for us. May we also be thankful today for how He chose to serve to give us eternal freedom.

Some have chosen to dawn a different uniform in service to Him.
2 Timothy 2:3-4
"Thou therefore endure hardness, as a good soldier of Jesus Christ. No man that warreth entangleth himself with the affairs of this life; that he may please him who hath chosen him to be a soldier."

Each uniform looks a little different than a typical soldier. Some wear a suit and tie, some a modest dress. Some wear casual apparel as they walk on a foreign field telling others about Him. Some dawn a company logo as they so shine amongst their co-workers. Some are covered with the evidence of motherhood as they raise their children. Some stay behind the scenes with no desire to be seen of anyone but Him. **Whatever your uniform of service to Him looks like, wear it with a thankful heart of why we serve Him.**

Acts 27:23-24
"For there stood by me this night the angel of God, whose I am, and whom I serve, Saying, Fear not, Paul; thou must be brought before Caesar: and, lo, God hath given thee all them that sail with thee."

Be a good soldier for Him today. Thank Him for the opportunity to serve.

Bible Reading
Ezekiel 1-2 | Psalm 71-73

11.12 | November 12

Thankful To Be Enabled.

1 Timothy 1:12
"And I thank Christ Jesus our Lord, who hath enabled me, for that he counted me faithful, putting me into the ministry;"

As children of God, each of us have been entrusted with the glorious Gospel of Jesus Christ.

1 Timothy 1:11
"According to the glorious gospel of the blessed God, which was committed to my trust."

Whether or not we have a ministry title beside our name, each of His children have a responsibility to further the Gospel. He does not intend for us to try this on our own, for He knows we are nothing without Him.

2 Corinthians 3:5
"Not that we are sufficient of ourselves to think any thing as of ourselves; but our sufficiency is of God;"

Along with the entrustment, comes His enabling.
He is our Enabler.
Philippians 4:13
"I can do all things through Christ which strengtheneth me."

He enables us to plant the Seed of the Word of God, and water those Seeds that have already been planted. Then He alone gives the increase.

How faithful are we to plant and water?
Do we allow the things of this world to distract us from our purpose?

Acts 20:24
"But none of these things move me, neither count I my life dear unto myself, so that I might finish my course with joy, and the ministry, which I have received of the Lord Jesus, to testify the gospel of the grace of God."

**Depend on His enabling today
as you set out to further the Gospel.**

Thank Him for allowing you the opportunity to be counted faithful for His glory.

Bible Reading
Ezekiel 3-4 | Psalm 74-76

Thankful That He Hears.

John 11:41
*"Then they took away the stone from the place where the dead was laid.
And Jesus lifted up his eyes, and said,
Father, I thank thee that thou hast heard me."*

Jesus was standing at the grave of His friend, Lazarus, who had been dead four days. He continued His prayer explaining why He had thanked the Father for hearing Him.

John 11:42
"And I knew that thou hearest me always: but because of the people which stand by I said it, that they may believe that thou hast sent me."

Perhaps if we realized how our thankfulness affects other people, we would thank Him more.

He was groaning within Himself, weeping over His friend. He heard the rebuke of Martha as she told Him the impossibility of the situation now that her brother was dead, then He reminded her of what He had already said.

John 11:40
"Jesus saith unto her, Said I not unto thee, that, if thou wouldest believe, thou shouldest see the glory of God?"

She either forgot what He said, or simply chose not to believe Him. Is that not what we do on a regular basis? We have the perfect Word of God at our fingertips. The answer to every situation lies within the Words on the pages. Yet, so often, we choose to ignore or forget what He said.

Whatever seemingly impossible situation lies in front of you today, He is Able.

Ephesians 3:20
"Now unto him that is able to do exceeding abundantly above all that we ask or think, according to the power that worketh in us,"

As much as He is Able to provide a solution, He is also waiting for us to cry unto Him for help. He desires for us to call upon Him.

Jeremiah 33:3
"Call unto me, and I will answer thee, and shew thee great and mighty things, which thou knowest not."

When the task in front of us seems impossible, the Lord hears the cry of His children.

Bible Reading
Ezekiel 5-6 | Psalm 77-79

11.14 | November 14

Thankful To Remember.

1 Thessalonians 1:2-3
*"We give thanks to God always for you all,
making mention of you in our prayers; Remembering without ceasing
your work of faith, and labour of love, and patience of hope in our
Lord Jesus Christ, in the sight of God and our Father;"*

Consider for a moment what it is that makes you thankful for someone. Is it something that they have done for you? Is it simply who they are?

Paul, Silas and Timothy were giving thanks for the people of the church at Thessalonica. **They made it a priority to pray for these people that were dear to their hearts.**

They were so thankful for them that they remembered them constantly. *"Remembering without ceasing…"*

Has anyone ever made that kind of impact on you?

We find three specific reasons
they were thankful for them in these verses.

"your work of faith"

"labour of love"

"patience of hope"

Each of these reasons were rooted in Christ.
"… in our Lord Jesus Christ, in the sight of God and our Father;"
He was their motive for all that they did.

Could someone say that of us?
And if so, enough for them to thank the Lord
remembering us in their prayers?

What a convicting thought.
May we all strive to live with such a testimony.

Bible Reading
Ezekiel 7-8 | Psalm 80-82

Thank Him For Growth.

2 Thessalonians 1:3
"We are bound to thank God always for you, brethren, as it is meet, because that your faith groweth exceedingly, and the charity of every one of you all toward each other aboundeth;"

Paul, Silas and Timothy pinned a second letter to the church of Thessalonica, and they began once again by thanking God for the people. But this time, they specifically noticed their spiritual growth.
"because that your faith groweth exceedingly"
Is your faith growing?
Or perhaps you have found yourself in somewhat of a spiritual rut lately. We've all been there. The best way to get out of a rut, and continue to grow is to drown yourself with the Word of God.

1 Peter 2:2-3
"As newborn babes, desire the sincere milk of the word, that ye may grow thereby: If so be ye have tasted that the Lord is gracious."
A taste of His Word can change our perspective and our position.

2 Peter 3:18
"But grow in grace, and in the knowledge of our Lord and Saviour Jesus Christ. To him be glory both now and for ever. Amen."

They also noticed growth in the people's love for one another.
"and the charity of every one of you all toward each other aboundeth;"
Are you investing in others?
That is a true sign of love toward one another.

John 13:34-35
"A new commandment I give unto you, That ye love one another; as I have loved you, that ye also love one another. By this shall all men know that ye are my disciples, if ye have love one to another."

It is easy to be so focused on ourselves and what we need that we miss out on being a blessing to others.

Philippians 2:4
"Look not every man on his own things, but every man also on the things of others."

Thank Him today for those who have invested in you so that you could grow. Where would you be if someone had not shown the love of Christ to you? May remembering them cause you to desire to invest in someone else.

Bible Reading
Ezekiel 9-10 | Psalm 83-85

11.16 | November 16

Thank Him For His Word.

Psalm 119:62
*"At midnight I will rise to give thanks unto thee
because of thy righteous judgments."*

When the storms of life rage around us, His Word can bring us comfort and peace. Knowing His Word in the midst of our storm allows us to give thanks to Him even in our darkest hour.

**Unless we know His Word,
we cannot give Him thanks for what He has done.**
Psalm 119:75
*"I know, O LORD, that thy judgments are right,
and that thou in faithfulness hast afflicted me."*

In the midst of our affliction, we have to decide whether to allow the circumstances to distract us or remind us of what God's Word says. He brings situations to pass so that we can learn Who He is in the middle of our suffering.

Unless we know His Word, we cannot give Him the praise He deserves.
Psalm 119:7
*"I will praise thee with uprightness of heart,
when I shall have learned thy righteous judgments."*

Our hearts cannot be right with Him, if we are not spending time in the Scriptures. Studying the Word shows us Who God is, and why He alone deserves our praise.

**Unless we know His Word, we cannot understand
the difference between right and wrong.**
Psalm 119:128
*"Therefore I esteem all thy precepts concerning all things to be right;
and I hate every false way."*

In order to know which way is wrong, we must first know the right Way. Jesus Christ alone is the Way, the Truth, and the Life. We cannot be on the right way, have the Truth, or experience real life without Him.

All of this begins with knowing His Word.
Before we praise the Lord, we must know why He deserves our praise.
Before we thank the Lord, we must know what He has done for us.
Thank Him for His Word today by seeking to know Him more.

Bible Reading
Ezekiel 11-12 | Psalm 86-88

November 17 | 11.17

Thankfully Effectual.

1 Thessalonians 2:13
*"For this cause also thank we God without ceasing, because,
when ye received the word of God which ye heard of us,
ye received it not as the word of men, but as it is in truth,
the word of God, which effectually worketh also in you that believe."*

In our walk with the Lord, we read His Word, we listen to preaching and we glean from the people He has placed in our lives. If we are not careful, we can slowly begin to focus on the words of others more closely than the Word of God. We must remind ourselves from time to time that any advice we receive from someone should be rooted in the Word.

His Word is Powerful.

Hebrews 4:12
*"For the word of God is quick, and powerful, and sharper than any twoedged sword, piercing even to the dividing asunder
of soul and spirit, and of the joints and marrow, and is a discerner
of the thoughts and intents of the heart."*

His Word makes the difference.

Isaiah 55:11
*"So shall my word be that goeth forth out of my mouth:
it shall not return unto me void, but it shall accomplish that which I please,
and it shall prosper in the thing whereto I sent it."*

When we are asked to give an answer to the reason for the Hope that lies within us, we must simply point them to the Word.

Remember the parable of the Sower…some of the Seed fell on the wayside, and ended up eaten by the fowls…some fell upon a rock, and withered away…some fell among thorns, and choked…and other fell on good ground, and bare fruit. **The sower was to just sow the Seed of the Word of God and allow the Lord to do the rest.**

Thankfully, it is not our job to persuade or guide.
It is simply our responsibility to point them to the effectual Word of God.

Philemon 6
*"That the communication of thy faith may become effectual
by the acknowledging of every good thing
which is in you in Christ Jesus."*

Bible Reading
Ezekiel 13-14 | Psalm 89-91

11.18 | November 18

Thankful Despite Persecution.

Daniel 6:10
"Now when Daniel knew that the writing was signed, he went into his house; and his windows being open in his chamber toward Jerusalem, he kneeled upon his knees three times a day, and prayed, and gave thanks before his God, as he did aforetime."

There had been a decree signed by King Darius that prohibited anyone from asking a petition of any God or man except the king for thirty days.

Daniel 6:7
"All the presidents of the kingdom, the governors, and the princes, the counsellors, and the captains, have consulted together to establish a royal statute, and to make a firm decree, that whosoever shall ask a petition of any God or man for thirty days, save of thee, O king, he shall be cast into the den of lions."

That meant it was unlawful for Daniel to pray to his God. If he continued to faithfully pray to God, he would be cast into the den of lions. **He had a choice to make.** Would he do what he knew in his heart was right or would he concede to the demands of the government?

Daniel 6:11
"Then these men assembled, and found Daniel praying and making supplication before his God."

Despite what was now the law of the land, he chose to be faithful to God. He did not even try to hide. He prayed with the windows open, unashamed of his faith.

There is coming a day, and for some it has already come, that we will be forced to choose who we will obey. What will we choose when we are threatened with a den of lions? There may not be literal lions waiting for us, but there is a lion who walks about seeking to devour anyone who has placed their faith in Jesus Christ. 1 Peter 5:8-9

Will we continue to pray?
Will we continue to give thanks to the One Who gives us all things?
Or will we bend out of fear of the consequences?

Acts 5:29
"Then Peter and the other apostles answered and said, We ought to obey God rather than men."

Bible Reading
Ezekiel 15-16 | Psalm 92-94

November 19 | 11.19

Thankful Before The Miracle.

Matthew 15:36
"And he took the seven loaves and the fishes, and gave thanks, and brake them, and gave to his disciples, and the disciples to the multitude."

When you hear the words "the feeding of the…" most likely you finished that phrase with 5,000. What a miracle that was, Jesus took five loaves of bread and two fishes, and fed a multitude of at least 5,000 people. There remained 12 baskets of fragments left over, one for each disciple. Many times, we overlook a similar miracle found in Matthew 15.

Matthew 15:37-38
"And they did all eat, and were filled: and they took up of the broken meat that was left seven baskets full. And they that did eat were four thousand men, beside women and children."

He took seven loaves and a few little fishes, fed at least 4,000, and seven baskets full were left. A cynic may say, "well, He had more food to work with and fed less people…", all the while failing to see that it was still a miracle. The little supply that was available was brought to Jesus. Anything His hands touched resulted in a miracle taking place. But notice the first thing Jesus did when He received what was available…He gave thanks.

Jesus gave thanks to His Father for what they had before He broke the loaves and fishes into fragments. He knew what He was about to do. He knew the miracle that was about to happen. **Yet, He thanked God the Father before anything else happened.** Perhaps we should follow His example and thank the Lord for what we have and what we believe He will do before we do anything else to help our situation.

Matthew 6:33
"But seek ye first the kingdom of God, and his righteousness; and all these things shall be added unto you."

He may already be working on the problem.
He may have a miracle waiting for us.

Perhaps He is only waiting for us to be thankful for what we have now.

Ephesians 5:20
"Giving thanks always for all things unto God and the Father in the name of our Lord Jesus Christ;"

Maybe He desires us to thank Him in faith believing He will come through.
Choose to be thankful today for the miracle that could happen tomorrow.

Bible Reading
Ezekiel 17-18 | Psalm 95-97

11.20 | November 20

Thankful To Speak Of Him.

Luke 2:38
"And she coming in that instant gave thanks likewise unto the Lord, and spake of him to all them that looked for redemption in Jerusalem."

Anna is one of the women of the Bible that is often overlooked. Her story is found within what we refer to as "The Christmas Story" in Luke 2. Only three verses are written about her; yet, she is a great example of who we should all strive to be.

Luke 2:36-37
"And there was one Anna, a prophetess, the daughter of Phanuel, of the tribe of Aser: she was of a great age, and had lived with an husband seven years from her virginity; And she was a widow of about fourscore and four years, which departed not from the temple, but served God with fastings and prayers night and day."

Even in her old age, she was faithful.
She faithfully served God night and day in the temple.
Anna was devoted to serving the Lord.
"and spake of him to all them that looked for redemption in Jerusalem."
But before she spake of Him to others, she thanked Him.

She knew He was coming soon. She wanted to share the Good News with those who needed redemption. Her faith would soon become sight as she saw Jesus, and she would spend the rest of her days telling others about Him.

Though she was looking for His first coming, does her story not sound like how we should be today? He is coming again soon. This time He will not be found as a baby in a manger, but rather as the King of Kings and Lord of Lords. Soon it will be too late to receive Him as Saviour.

What a privilege we have to be entrusted with the Gospel of Jesus Christ! With that great privilege comes a humbling responsibility. How often do we take the Gospel for granted? If we are not faithfully sharing the Good News with others, do we really know Him? We cannot speak of Someone we do not know.

Thank Him for the opportunity to speak of Him today. Thank Him that He made salvation possible. Thank Him that He was willing to die for you. Thank Him today for His first coming, then go tell someone else about why He came.

Bible Reading
Ezekiel 19-20 | Psalm 98-99

November 21 | 11.21

Be Thankful Unto Him.

Psalm 100
"Make a joyful noise unto the LORD, all ye lands. Serve the LORD with gladness: come before his presence with singing. Know ye that the LORD he is God: it is he that hath made us, and not we ourselves; we are his people, and the sheep of his pasture. Enter into his gates with thanksgiving, and into his courts with praise: be thankful unto him, and bless his name. For the LORD is good; his mercy is everlasting; and his truth endureth to all generations."

One of the most quoted Psalms. It has only five short verses, but is filled with so much Truth. Within those five verses are seven principles that we can apply in order to maintain a thankful heart within us.

"Make a joyful noise unto the LORD"
Regardless of how well we think our voice sounds,
we can all sing praises unto Him.

"Serve the LORD with gladness"
The purpose of our lives is to serve, honor and glorify Him.
Why not do it gladly with the unspeakable joy that only He can give?

"come before his presence with singing."
Singing is simply praise to Him. We can come boldly before Him with praise in our hearts and find grace to help in our time of need.

"Know ye that the LORD he is God"
How comforting it is to know that He is Who He said He is.
There is simply no one like Him!

"Enter into his gates with thanksgiving, and into his courts with praise"
From the moment we come before Him, our hearts should be giving thanks that He even hears a word we say.

"be thankful unto him"
This is the only place within the Scripture where this phrase is found. No one else deserves our thankfulness. No one else deserves our praise.

"and bless his name."
The phrase implies a bent knee, signifying humility and reverence.

Why should we strive to apply all these things? The last verse gives the answer. Psalm 100:5. Has He not been good to you? Has He not shown you mercy? **Be thankful unto Him today for all that He has given you.**

Bible Reading
Ezekiel 21-22 | Psalm 100

11.22 | November 22

The Cause Of Thanksgiving.

2 Corinthians 9:11
"Being enriched in every thing to all bountifulness, which causeth through us thanksgiving to God."

If we take time to pause and reflect on just how good God has been to us, it is overwhelmingly evident just how blessed we are. The hymn "Count Your Blessings" comes to mind.

Despite any circumstance we may be struggling through or dealing with at the moment, none of that can change the fact that God is Good, and He has blessed us abundantly.

Have you ever considered what it is that enriches your life?

Yes, of course, it is God. But consider for a moment how He enriches us *"in every thing to all bountifulness"*…the answer lies a few verses above our verse today.

2 Corinthians 9:8
"And God is able to make all grace abound toward you; that ye, always having all sufficiency in all things, may abound to every good work:"

Everything we have is because of His grace.
His grace abounds towards us
and is always sufficient for our every need.

2 Corinthians 12:9
"And he said unto me, My grace is sufficient for thee: for my strength is made perfect in weakness. Most gladly therefore will I rather glory in my infirmities, that the power of Christ may rest upon me."

When we think about His grace towards us,
does it not cause your heart to be overwhelmed
with thanksgiving to Him?

Psalm 84:11
"For the LORD God is a sun and shield: the LORD will give grace and glory: no good thing will he withhold from them that walk uprightly."

Thank Him today for how He has enriched your life by His grace.

Bible Reading
Ezekiel 23-24 | Psalm 101-103

Thank Him For His Gift.

2 Corinthians 9:15
"Thanks be unto God for his unspeakable gift."

Have you ever received a gift that made you speechless when you opened it? Maybe you hoped it was a prank or maybe it was just what you had wanted.

With the Christmas season around the corner, perhaps you've made a list of the things you hope to receive or give this year.

Who is on your list?
Beside the names of those you love most are likely some material things you plan to give them.

**But has each person on your list
received the Unspeakable Gift?**

Romans 6:23
*"For the wages of sin is death; but the gift of God
is eternal life through Jesus Christ our Lord."*

The Unspeakable Gift of God is Jesus, His only begotten Son.

John 3:16
*"For God so loved the world,
that he gave his only begotten Son,
that whosoever believeth in him should not perish,
but have everlasting life."*

It is only through Him that we can have what truly matters.

2 Corinthians 2:14
*"Now thanks be unto God, which always causeth us to triumph in Christ,
and maketh manifest the savour of his knowledge by us in every place."*

**Those on your list that do not know Him
need to hear of their need for Him.**

Give them the Gift of the Gospel of Jesus Christ this season.
Then you can both be thankful for the Unspeakable Gift of God.

Thank Him for His Gift, today and every day.

Bible Reading
Ezekiel 25-26 | Psalm 104-106

11.24 | November 24

Thank Him For His Goodness.

Psalm 107:1
*"O give thanks unto the LORD, for he is good:
for his mercy endureth for ever."*

This psalm begins with a single letter word that is found all throughout the Bible.

"O"

Have you ever considered why this word is used so often?
It is found most often within the Book of Psalms, and mostly used to convey a groaning of the heart. This word connects the Truths that follow it with an intense feeling of heartfelt importance.

Far too often we lose our heart of thanksgiving.
Perhaps because the intense feeling of importance has somehow been neglected as we read over familiar verses of Scripture that we have heard over and over again.

"O give thanks unto the LORD, for he is good"
Six times within the pages of Scripture we find this exact phrase. If the Lord says it once it is true and important; but when He repeats Himself over and over, we had better take notice.

"for he is good"
**May we never forget to give thanks,
but may we also never forget the simple reason that He is Good.**

How good has He been to you?
Why not thank Him today specifically for His goodness?

Psalm 107:8
*"Oh that men would praise the LORD for his goodness,
and for his wonderful works to the children of men!"*

This verse is repeated four times within Psalm 107.

**May we praise Him today, and every day,
for His goodness and His wonderful works towards us!**

Bible Reading
Ezekiel 27-28 | Psalm 107

November 25 | 11.25

A Good Thing To Give Thanks.

Psalm 92:1-5
"It is a good thing to give thanks unto the LORD, and to sing praises unto thy name, O most High: To shew forth thy lovingkindness in the morning, and thy faithfulness every night, Upon an instrument of ten strings, and upon the psaltery; upon the harp with a solemn sound. For thou, LORD, hast made me glad through thy work: I will triumph in the works of thy hands. O LORD, how great are thy works! and thy thoughts are very deep."

The Lord is Good, and His Word tells us that it is a good thing to thank Him and praise His Name. Psalm 92 even tells us how to thank and praise Him.

"To shew forth thy lovingkindness in the morning"

We can show His lovingkindness to others by being rooted and grounded in His love.

Ephesians 3:17-19
"That Christ may dwell in your hearts by faith; that ye, being rooted and grounded in love, May be able to comprehend with all saints what is the breadth, and length, and depth, and height; And to know the love of Christ, which passeth knowledge, that ye might be filled with all the fulness of God."

"and thy faithfulness every night"

May we be faithful to thank Him for how faithful He has been to us.

Lamentations 3:22-23
"It is of the LORD'S mercies that we are not consumed, because his compassions fail not. They are new every morning: great is thy faithfulness."

How have you thanked Him today?
He has placed a song in our hearts that we may sing it back to Him.

Psalm 28:7
"The LORD is my strength and my shield; my heart trusted in him, and I am helped: therefore my heart greatly rejoiceth; and with my song will I praise him."

Bible Reading
Ezekiel 29-30 | Psalm 108

11.26 | November 26

The Trade For Thankfulness.

Philippians 4:6
"Be careful for nothing; but in every thing by prayer and supplication with thanksgiving let your requests be made known unto God."

When trouble and anxiety take hold of us, we have traded our faith for worry and confusion. Martha experienced this when she chose to be cumbered about with so many things that she questioned whether Jesus cared about her.

Luke 10:40-42
"But Martha was cumbered about much serving, and came to him, and said, Lord, dost thou not care that my sister hath left me to serve alone? bid her therefore that she help me. And Jesus answered and said unto her, Martha, Martha, thou art careful and troubled about many things: But one thing is needful: and Mary hath chosen that good part, which shall not be taken away from her."

The Scripture tells us to be careful about one thing…nothing.
"Be careful for nothing"

Instead, the Lord desires that we trade our carefulness for placing our faith in Him.
Matthew 6:33-34

When we take every thing to Him by prayer and supplication, our hearts can focus on being thankful for all He has done as we make our requests known unto Him. **The trade for thankfulness then brings peace.** Just as He calmed the raging winds and waves, He can speak peace to our troubled hearts.

Philippians 4:7
"And the peace of God, which passeth all understanding, shall keep your hearts and minds through Christ Jesus."

When we thank Him in every thing He gives the peace which passeth all understanding that only comes from Him. We can choose to be thankful in every situation, regardless of what comes our way, simply because we know that God is working every thing together for our good and His glory.

Colossians 3:15 & Romans 8:28

Decide today to be careful for nothing, and instead…
Take every thing to God in prayer trading your trouble for thankfulness as you make your requests.

Bible Reading
Ezekiel 31-32 | Psalm 109-110

November 27 | 11.27

The Blessing Of Thanksgiving.

Psalm 34:1
*"I will bless the LORD at all times:
his praise shall continually be in my mouth."*

Even when distress brings us to our knees, we can choose to allow our discomfort to cause us to bless and praise the Lord. **If our trials cause us to seek to know Him more, should we not be thankful for them?**

David promised to bless the Lord at all times…constantly…while also vocalizing his praise continually.

Psalm 71:8
"Let my mouth be filled with thy praise and with thy honour all the day."

No matter what or who tried to stand in his way, he trusted the Lord.

When we realize that anything that touches our lives has been filtered by Him, we can choose to be thankful even in the middle of our storm.

He allows every thing, even our trials, to bring praise unto Him.

1 Peter 1:7-8
"That the trial of your faith, being much more precious than of gold that perisheth, though it be tried with fire, might be found unto praise and honour and glory at the appearing of Jesus Christ: Whom having not seen, ye love; in whom, though now ye see him not, yet believing, ye rejoice with joy unspeakable and full of glory:"

**When a thankful heart becomes our priority,
it will change us.**

It strengthens our faith.
It helps us show mercy to others.
It changes our perspective.

It allows us to praise the Lord regardless of our circumstances.

The blessing of thanksgiving in the life of a believer
is the opportunity to bless and praise Him.

Bible Reading
Ezekiel 33-34 | Psalm 111-112

11.28 | November 28

The Hope Of Thanksgiving.

Psalm 71:14
"But I will hope continually, and will yet praise thee more and more."

Hope is found within the Foundation of our faith.
The more thankful we are, the more hope we will have in Him.
Psalm 39:7
"And now, Lord, what wait I for? my hope is in thee."

**The Hope of Thanksgiving in the life of a believer
is impossible to keep to ourselves.**
Psalm 71:15
*"My mouth shall shew forth thy righteousness
and thy salvation all the day; for I know not the numbers thereof."*

How can those who truly possess the hope of salvation in Jesus Christ not share that Gift with others? What a comfort to know that when we share the Gift of Hope, He enables us to so!
Romans 15:13
*"Now the God of hope fill you with all joy and peace in believing,
that ye may abound in hope, through the power of the Holy Ghost."*

The devil will try anything he can to keep us from sharing Hope with others. Whatever trial or storm you are facing today, remind yourself that although the Lord allowed it, any discomfort ultimately comes from the enemy.
Ephesians 6:11-12
*"Put on the whole armour of God, that ye may be able to stand against
the wiles of the devil. For we wrestle not against flesh and blood,
but against principalities, against powers, against the rulers
of the darkness of this world, against spiritual wickedness in high places."*

We can stand thankful because of what the Lord has done for us.
He protects us even from those things we cannot see,
while strengthening us for another day.
Psalm 71:18
*"Now also when I am old and grayheaded, O God, forsake me not;
until I have shewed thy strength unto this generation,
and thy power to every one that is to come."*

Praise Him today for the Hope that is found in Him,
and then ask Him to help you share that Gift
with someone who needs Him.

Bible Reading
Ezekiel 35-36 | Psalm 113-114

November 29 | 11.29

Thanks Given For Others.

2 Corinthians 1:11
*"Ye also helping together by prayer for us,
that for the gift bestowed upon us by the means of many persons
thanks may be given by many on our behalf."*

Sometimes the distresses of life can press us in such a way that we are unable to give thanks unto the Lord ourselves.

Paul and Timothy experienced this.
2 Corinthians 1:8
*"For we would not, brethren, have you ignorant of our trouble
which came to us in Asia, that we were pressed out of measure,
above strength, insomuch that we despaired even of life:"*

They were in despair and without strength because of their trouble; but God used it to remind them of Who they could trust.
2 Corinthians 1:9-10
*"But we had the sentence of death in ourselves,
that we should not trust in ourselves, but in God which raiseth the dead:
Who delivered us from so great a death, and doth deliver:
in whom we trust that he will yet deliver us;"*

**When others fail us, we must remember
to trust in the only One Who never will.**

Deuteronomy 31:6
*"Be strong and of a good courage, fear not, nor be afraid of them:
for the LORD thy God, he it is that doth go with thee;
he will not fail thee, nor forsake thee."*

They were thankful for those who gave thanks when they could not.
"…thanks may be given by many on our behalf."

If we can relate with their need in the time of trouble,
may it cause us to also give thanks on the behalf of others.

Galatians 6:2
"Bear ye one another's burdens, and so fulfil the law of Christ."

Give thanks today for those who have given thanks on your behalf.

Bible Reading
Ezekiel 37-38 | Psalm 115-116

11.30 | November 30

Thankful For The Victory.

1 Corinthians 15:57
"But thanks be to God, which giveth us the victory through our Lord Jesus Christ."

**All throughout the Bible,
we see the victories won through the power of God.**
David over Goliath.
Jericho.
The Red Sea.
The Feeding of the 5,000.
The Prodigal Son.
Lazarus.
The Garden Tomb.

Miracle after miracle is preserved for us to read in order that we might have faith that the same God can do the impossible within our lives. He never changes. **What He did then, He can still do today.**

2 Corinthians 2:14
"Now thanks be unto God, which always causeth us to triumph in Christ, and maketh manifest the savour of his knowledge by us in every place."

Whatever battle you are facing…He is the Answer.
Victory is found by knowing Him.

2 Corinthians 9:15
"Thanks be unto God for his unspeakable gift."

That Gift which God has freely given to us is His Son,
Jesus Christ, through Whom we have eternal life.

Romans 6:23
"For the wages of sin is death; but the gift of God is eternal life through Jesus Christ our Lord."

Every victory we have, is because of Him.
Thank Him today, and every day.

Bible Reading
Ezekiel 39-40 | Psalm 117-118

December 1 | 12.01

The Word.

Psalm 119:1
"Blessed are the undefiled in the way, who walk in the law of the LORD."

Psalm 119 is the longest chapter in the Scriptures.
It is found almost right in the middle of our Bibles.
The common theme is woven throughout almost every verse,
using 13 different words to describe or refer to the Word of God.

The Law of the Lord is the Word of God.
In the New Testament, we find out Who is the Word of God.

John 1:1
"In the beginning was the Word, and the Word was with God,
and the Word was God."

John 1:14
"And the Word was made flesh, and dwelt among us,
(and we beheld his glory, the glory as of the only begotten of the Father,)
full of grace and truth."

Jesus Christ, the Son of God, is the Word.
The Word was born into this world as that Baby lying in a manger.

The Word was named Jesus,
meaning Jehovah is Salvation, to tell of His purpose.

Matthew 1:21
"And she shall bring forth a son, and thou shalt call his name JESUS:
for he shall save his people from their sins."

The Word walked amongst His creation so that He could redeem those who believed in Him. **The longest chapter in the Bible is all about Him.**

He is the Lamp unto our feet.
He is the Light unto our path.

We are promised to be blessed when we walk with Him.

Psalm 119:2
"Blessed are they that keep his testimonies,
and that seek him with the whole heart."

Are you walking with the Word today?

Bible Reading
Psalm 119

| 343

12.02 | December 2

God With Us.

Isaiah 7:14
"Therefore the Lord himself shall give you a sign; Behold, a virgin shall conceive, and bear a son, and shall call his name Immanuel."

It had never happened before, it has never happened since, nor will it ever happen again. Isaiah prophesized what would happen long before it did.

The sign was Mary, a virgin, having a child.

Matthew 1:22-23
"Now all this was done, that it might be fulfilled which was spoken of the Lord by the prophet, saying, Behold, a virgin shall be with child, and shall bring forth a son, and they shall call his name Emmanuel, which being interpreted is, God with us."

God chose to take on a robe of humanity in order to dwell with us.

Colossians 2:9
"For in him dwelleth all the fulness of the Godhead bodily."

He dwelt among us so that we could walk with Him.

John 1:14
"And the Word was made flesh, and dwelt among us, (and we beheld his glory, the glory as of the only begotten of the Father,) full of grace and truth."

Though He is no longer bodily on the earth,
He has left us a Comforter to dwell in us and teach us His Word.

John 14:26
"But the Comforter, which is the Holy Ghost, whom the Father will send in my name, he shall teach you all things, and bring all things to your remembrance, whatsoever I have said unto you."

His Word is with us today so that we may know Him more.

This Christmas season,
seek Him through His Word like you never have before.

Bible Reading
Ezekiel 41-43 | Psalm 120-121

December 3 | 12.03

For Unto Us.

Isaiah 9:6
"For unto us a child is born, unto us a son is given: and the government shall be upon his shoulder: and his name shall be called Wonderful, Counsellor, The mighty God, The everlasting Father, The Prince of Peace."

Each year we look toward Christmas with great wonder and expectation of what the holiday season will bring. Some focus on what they will get rather than what they can give. Do we do this when it comes to the real meaning of Christmas as well? Sure we say that it's all about Jesus…but is it really? **Many times, we are so focused on what we receive in Jesus rather than what God gave.**

John 3:16
"For God so loved the world, that he gave his only begotten Son, that whosoever believeth in him should not perish, but have everlasting life."

He gives salvation and so much more to all who believe in Him.
Romans 8:32
"He that spared not his own Son, but delivered him up for us all, how shall he not with him also freely give us all things?"

It's hard to imagine what it would have been like to wait in anticipation of the Messiah coming the first time, even though we now wait for His second coming. The Child that was lying in a manger was the Son of God wrapped not only in swaddling clothes, but in human flesh. He was the Messiah that the prophet Isaiah said would come. Isaiah gave us five names for Jesus Christ hundreds of years before He drew His first earthly breath as that Baby born of Mary. Yet, because He never changes, those Names apply just as much today as they did then.

He is still Wonderful.
He is still our Counsellor.
He is still The mighty God.
He is still The everlasting Father.
He is still The Prince of Peace.
And He always will be.

Isaiah 9:6
"For unto us a child is born, unto us a son is given…"

He was given for us.

Bible Reading
Ezekiel 44-46 | Psalm 122

12.04 | December 4

Herein Is Love.

1 John 4:10
"Herein is love, not that we loved God, but that he loved us, and sent his Son to be the propitiation for our sins."

Before Adam drew his first breath, God knew that He would send His Son as that Baby lying in a manger.

1 John 4:9
"In this was manifested the love of God toward us, because that God sent his only begotten Son into the world, that we might live through him."

This is love in its highest, purest and truest form.

John 15:13
"Greater love hath no man than this, that a man lay down his life for his friends."

Romans 5:8
"But God commendeth his love toward us, in that, while we were yet sinners, Christ died for us."

He loved us first; even though we are so unworthy of His love.

1 John 4:19
"We love him, because he first loved us."

We love celebrating the birth of Christ this time of year, and we should; but may we never forget the ultimate reason He came.

He was born in a cradle so that He could die on a cross.

1 John 2:2
"And he is the propitiation for our sins: and not for ours only, but also for the sins of the whole world."

Bible Reading
Ezekiel 47-48 | Psalm 123

December 5 | 12.05

Highly Favoured.

Luke 1:28
"And the angel came in unto her, and said, Hail, thou that art highly favoured, the Lord is with thee: blessed art thou among women."

Out of all the women ever created, God chose Mary to be the mother of Jesus.

Luke 1:26-27
"And in the sixth month the angel Gabriel was sent from God unto a city of Galilee, named Nazareth, To a virgin espoused to a man whose name was Joseph, of the house of David; and the virgin's name was Mary."

She was highly favoured, which refers to obtaining grace. Mary had been found to be graciously accepted to birth God in the flesh.

She had not known a man, because the blood of man could not be involved in the redeeming of the souls of mankind. The Holy Ghost came upon her to conceive within her the blood of the Father required to redeem us from our sins.

1 John 4:9
"In this was manifested the love of God toward us, because that God sent his only begotten Son into the world, that we might live through him."

God had chosen her to be the vessel who carried the Son of God into the world so that we might have life in Him. We are accepted through the blood of Jesus.

Mary was the first to carry the Gospel.
The Living Word literally grew inside of her, just as God desires the Word of God to grow within us.

May we carry the Gospel of Jesus Christ today to those around us.

Bible Reading
Daniel 1-2 | Psalm 124

12.06 | December 6

Favour Over Fear.

Luke 1:30
*"And the angel said unto her, Fear not, Mary:
for thou hast found favour with God."*

Can you imagine how Mary must have felt to hear that she had been chosen by God? **Any thing we have the privilege to do for Him should remind us of how unworthy we are to be used for His glory.**

Luke 1:31
*"And, behold, thou shalt conceive in thy womb,
and bring forth a son, and shalt call his name JESUS."*

She was chosen to be the vessel to bring forth the Son of God into this world. The angel then told her a little bit about the Son she would be carrying within her.

Luke 1:32-33
*"He shall be great, and shall be called the Son of the Highest:
and the Lord God shall give unto him the throne of his father David:
And he shall reign over the house of Jacob for ever;
and of his kingdom there shall be no end."*

**Fear must have gripped ahold of her tender heart
when she heard those words.**

The devil will try to convince us that any task we are given is impossible. He will send distractions and discouragement to try and defeat us before the work even begins.

Mary needed to realize and be reminded of the favour that God had shown her in order to push out the fear within her heart.

Whatever situation has you consumed with fear, choose today to remind yourself of the favour that God has shown you. You are His vessel to be used by Him for one purpose…His glory. Nothing else matters. He is there with you. He desires to help you. When the devil fights, fight back by choosing to rely on the Lord to strengthen you and do the work in and through you. **Allow Him to fight your fear with His favour.**

Isaiah 41:10
*"Fear thou not; for I am with thee: be not dismayed; for I am thy God:
I will strengthen thee; yea, I will help thee; yea, I will uphold thee
with the right hand of my righteousness."*

Bible Reading
Daniel 3-4 | Psalm 125

December 7 | 12.07

Faith Over Fear.

Luke 1:34
*"Then said Mary unto the angel,
How shall this be, seeing I know not a man?"*

Mary's response to being told that God had a purpose to do a work in and through her is much like how any other person would react.

She immediately questioned and deemed it impossible.
"How shall this be"

Whenever we feel God prompting us to do something for Him, our first reaction is often to make excuses out of doubt.

The patience of the angel is clearly seen as they explained how the Lord Jesus would be conceived.

Luke 1:35
"And the angel answered and said unto her, The Holy Ghost shall come upon thee, and the power of the Highest shall overshadow thee: therefore also that holy thing which shall be born of thee shall be called the Son of God."

Mary had nothing to do with this miracle. The Holy Ghost would do the work within her. She was simply the vessel that God chose to use.

Isn't that just like anything the Lord does within us?
He uses us in spite of our doubt and questions.

Are you full of doubt today? Do you have questions even though the Lord has made His direction clear? **Look within the pages of the Scriptures to find the Truth.** He may not answer with as much detail as He did Mary, but the Answer is there.

Matthew 17:20
"And Jesus said unto them, Because of your unbelief: for verily I say unto you, If ye have faith as a grain of mustard seed, ye shall say unto this mountain, Remove hence to yonder place; and it shall remove; and nothing shall be impossible unto you."

Mark 9:24
"…Lord, I believe; help thou mine unbelief."

**Conquer your unbelief today
by choosing to have faith over the fear that is fueled by your flesh.**

Bible Reading
Daniel 5-6 | Psalm 126

12.08 | December 8

From Barren To Blessed.

Luke 1:36
"And, behold, thy cousin Elisabeth, she hath also conceived a son in her old age: and this is the sixth month with her, who was called barren."

Elisabeth was the cousin of Mary the Mother of Jesus. God used her as an example to help Mary see that the Lord was about to do what was considered impossible.

Mary conceived as a virgin. She conceived in her old age.

Luke 1:37
"For with God nothing shall be impossible."

This verse is often quoted in reference to Mary, and although the Truth of the verse certainly applies, the context refers to Elisabeth. **Her testimony helped Mary believe that if God could do the impossible in Elisabeth, He could do the same within her.**

Luke 1:41-42
"And it came to pass, that, when Elisabeth heard the salutation of Mary, the babe leaped in her womb; and Elisabeth was filled with the Holy Ghost: And she spake out with a loud voice, and said, Blessed art thou among women, and blessed is the fruit of thy womb."

A baby was the first to rejoice over the presence of Jesus.
She was overwhelmed that the mother of her Saviour was in her house.

Luke 1:43-44
"And whence is this to me, that the mother of my Lord should come to me? For, lo, as soon as the voice of thy salutation sounded in mine ears, the babe leaped in my womb for joy."

She went from barren to overwhelmingly blessed.

Elisabeth is a humble example of how
His presence changes everything.

Bible Reading
Daniel 7-8 | Psalm 127

December 9 | 12.09

Be It Unto Me.

Luke 1:38
*"And Mary said, Behold the handmaid of the Lord;
be it unto me according to thy word. And the angel departed from her."*

What if we always responded to what the Lord
would have us to do the way Mary did?
"…be it unto me according to thy word."

May this be our response to anything and everything He tells us to do.

Mary was willing to bear the burden of carrying the Saviour of the world. She was willing to endure the pain that would come in His birth. She was willing to accept the sorrow that would come in His death.

What if we knew how it would end beforehand? Would we still be willing to endure the suffering He had in store in order for us to be more like Him?

When she submitted to what God would have
to take place in her life, she knew how it would end.
Yet, she was still willing.

She went from questioning
"How shall this be"
to proclaiming
"be it unto me".

She humbly desired for the Lord's will to be done in her life.

"according to thy word"
**Her fear turned to faith because
she believed what the Lord had said.**

Luke 1:45
*"And blessed is she that believed:
for there shall be a performance of those things
which were told her from the Lord."*

That is true faith.
No wonder she was highly favoured.

**Decide today to take the Lord at His Word
and then be willing to follow His direction.**

Bible Reading
Daniel 9-10 | Psalm 128

12.10 | December 10

On This Wise.

Matthew 1:18
"Now the birth of Jesus Christ was on this wise: When as his mother Mary was espoused to Joseph, before they came together, she was found with child of the Holy Ghost."

From the beginning, God knew that His Son would one day be born of a virgin, named Mary. This is how God had planned for everything to occur. **Sometimes we need to remind ourselves that even when things do not make sense to us, the Lord has everything under control.** He knows and He alone has a plan for how He sees fit to bring His will to pass.

Matthew 1:19
"Then Joseph her husband, being a just man, and not willing to make her a publick example, was minded to put her away privily."

Joseph found out about Mary's condition before he understood the whole story. Isn't his reaction just like we react sometimes? We often begin to consider what we should do and how to handle a situation before we have all the details.

Matthew 1:20-21
"But while he thought on these things, behold, the angel of the Lord appeared unto him in a dream, saying, Joseph, thou son of David, fear not to take unto thee Mary thy wife: for that which is conceived in her is of the Holy Ghost. And she shall bring forth a son, and thou shalt call his name JESUS: for he shall save his people from their sins."

Just as an angel had appeared unto Mary, the angel of the Lord appeared unto Joseph. The angel knew he was fearful to take Mary as his wife and informed him of the great purpose the Lord had for the Son she would bring forth. Joseph displayed patience and grace when he had just cause to refuse to be a part of the Christmas story. His willingness allowed him to be the one to call His name Jesus. He was the first to speak the Name above every name after He was born. Philippians 2:9

God had chosen him, a carpenter, to be the earthly father of the One Who would one day carry a wooden cross to save His people from their sins.

Sometimes we need to be patient as we wait to see God's amazing plan for our lives unfold according to His will.

Bible Reading
Daniel 11-12 | Psalm 129

December 11 | 12.11

Magnify Him.

Luke 1:46-47
*"And Mary said, My soul doth magnify the Lord,
And my spirit hath rejoiced in God my Saviour."*

Magnify: to make bigger, to increase, to make great, to get glory and praise.

We all magnify something or someone at any given moment of our lives. It is as if each of us have a magnifying glass that we carry around within us, carefully choosing what or who to increase.

Mary chose to magnify the Lord.

She could have easily used the opportunity she was given to attempt to receive the glory herself. She did indeed carry the Saviour of the world inside of her for 9 months. As He grew within her womb, we have to conclude that she grew spiritually. Her only desire was that she be used for His glory.

She knew that in her dwelleth no good thing, but Him.

Luke 1:48-49
*"For he hath regarded the low estate of his handmaiden:
for, behold, from henceforth all generations shall call me blessed.
For he that is mighty hath done to me great things; and holy is his name."*

Nothing that we do or try to be could ever justify us magnifying ourselves.
May we choose today to magnify Him alone.

Mary's choice to magnify Him caused her to rejoice.

**When we desire for others to see Him instead of us,
we too can rejoice that He is glorified in us.**

Philippians 4:4
"Rejoice in the Lord alway: and again I say, Rejoice."

Psalm 34:3
*"O magnify the LORD with me,
and let us exalt his name together."*

Bible Reading
Hosea 1-3 | Psalm 130

12.12 | December 12

Raised To Be Bold.

Luke 1:57
"Now Elisabeth's full time came that she should be delivered; and she brought forth a son."

Mary had stayed with Elisabeth for three months before returning to her own house. Shortly after she departed, Elisabeth gave birth to a son in her old age.

Luke 1:58
"And her neighbours and her cousins heard how the Lord had shewed great mercy upon her; and they rejoiced with her."

She was the mother of John the Baptist, the forerunner of Christ. **She knew that there was something different about her son.**

Luke 1:66
"And all they that heard them laid them up in their hearts, saying, What manner of child shall this be! And the hand of the Lord was with him."

She raised him to have boldness for the Lord.
He was the voice in the wilderness proclaiming that Christ would come.

Matthew 3:7
"But when he saw many of the Pharisees and Sadducees come to his baptism, he said unto them, O generation of vipers, who hath warned you to flee from the wrath to come?"

She raised him to point others to Christ.
He never drew attention to himself,
but always led his followers to look for the only One Who truly worthy.

Matthew 3:11
"I indeed baptize you with water unto repentance: but he that cometh after me is mightier than I, whose shoes I am not worthy to bear: he shall baptize you with the Holy Ghost, and with fire:"

John 1:29
"The next day John seeth Jesus coming unto him, and saith, Behold the Lamb of God, which taketh away the sin of the world."

If you have children, consider how Elisabeth raised her son to be used by God and what we can learn from her example. **Sometimes our greatest ministry is in not what we do, but who we raise.**

Bible Reading
Hosea 4-6 | Psalm 131

December 13 | 12.13

There Came Wise Men.

Matthew 2:1-2
"Now when Jesus was born in Bethlehem of Judaea in the days of Herod the king, behold, there came wise men from the east to Jerusalem, Saying, Where is he that is born King of the Jews? for we have seen his star in the east, and are come to worship him."

The wise men from the east saw a star they believed to be leading them to Jesus. Every other reference that we find of the *"King of the Jews"* is spoken during His trial and crucifixion. The wise men were the first to use this title for Him.

Many place them within or beside the stable in nativity scenes, however they arrived much later in the Christmas story when Jesus was no longer a baby.

Matthew 2:9
"When they had heard the king, they departed; and, lo, the star, which they saw in the east, went before them, till it came and stood over where the young child was."

But why were they called wise men?
Wisdom begins with a fear of the Lord.
Proverbs 9:10
"The fear of the LORD is the beginning of wisdom: and the knowledge of the holy is understanding.

Perhaps they were called wise men because they already had a healthy fear of Who He is.
Matthew 2:10-11
"When they saw the star, they rejoiced with exceeding great joy. And when they were come into the house, they saw the young child with Mary his mother, and fell down, and worshipped him: and when they had opened their treasures, they presented unto him gifts; gold, and frankincense, and myrrh."

It is up to us to shine so that others will see their need to come to Him for salvation. Many are still seeking Him today, only they have no star to guide them. **It is wise to shine our Light for Him today, and every day.**
Matthew 5:16
"Let your light so shine before men, that they may see your good works, and glorify your Father which is in heaven."

Bible Reading
Hosea 7-9 | Psalm 132

12.14 | December 14

The Days Were Accomplished.

Luke 2:4-6
"And Joseph also went up from Galilee, out of the city of Nazareth, into Judaea, unto the city of David, which is called Bethlehem; (because he was of the house and lineage of David:) To be taxed with Mary his espoused wife, being great with child. And so it was, that, while they were there, the days were accomplished that she should be delivered."

Mary and Joseph were brought to Bethlehem as a result of the decree from Caesar Augustus that all the world should be taxed. God used a politician to help orchestrate His perfect plan.

It had been prophesied that Christ would be born in Bethlehem.

Micah 5:2
"But thou, Bethlehem Ephratah, though thou be little among the thousands of Judah, yet out of thee shall he come forth unto me that is to be ruler in Israel; whose goings forth have been from of old, from everlasting."

While they were in Bethlehem, the days were accomplished for Mary to give birth to Jesus. The time had come for the purpose of her being highly favoured to come to pass. Her *"for such a time as this"* moment had arrived. The work that God had begun in her nine months before was about to be born.

Philippians 1:6
"Being confident of this very thing, that he which hath begun a good work in you will perform it until the day of Jesus Christ:"

Each of us has been given a divine purpose for our lives. For Mary, it was to give birth to our Saviour. She was the vessel that the Lord chose to bring His Son to dwell among us.

At some point, the days will be accomplished for our purpose.
Will we faint before that day comes?

Galatians 6:9
"And let us not be weary in well doing: for in due season we shall reap, if we faint not."

1 Corinthians 15:58
"Therefore, my beloved brethren, be ye stedfast, unmoveable, always abounding in the work of the Lord, forasmuch as ye know that your labour is not in vain in the Lord."

Bible Reading
Hosea 10-12 | Psalm 133

December 15 | 12.15

Let Him In.

Luke 2:7
"And she brought forth her firstborn son, and wrapped him in swaddling clothes, and laid him in a manger; because there was no room for them in the inn."

Rather than dwelling on the innkeeper, consider for a moment… **How much do we let Christ into every area of our life?** Every relationship. Every opportunity. Every moment of every day. Too often we want our walk with Him to focus on us. What we need. What we want. What we think should happen. But really, our walk with Him should be all about Him.

Yes, He wants to hear from us in prayer.
1 Thessalonians 5:17
"Pray without ceasing."
But if we do all the talking, who is really leading our lives?

Maybe we make room for us to talk to Him sometimes…
But how much room do we make for Him to talk to us?

Jesus Christ, the Son of God, is the Word. He was born into this world as that Baby lying in a manger. He dwells with us today through the Word we hold in our hands. But far too often, we get distracted by the wonder of what we have made Christmas about.

When that happens…we trade the Word for the wonder.
Luke 2:7
"…because there was no room for them in the inn."

We cannot let Him in if we are already full of worry, confusion, doubt, ourselves, busyness, etc. **We must first empty ourselves.** Sometimes, if we are not willing to empty ourselves, He will do it for us through trials and affliction.

Psalm 119:71
"It is good for me that I have been afflicted; that I might learn thy statutes."

Psalm 119:11
"Thy word have I hid in mine heart, that I might not sin against thee."

Every time we open our Bibles, our prayer should be…
Psalm 119:18
"Open thou mine eyes, that I may behold wondrous things out of thy law."

Let Him in today, and every day.

Bible Reading
Hosea 13-14 | Psalm 134

12.16 | December 16

Good Tidings Of Great Joy.

Luke 2:8-10
"And there were in the same country shepherds abiding in the field, keeping watch over their flock by night. And, lo, the angel of the Lord came upon them, and the glory of the Lord shone round about them: and they were sore afraid. And the angel said unto them, Fear not: for, behold, I bring you good tidings of great joy, which shall be to all people."

Can you imagine what the sky looked like that night? As ordinary shepherds were abiding in their fields, watching over their flock in the dark hours, suddenly they saw an angel in the sky. This was not just any angel, it was *"the angel of the Lord"*. No wonder they were sore afraid. The angel spoke peace to their fearful hearts, and assured them there was *"good tidings of great joy"*.

Those *"good tidings"* were none other than the Gospel of Jesus Christ. It is Him alone Who brings great joy, and He makes it available to all people.

Romans 10:13-14
"For whosoever shall call upon the name of the Lord shall be saved. How then shall they call on him in whom they have not believed? and how shall they believe in him of whom they have not heard? and how shall they hear without a preacher?"

The only reason you have heard *"good tidings of great joy"* is because someone took the time to share the Gospel with you.

Romans 10:15
"And how shall they preach, except they be sent? as it is written, How beautiful are the feet of them that preach the gospel of peace, and bring glad tidings of good things!"

Every person who has trusted in the free Gift of the Gospel of Jesus Christ is responsible for sharing the Good News with others.

How else will your friend hear?
How will that family member trust Christ
if someone does not tell them?
Maybe that someone is you.

Share *"good tidings of great joy"* this Christmas season.

Bible Reading
Joel | Psalm 135

December 17 | 12.17

A Saviour.

Luke 2:11
"For unto you is born this day in the city of David a Saviour, which is Christ the Lord."

In all the world, there is only one Saviour. He alone is our Deliverer, our Preserver. The shepherds in the field heard *"good tidings of great joy"* that their Saviour had been born for them.

"For unto you…"
He came for them, and He came for us.

1 Timothy 4:10
"For therefore we both labour and suffer reproach, because we trust in the living God, who is the Saviour of all men, specially of those that believe."

He was born the Saviour of all men, yet He can only be Saviour effectually to those who choose to believe and place their faith in Him.

Luke 1:46-47
"And Mary said, My soul doth magnify the Lord, And my spirit hath rejoiced in God my Saviour."

Mary knew that she was carrying her Saviour so that He could be the same for so many others.

1 John 4:14
"And we have seen and do testify that the Father sent the Son to be the Saviour of the world."

Is He your Saviour today?
How well do you know Him?

2 Peter 3:18
"But grow in grace, and in the knowledge of our Lord and Saviour Jesus Christ. To him be glory both now and for ever. Amen."

Having Him as our Saviour should compel us to share with others how they can know Him too.

Bible Reading
Amos 1-4 | Psalm 136

12.18 | December 18

Wrapped With Love.

Luke 2:12
"And this shall be a sign unto you; Ye shall find the babe wrapped in swaddling clothes, lying in a manger."

The angel told the shepherds of a sign that they would find the Baby, a Saviour, which is Christ the Lord. Jews often require a sign to believe. They were told He was wrapped in swaddling clothes, grave clothes.

Mary, who had given birth to Him,
wrapped Him in clothes that signified His death.

Romans 5:8
"But God commendeth his love toward us, in that, while we were yet sinners, Christ died for us."

He was lying in a manger, surely where no baby had ever laid before. Much like His tomb.

His first and last days on earth were spent wrapped with His purpose.
The reason He came was, and is, always evident.

He did not come so that He could live.
He came so that He could die, that we might have eternal life.

John 3:15
"That whosoever believeth in him should not perish, but have eternal life."

John 20:31
"But these are written, that ye might believe that Jesus is the Christ, the Son of God; and that believing ye might have life through his name."

Why do we wrap the presents we give to those we love?
Perhaps because the Saviour was wrapped up
in the purpose of why He came.

1 John 4:10
"Herein is love, not that we loved God, but that he loved us, and sent his Son to be the propitiation for our sins."

Bible Reading
Amos 5-9 | Psalm 137

December 19 | 12.19

Luke 2:13-14
"And suddenly there was with the angel a multitude of the heavenly host praising God, and saying, Glory to God in the highest, and on earth peace, good will toward men."

One angel would have been amazing enough, yet suddenly there was a multitude of them praising God together.
Psalm 34:3
"O magnify the LORD with me, and let us exalt his name together."

They all said the same thing in unison.
"Glory to God in the highest, and on earth peace, good will toward men."

If only every believer would live by this same phrase.
The entire purpose of our lives is to glorify Him.
Revelation 4:11
"Thou art worthy, O Lord, to receive glory and honour and power: for thou hast created all things, and for thy pleasure they are and were created."

Jesus was born as that Baby lying in a manger
for the purpose of bringing glory to God.
Isaiah 9:6
"For unto us a child is born, unto us a son is given: and the government shall be upon his shoulder: and his name shall be called Wonderful, Counsellor, The mighty God, The everlasting Father, The Prince of Peace."

He brings peace on earth as the Prince of Peace.
He brings good will toward men as the mighty God.
Luke 18:27
"And he said, The things which are impossible with men are possible with God."

When situations seem impossible, it simply leaves opportunity for all the glory to be given to Him. He is Able and willing to do the impossible in our lives, if only we are willing to give Him the glory He alone deserves.
Ephesians 3:20-21
"Now unto him that is able to do exceeding abundantly above all that we ask or think, according to the power that worketh in us, Unto him be glory in the church by Christ Jesus throughout all ages, world without end. Amen."
How is your life bringing glory to Him?

Bible Reading
Obadiah | Psalm 138

12.20 | December 20

Let Us Now Go.

Luke 2:15
"And it came to pass, as the angels were gone away from them into heaven, the shepherds said one to another, Let us now go even unto Bethlehem, and see this thing which is come to pass, which the Lord hath made known unto us."

Sometimes, people try to talk us out of going where we know we need to go. Sometimes, we even talk ourselves out of doing what we know is right. Sometimes, we find the faith to go…no matter the cost.

Psalm 111:2
"The works of the LORD are great, sought out of all them that have pleasure therein."

For the shepherds that night, their steps of faith led them straight to the One Who was, and is, the Answer to every situation. Instead of questioning if they should go, or making excuses of why they shouldn't, they went in faith knowing for certain Who they would find.

"Let us now go"
That is true faith. The Lord had made known unto the shepherds that Jesus the Saviour had come. They chose to go where He was.

Hebrews 11:8
"By faith Abraham, when he was called to go out into a place which he should after receive for an inheritance, obeyed; and he went out, not knowing whither he went."
Whether or not we know exactly where He is leading, it is simply our responsibility to go in faith.

"even unto"
Sometimes He directs us to the most unlikely places, but it is even there that we will find Him providing for our every need.

Psalm 139:10
"Even there shall thy hand lead me, and thy right hand shall hold me."
Even when we do not know the question He is asking of us, we can still choose to follow Him in faith.

Isaiah 6:8
"Also I heard the voice of the Lord, saying, Whom shall I send, and who will go for us? Then said I, Here am I; send me."

Bible Reading
Jonah | Psalm 139

Made Known.

Luke 2:16-17
"And they came with haste, and found Mary, and Joseph, and the babe lying in a manger. And when they had seen it, they made known abroad the saying which was told them concerning this child."

After the shepherds found Jesus lying in a manger just as the angel had said, they went to tell others what they had seen. They were the first evangelists. The *"saying"* which they were told concerning Him was that He was Christ the Lord.

The Lord had made it known unto them,
and now it was their turn to go and tell.

Every believer has the same responsibility.

Matthew 28:19-20
*"Go ye therefore, and teach all nations, baptizing them
in the name of the Father, and of the Son, and of the Holy Ghost: Teaching them to observe all things whatsoever I have commanded you: and, lo, I am with you alway, even unto the end of the world. Amen."*

Mark 16:15
*"And he said unto them, Go ye into all the world,
and preach the gospel to every creature."*

If the Great Commission seems like a daunting task,
rest in the Truth that He will empower us to be a Light for Him.

Acts 1:8
"But ye shall receive power, after that the Holy Ghost is come upon you: and ye shall be witnesses unto me both in Jerusalem, and in all Judaea, and in Samaria, and unto the uttermost part of the earth."

We can make known abroad
the Gospel of Jesus Christ through His power.

Make Him known today, and every day.

Bible Reading
Micah 1-4 | Psalm 140

12.22 | December 22

They That Heard.

Luke 2:18
*"And all they that heard it wondered at those things
which were told them by the shepherds."*

The Gospel fills hearts with wonder. When the Shepherds made known abroad what had taken place, those that heard the Good News wondered at what they were told.

The Saviour was born as a Baby in a stable instead of a palace.
The Angels told shepherds instead of kings.
Jesus was born of a virgin, as the Son of God.
He was born to die.

Matthew 1:21
"And she shall bring forth a son, and thou shalt call his name JESUS: for he shall save his people from their sins."

Romans 5:8
"But God commendeth his love toward us, in that, while we were yet sinners, Christ died for us."

Romans 6:23
"For the wages of sin is death; but the gift of God is eternal life through Jesus Christ our Lord."

Romans 10:9
"That if thou shalt confess with thy mouth the Lord Jesus, and shalt believe in thine heart that God hath raised him from the dead, thou shalt be saved."

If we only wonder at the Gospel instead of believing, we have missed out on the Gift.

Romans 10:13-14
"For whosoever shall call upon the name of the Lord shall be saved. How then shall they call on him in whom they have not believed? and how shall they believe in him of whom they have not heard? and how shall they hear without a preacher?"

If the Shepherds kept the news to themselves, how would people have heard? In order for someone to hear it, someone has to tell it. **Tell the Good News of the Gospel so that someone will hear today, and every day.**

Bible Reading
Micah 5-7 | Psalm 141

December 23 | 12.23

Keep & Ponder.

Luke 2:19
"But Mary kept all these things, and pondered them in her heart."

What are the things that Mary kept and pondered?
She was simply in awe of what God had done in and through her. She was highly favoured, willing, and full of faith in the Lord Who had performed *"those things"*.

Luke 1:45
"And blessed is she that believed: for there shall be a performance of those things which were told her from the Lord."

What are you pondering in your heart this Christmas?
Perhaps the wonder of the lights, the presents, Santa and his elves tends to distract you from the Reason for the Season.

Choose to stand in awe this Christmas.
Psalm 4:4
"Stand in awe, and sin not: commune with your own heart upon your bed, and be still. Selah."

Psalm 119:161
"Princes have persecuted me without a cause: but my heart standeth in awe of thy word."

Instead of "Carol Of The Bells" choose "O Come Let Us Adore Him".
Rather than "Jingle Bells" sing "Joy To The World".

Joy to the world, the Lord is come
Let earth receive her King
Let every heart prepare Him room
Isaac Watts

Is there room in your heart for Him?
At the end of Luke 2, Jesus is 12 years old… and Mary is still pondering over what God had done through her.

Luke 2:51
"And he went down with them, and came to Nazareth, and was subject unto them: but his mother kept all these sayings in her heart."

Here we see that it was not just the *"things"* that she kept in her heart, it was *"these sayings"*. **Are you keeping the Word of God in your heart?**

Bible Reading
Nahum | Psalm 142

12.24 | December 24

Luke 2:20
"And the shepherds returned, glorifying and praising God for all the things that they had heard and seen, as it was told unto them."

Their journey began full of fear in their field as they kept watch over their flock. They were led to the city of David where they found their Saviour wrapped in swaddling clothes and laying in a manger. Now, they returned to the field, but things were different. **What they had heard and seen had changed them.**

2 Corinthians 5:17
"Therefore if any man be in Christ, he is a new creature: old things are passed away; behold, all things are become new."

Once you have experienced the presence of the Lord, you will never be the same.

They heard the angel bring good tidings of great joy.
What we hear affects our faith.
Romans 10:17
"So then faith cometh by hearing, and hearing by the word of God."

They saw the Saviour, as a Baby in a manger.
What we do not see strengthens our faith.
2 Corinthians 5:7
"(For we walk by faith, not by sight:)"

What they had heard and seen changed everything, both for them and for all of us. How could they not glorify and praise God for what He had done? Yet, every moment we are given the same opportunity and often choose to glorify and praise anything and anyone but Him.

Glorify Him today.
Matthew 5:16
"Let your light so shine before men, that they may see your good works, and glorify your Father which is in heaven."

Praise His Name for the wonderful things He has done!
Isaiah 25:1
"O LORD, thou art my God; I will exalt thee, I will praise thy name; for thou hast done wonderful things; thy counsels of old are faithfulness and truth."

Bible Reading
Habakkuk | Psalm 143

December 25 | 12.25

His Name Was Called.

Luke 2:21
"And when eight days were accomplished for the circumcising of the child, his name was called JESUS, which was so named of the angel before he was conceived in the womb."

Isaiah told that His Name would be called Wonderful, Counsellor, The mighty God, The everlasting Father, The Prince of Peace, and Immanuel. Yet none of those compare to His given Name.

"his name was called JESUS."

Gabriel had told Mary before she conceived.
Luke 1:31
"And, behold, thou shalt conceive in thy womb, and bring forth a son, and shalt call his name JESUS."

The angel of the Lord had also foretold it to Joseph in a dream.
Matthew 1:21
"And she shall bring forth a son, and thou shalt call his name JESUS: for he shall save his people from their sins."

JESUS.
Jehovah is Salvation.

The Reason He came is woven throughout His Name.
John 20:31
"But these are written, that ye might believe that Jesus is the Christ, the Son of God; and that believing ye might have life through his name."

JESUS.
The Name above all names.

Philippians 2:9-11
"Wherefore God also hath highly exalted him, and given him a name which is above every name: That at the name of Jesus every knee should bow, of things in heaven, and things in earth, and things under the earth; And that every tongue should confess that Jesus Christ is Lord, to the glory of God the Father."

JESUS.
There is just something about His Name.

Bible Reading
Zephaniah | Psalm 144

12.26 | December 26

Seeking Him.

Luke 2:49
"And he said unto them, How is it that ye sought me? wist ye not that I must be about my Father's business?"

Jesus and His parents returned into Galilee, to Nazareth, after sometime, and then made yearly trips to Jerusalem for the feast of the Passover. When He was twelve, Jesus tarried behind in Jerusalem while His parents travelled home.

Luke 2:43
"And when they had fulfilled the days, as they returned, the child Jesus tarried behind in Jerusalem; and Joseph and his mother knew not of it."

They returned back to Jerusalem after three days and found Him in the temple sitting in the midst of the doctors asking them questions that amazed everyone.

In the first recorded Words of Jesus, the Son of God, He asked two questions of His seeking parents. *"How is it that ye sought me? wist ye not that I must be about my Father's business?"*

They looked for Him in all the wrong places.
It took them three days to find Him.
How are you seeking Him?
It is easy to seek Him in all the wrong places, just as His parents did.

Matthew 6:33
"But seek ye first the kingdom of God, and his righteousness; and all these things shall be added unto you."

He must be our first priority, if we are to live as He intends.
1 Chronicles 22:19
"Now set your heart and your soul to seek the LORD your God…"

What is your heart set on today?
Colossians 3:2
"Set your affection on things above, not on things on the earth."

Matthew 6:21
"For where your treasure is, there will your heart be also."

What is in our hearts determines what we do, how we act, and who we are. If we are to be like Christ, we too must be about our Father's business.
Seek Him with your whole heart today, and every day.

Bible Reading
Haggai | Psalm 145

December 27 | 12.27

Purged To Be More Fruitful

2 Corinthians 4:17-18
"For our light affliction, which is but for a moment, worketh for us a far more exceeding and eternal weight of glory; While we look not at the things which are seen, but at the things which are not seen: for the things which are seen are temporal; but the things which are not seen are eternal."

As this crazy and chaotic year draws to an end, may it cause us to dwell on the fact that although most of this year did not go as we had planned, nothing was a surprise to the Lord. **He allowed every situation, and has given us unique opportunities to use for His glory.**

Romans 8:18
"For I reckon that the sufferings of this present time are not worthy to be compared with the glory which shall be revealed in us."

Sometimes He has to purge away some things in order to make us more fruitful. Amidst all the uncertainties and trials, the Lord gives more fruit.

John 15:2
"Every branch in me that beareth not fruit he taketh away: and every branch that beareth fruit, he purgeth it, that it may bring forth more fruit."

Anything that makes us more fruitful is a blessing from Him.

1 Peter 5:10
"But the God of all grace, who hath called us unto his eternal glory by Christ Jesus, after that ye have suffered a while, make you perfect, stablish, strengthen, settle you."

Regardless of what this year has brought your way, choose to allow Him to enable you to be more fruitful and bring Him glory. The choice is up to each of us. We can hide in fear or press forward in faith. He is in control. He knows best.

Proverbs 29:25
"The fear of man bringeth a snare: but whoso putteth his trust in the LORD shall be safe."

Romans 8:31
"What shall we then say to these things? If God be for us, who can be against us?"

Trust Him today, and allow Him to make you fruitful for His glory.

Bible Reading
Zechariah 1-3 | Psalm 146

12.28 | December 28

Broken & Binded.

Psalm 147:3
"He healeth the broken in heart, and bindeth up their wounds."

The purging of branches often involves a painful experience.
This is a vital part of preparing for more fruit to be produced.
John 15:2
"Every branch in me that beareth not fruit he taketh away: and every branch that beareth fruit, he purgeth it, that it may bring forth more fruit."

Purging means something has to be broken.
Psalm 34:18
"The LORD is nigh unto them that are of a broken heart; and saveth such as be of a contrite spirit."

A broken heart can bring us closer to Him.
When we feel as if our world has been crushed,
it gives opportunity for Him to bring healing.

"He healeth the broken in heart, and bindeth up their wounds."

Allow Him to bind up your wounds today.
The healing you need can be found within the pages of His Word.
Psalm 107:19-20
"Then they cry unto the LORD in their trouble, and he saveth them out of their distresses. He sent his word, and healed them, and delivered them from their destructions."

He has sent us His Word, so that we may be healed.
Despite our circumstances, our perspective
can change if we will allow our affliction to drive us to the Word.
Psalm 119:50
"This is my comfort in my affliction: for thy word hath quickened me."
Psalm 119:71
"It is good for me that I have been afflicted; that I might learn thy statutes."

His Word can fix what is broken,
if only we will let Him.

Allow His Word to bind up your wounds today, and every day.

Bible Reading
Zechariah 4-7 | Psalm 147

December 29 | 12.29

Prepared To Trust.

Isaiah 26:4
*"Trust ye in the LORD for ever:
for in the LORD JEHOVAH is everlasting strength:"*

How we conduct ourselves in times of struggle depends on how we have prepared our hearts before they are broken.

Isaiah 12:2
"Behold, God is my salvation; I will trust, and not be afraid: for the LORD JEHOVAH is my strength and my song; he also is become my salvation."

**The best way to prepare ourselves
is to trust Him before the storm comes.**
2 Samuel 22:31
*"As for God, his way is perfect; the word of the LORD is tried:
he is a buckler to all them that trust in him."*

Trust is found within the pages of His Word.
Proverbs 30:5
*"Every word of God is pure:
he is a shield unto them that put their trust in him."*

When we trust Him, there is no reason to fear anything or anyone else.
Psalm 118:6
"The LORD is on my side; I will not fear: what can man do unto me?"

When we trust Him, there is everlasting strength.
Psalm 18:2
*"The LORD is my rock, and my fortress, and my deliverer;
my God, my strength, in whom I will trust; my buckler,
and the horn of my salvation, and my high tower."*

**When we trust Him, there is not just any kind of peace,
but perfect peace.**
Isaiah 26:3
*"Thou wilt keep him in perfect peace, whose mind is stayed on thee:
because he trusteth in thee."*

What is your mind stayed on today?
If it is anything or anyone else but Him, you will have anything but peace.

**Regardless of the situation you are facing,
choose to trust Him today, and every day.**

Bible Reading
Zechariah 8-10 | Psalm 148

12.30 | December 30

Seeking Peace.

Philippians 4:7
"And the peace of God, which passeth all understanding, shall keep your hearts and minds through Christ Jesus."

Everyone is searching for peace amidst the chaos and confusion of the world in which we are living. The Truth of the matter is that most are looking in all the wrong places. When we need a break, or to find some peace, we often look to the things of the world. Any form of stress reliever that we can buy or schedule will only give temporary results.

Philippians 4:6
"Be careful for nothing; but in every thing by prayer and supplication with thanksgiving let your requests be made known unto God."

Anxiety is rampant today.
We seek peace and comfort from everywhere else but where the Scriptures tell us it is found.

Isaiah 26:3
"Thou wilt keep him in perfect peace, whose mind is stayed on thee: because he trusteth in thee."

The perfect peace that is found in Him *"passeth all understanding"*. No matter how hard we try, it is impossible for us to comprehend or understand it. Our finite minds simply cannot fully grasp the concept, no matter how spiritual we may consider ourselves. Yet, it is available to us when we come to God through Christ Jesus. He keeps our hearts and minds secure through peace that only He can give.

Colossians 3:15-16
"And let the peace of God rule in your hearts, to the which also ye are called in one body; and be ye thankful. Let the word of Christ dwell in you richly in all wisdom; teaching and admonishing one another in psalms and hymns and spiritual songs, singing with grace in your hearts to the Lord."

Instead of searching everywhere else before you pick up your Bible, why not finish out this hectic year seeking peace in Him?

John 16:33
"These things I have spoken unto you, that in me ye might have peace. In the world ye shall have tribulation: but be of good cheer; I have overcome the world."

Bible Reading
Zechariah 11-14 | Psalm 149

December 31 | 12.31

Delight In Peace.

Psalm 37:11
*"But the meek shall inherit the earth;
and shall delight themselves in the abundance of peace."*

Christ spoke of the meek, calling them blessed, in His sermon on the mount, when He was referring to this Psalm.

Matthew 5:5
"Blessed are the meek: for they shall inherit the earth."

Many consider themselves to be meek without realizing what it requires.
The Meek are they who are poor and afflicted for His purpose.

Psalm 119:71
"It is good for me that I have been afflicted; that I might learn thy statutes."

Any affliction that we endure which causes us to know His Word is worth the pain. If the circumstances of this year have driven you to the Word of God more, thank Him. If the pain you experienced has sent you to your knees in prayer, thank Him.

**Peace is found when we come to Him,
for He is the Abundance of Peace.**

Just as He spoke peace to the wind and waves,
let Him speak peace to your storm.

Mark 4:39
"And he arose, and rebuked the wind, and said unto the sea, Peace, be still. And the wind ceased, and there was a great calm."

His Word is powerful.
His Word can turn pain into praise.
His Word brings peace to a troubled soul.

**Choose to end this year and begin the new year
delighting in the Abundance of Peace through His Word.**

Psalm 119:47
"And I will delight myself in thy commandments, which I have loved."

Delight in Him today, and every day.

Bible Reading
Malachi | Psalm 150

Index

January

01.01 - Where God Guides.
Isaiah 58:11

01.02 - Doubting Nothing.
Acts 10:20

01.03 - Most Unlikely.
1 Corinthians 1:26-27

01.04 - Speechless.
Acts 4:14

01.05 - Counted Worthy.
Acts 5:41

01.06 - Great Fear.
Acts 5:11

01.07 - Speak His Name.
Acts 4:20

01.08 - Declare His Name.
Romans 9:17

01.09 - Baptism.
Acts 8:36

01.10 - Justified.
Romans 3:24

01.11 - The Lord Hath Heard.
Psalm 6:9

01.12 - The Promise Of Salvation.
Romans 10:13

01.13 - Willing To Lose.
Philippians 3:7

01.14 - The Reason To Lose.
Philippians 3:8-11

01.15 - The Cost Of Being Fruitful.
John 15:1-2

01.16 - His Ways.
Isaiah 55:8-9

01.17 - Ready.
Romans 1:15

01.18 - But Thou, O LORD.
Psalm 3:3

01.19 - Clearly Seen.
Romans 1:20

01.20 - Burdens To Blessings.
Psalm 55:22

01.21 - The Hedge.
Job 1:10

01.22 - We Know.
Romans 8:28

01.23 - Fully Persuaded.
Romans 4:21

01.24 - Seeking To Devour.
1 Peter 5:8-9

01.25 - Wonderfully Made.
Psalm 139:14

01.26 - Divine Appointments.
Psalm 37:23

01.27 - Divine Protection.
Psalm 91:1-2

01.28 - Praying For Others.
Colossians 1:3

01.29 - When We Pray.
Acts 4:31-32

01.30 - Drinking From The Saucer.
Psalm 23:5

01.31 - What Do You Battle?
Ephesians 6:12

February

02.01 - The Battle Is The LORD's.
1 Samuel 17:47

02.02 - He Fights For Us.
Exodus 14:14

02.03 - Who Can Be Against Us?
Romans 8:31

02.04 - Communication.
Jeremiah 33:3

02.05 - Waiting To Be Led.
Psalm 25:4-5

02.06 - He Is Our Help.
Psalm 28:7

02.07 - Overwhelmed.
Psalm 61:2

02.08 - My Heart's Desire.
Romans 10:1

02.09 - The Worth Of A Soul.
Psalm 126:5-6

02.10 - Only Believe.
Mark 5:36

02.11 - God Given Power.
Matthew 28:18-20

02.12 - Witnessing The Gospel.
1 Corinthians 15:3-4

Index

February

02.13 - Wait.
Psalm 39:7

02.14 - The More Excellent Way.
1 Corinthians 12:31

02.15 - But If Not.
Daniel 3:18

02.16 - Changed At His Feet.
Luke 7:38

02.17 - The Choice At His Feet.
Luke 10:39

02.18 - A Cure At His Feet.
John 11:32

02.19 - Reminded.
Isaiah 40:28

02.20 - Redeem The Time.
Ephesians 5:16

02.21 - Understanding His Will.
Ephesians 5:17

02.22 - His Way Is The Way.
Psalm 5:8

02.23 - I Will.
Psalm 9:1-2

02.24 - Now Unto Him.
Ephesians 3:20

02.25 - By Strength Of Hand.
Exodus 13:3

02.26 - His Foresight.
Exodus 14:1-2

02.27 - Forward.
Exodus 14:15

02.28 - The Word Divides.
Exodus 14:16

02.29 - The Midst Of The Sea.
Exodus 14:22

March

03.01 - Resort & Rest.
Exodus 15:27

03.02 - Prove It.
1 Thessalonians 5:21

03.03 - Refresh.
Acts 27:3

03.04 - The Source Of Refreshment.
Proverbs 25:13

03.05 - Before Goliath.
1 Samuel 17:4

03.06 - Finding Grace In The Brook.
1 Samuel 17:40

03.07 - Pearls Of Promise.
1 Peter 4:12-13

03.08 - Without The Promises.
2 Peter 3:9

03.09 - A Limited Time.
Colossians 4:5

03.10 - The Choice Of Whosoever.
Revelation 20:15

03.11 - Affliction.
Psalm 88:9

03.12 - God Sees, Hears & Knows.
Exodus 3:7

03.13 - A Spiritual Rut.
Psalm 51:3

03.14 - The Domino Effect.
1 Timothy 4:12

03.15 - Sought Means.
Luke 5:18

03.16 - Come.
Revelation 22:17

03.17 - Get Your Hands Up.
Exodus 17:11

03.18 - Trust & Trace.
Esther 2:17

03.19 - Choosing To Suffer.
Hebrews 11:25-26

03.20 - Growing Pains.
Romans 8:18

03.21 - Choices.
Mark 8:34-35

03.22 - Why?
Matthew 27:46

03.23 - His Name.
Acts 4:12

03.24 - Our Whole Duty.
Ecclesiastes 12:13

03.25 - Built By Wisdom.
Proverbs 14:1

03.26 - Bold As A Lion.
Proverbs 28:1

Index

March
03.27 - Tolerance.
Isaiah 5:20-21
03.28 - An Appointment.
Hebrews 9:27
03.29 - The Purpose Of Things.
Philippians 1:12
03.30 - Keep Thy Heart.
Proverbs 4:23
03.31 - Life Found In The Word.
John 6:63

April
04.01 - Abide In Truth.
John 15:4
04.02 - The Word Came.
John 1:1
04.03 - Full Of Grace And Truth.
John 1:14
04.04 - The Way.
John 14:6
04.05 - The Truth.
John 8:32
04.06 - The Life.
John 11:25-26
04.07 - A Picture Of Jesus.
Acts 8:35
04.08 - Wise To Give.
John 3:16
04.09 - The Light Of The World.
John 12:46
04.10 - The Foundation For Everything.
Psalm 138:2
04.11 - Turn To The Word.
Matthew 4:16-17
04.12 - The Hour Is Come.
John 13:1
04.13 - Betrayed.
Matthew 26:20-21
04.14 - God Intervened.
Romans 5:8
04.15 - Make It Sure.
Matthew 27:65-66
04.16 - Waiting For The Miracle.
Matthew 12:40
04.17 - They Remembered.
Luke 24:8
04.18 - Lift Him Up.
John 12:32
04.19 - He Is Still Risen.
Luke 24:44
04.20 - Determined Doubt.
John 20:29
04.21 - Ye Shall Find.
John 21:6
04.22 - The Last Words.
Mark 16:15
04.23 - Follow Him.
Matthew 4:19
04.24 - Without Delay.
Matthew 4:20
04.25 - Ask For A Miracle.
Matthew 14:29
04.26 - Part Of A Miracle.
John 2:5
04.27 - A Silent Answer.
Luke 23:9
04.28 - Clean Through The Word.
John 15:3
04.29 - Fruit That Remains.
John 15:16
04.30 - Take No Thought.
Matthew 6:25

May
05.01 - Little Faith.
Matthew 6:30
05.02 - The Possession Of Faith.
Matthew 17:20
05.03 - The Practice Of Faith.
Mark 11:22
05.04 - The Priority Of Faith.
Matthew 6:33
05.05 - Intercessory Faith.
Mark 2:5
05.06 - Expecting Faith.
Matthew 9:28
05.07 - Finding Faith.
Matthew 10:39

Index

May

05.08 - Stretching Faith.
Matthew 12:13

05.09 - Searching Faith.
John 5:39

05.10 - Saving Faith.
Luke 7:50

05.11 - Ask The Question.
Acts 9:6

05.12 - The Sweetness Of Friendship.
Proverbs 27:9

05.13 - A Testimony Of Faith.
Matthew 14:36

05.14 - Silenced By Fear.
John 7:11

05.15 - It Fell On A Day.
2 Kings 4:8

05.16 - Better.
Psalm 84:10

05.17 - When I Heard These Words.
Nehemiah 1:4

05.18 - So I Prayed.
Nehemiah 2:4

05.19 - Rise Up And Build.
Nehemiah 2:18

05.20 - Nevertheless.
Nehemiah 4:9

05.21 - A Great Work.
Nehemiah 6:3

05.22 - Attentive Unto The Book.
Nehemiah 8:3

05.23 - Because Of All This.
Nehemiah 9:38

05.24 - Forsake Not The House Of God.
Nehemiah 10:39

05.25 - So Much The More.
Hebrews 10:25

05.26 - That Which Brings Joy.
1 John 1:1

05.27 - This Then Is The Message.
1 John 1:5

05.28 - For The Master's Use.
2 Timothy 2:21

05.29 - Out Of Them All.
2 Timothy 3:10-11

05.30 - Crumbs.
Matthew 15:27

05.31 - Recalled.
Lamentations 3:21

June

06.01 - The Cost Of Silence.
Matthew 21:27

06.02 - Hope In Him.
Lamentations 3:24

06.03 - Methods Of Waiting.
Lamentations 3:25-26

06.04 - Trust Not Traps.
Proverbs 29:25

06.05 - Marvel Not.
Ecclesiastes 5:8

06.06 - While It Is Day.
John 9:4

06.07 - Mightier Than The Waves.
Psalm 93:4

06.08 - Weigh It Against The Truth.
Proverbs 20:10

06.09 - Come & Rest.
Matthew 11:28

06.10 - Promises To Give.
Joshua 1:3

06.11 - Promises To Abide.
Joshua 1:5

06.12 - Promises To Hear.
Psalm 40:1

06.13 - Promises To Endure.
Exodus 18:23

06.14 - We Have Heard.
Joshua 2:10

06.15 - Uncharted Territory.
Joshua 3:4

06.16 - Take To Serve.
Exodus 10:26

06.17 - But God.
1 Corinthians 2:10

06.18 - By Him.
Colossians 1:16-17

06.19 - In Him.
Colossians 1:19-20

Index

June

06.20 - For Him.
Hebrews 9:28

06.21 - An Unlawful Choice.
Esther 4:14

06.22 - Willing To Perish.
Esther 4:16

06.23 - Confidence.
Philippians 3:4

06.24 - Forgetting Those Things.
Philippians 3:13-14

06.25 - Trust The Author.
Hebrews 12:2

06.26 - Depend On Him.
Philippians 1:6

06.27 - Why Can't We?
Matthew 17:19

06.28 - Our Stay.
2 Samuel 22:19

06.29 - Sing To The Deliverer.
2 Samuel 22:1

06.30 - The Fruit Of Calamity.
Psalm 18:1

July

07.01 - Asking For Wisdom.
1 Kings 3:9

07.02 - Entrusted.
1 Kings 3:12

07.03 - What Are You Asking For?
1 Kings 3:11

07.04 - Shine As Lights.
Philippians 2:15

07.05 - Let Thine Heart.
Proverbs 3:1

07.06 - Hate What He Hates.
Proverbs 8:13

07.07 - Wholly Follow.
Joshua 14:8

07.08 - As Strong This Day.
Joshua 14:11

07.09 - Completely.
Proverbs 3:5-6

07.10 - Renewed Mercies.
Lamentations 3:22-23

07.11 - Silent Faith.
Isaiah 53:7

07.12 - Each Day For A Year.
Numbers 14:34

07.13 - If So Be.
Joshua 14:12

07.14 - True Friendship.
Proverbs 17:17

07.15 - Forget It All.
Genesis 41:51

07.16 - Fruitful In Affliction.
Genesis 41:52

07.17 - Glory In This.
Jeremiah 9:23-24

07.18 - He Is In Control.
Proverbs 21:1

07.19 - Bind His Word.
Romans 7:18-20

07.20 - Integrity.
Proverbs 11:3

07.21 - Wise To Be Fruitful.
Proverbs 11:30-31

07.22 - Vision.
Proverbs 29:18

07.23 - Hear & Apply.
James 1:22-24

07.24 - The Result Of Refusing.
Proverbs 15:32

07.25 - Choosing Who To Obey.
Acts 5:29

07.26 - Great Things.
1 Samuel 12:23-24

07.27 - Let Him Hear.
Mark 4:9

07.28 - Every Word.
Proverbs 30:5

07.29 - His Word Is Sufficient.
Deuteronomy 4:2

07.30 - His Word Is The Solution.
Psalm 33:10

07.31 - Go Home.
Mark 5:19-20

Index

August

08.01 - Satisfied In The Wilderness.
Mark 8:4
08.02 - He Is Faithful.
1 Corinthians 1:9
08.03 - Let Us Come Boldly.
Hebrews 4:16
08.04 - Let Us Draw Near.
Hebrews 10:22
08.05 - Let Us Hold Fast.
Hebrews 10:23
08.06 - Let Us Consider.
Hebrews 10:24
08.07 - A Better Hope.
Hebrews 7:19
08.08 - An Immediate Change.
Mark 10:52
08.09 - Nothing But Leaves.
Mark 11:13
08.10 - Called To Mind.
Mark 14:72
08.11 - Willing To Content.
Mark 15:15
08.12 - Thorns.
Judges 2:3
08.13 - A Thorn In The Flesh.
2 Corinthians 12:7
08.14 - Lying Words.
Jeremiah 7:8
08.15 - Most Surely Believed.
Luke 1:1
08.16 - Sincerity & Truth.
Joshua 24:14
08.17 - God Is Able.
2 Corinthians 9:8
08.18 - If Thou Wouldest Believe.
John 11:40
08.19 - Filtered By Him.
Jeremiah 10:23
08.20 - Heavy Hands.
Exodus 17:12
08.21 - Search The Heart.
Jeremiah 17:10
08.22 - Fruit Bearing.
John 15:5
08.23 - Stedfastly Minded.
Ruth 1:18
08.24 - Happenstance.
Ruth 2:3
08.25 - Sit Still.
Ruth 3:18
08.26 - Redemption.
Ruth 4:8
08.27 - It Shall Not Return Void.
Isaiah 55:11
08.28 - Arise & Go.
Jeremiah 18:1-2
08.29 - He Wrought A Work.
Jeremiah 18:3
08.30 - Faith Without Works.
James 2:20
08.31 - Stablish Your Hearts.
James 5:8

September

09.01 - Cause Me To Know.
Psalm 143:8
09.02 - The Root Of Deception.
Luke 4:7
09.03 - Weighed By Him.
1 Samuel 2:2-3
09.04 - Take Your Journey.
Deuteronomy 1:40
09.05 - Rehearse It.
1 Samuel 8:21
09.06 - Reminded By His Word.
Jeremiah 32:17
09.07 - That We Might Have Hope.
Romans 15:4
09.08 - Strange Things.
Luke 5:26
09.09 - If It Had Not Been.
Psalm 124:1-2
09.10 - The Lord Is My Helper.
Hebrews 13:6
09.11 - Fear To Follow.
1 Samuel 12:14
09.12 - Idol Works & Idleness.
Jeremiah 44:8

Index

September

09.13 - Upheld By Him.
Isaiah 41:10

09.14 - Unless I Had Believed.
Psalm 27:13

09.15 - Watched.
Luke 6:7

09.16 - Separated.
Luke 6:22

09.17 - Distracted.
Deuteronomy 5:32

09.18 - Confused.
James 3:16

09.19 - Frustrated.
Galatians 2:21

09.20 - Say In A Word.
Luke 7:7

09.21 - Motivation.
2 Corinthians 5:14

09.22 - Determination.
Isaiah 26:3

09.23 - Procrastination.
Isaiah 40:31

09.24 - Expectation.
Isaiah 30:18

09.25 - Direction.
Psalm 32:8

09.26 - Pray For Them.
1 Samuel 12:23

09.27 - Shut The Door.
2 Kings 4:5

09.28 - Under His Wings.
Psalm 91:3-4

09.29 - In The Time Of Trouble.
Psalm 27:5

09.30 - In The Midst Of Trouble.
Psalm 138:7

October

10.01 - Yet.
Habakkuk 3:18

10.02 - He Knows What Is Best.
Proverbs 16:8-9

10.03 - The Gift Of Wisdom.
Proverbs 2:6

10.04 - Come & Buy.
Isaiah 55:1

10.05 - Think On These Things.
Philippians 4:8

10.06 - The Sword.
1 Kings 3:24-25

10.07 - Iron Friends.
Proverbs 27:17

10.08 - Thank God For Them.
Philippians 1:3-5

10.09 - What He Has Done.
Psalm 118:23

10.10 - He Prays For Us.
Luke 22:32

10.11 - This Man.
Matthew 13:54

10.12 - He Will Speak Peace.
Psalm 85:8

10.13 - The Other Side.
Mark 4:35

10.14 - The Bridge.
1 Timothy 2:5

10.15 - A Controlled Life.
Ephesians 5:18

10.16 - Full Of His Fruit.
Galatians 5:22-23

10.17 - He Will Guide.
John 16:13

10.18 - A True Servant.
Philippians 2:5-8

10.19 - Through.
Isaiah 43:2

10.20 - For A Season.
1 Peter 1:6

10.21 - As For Me.
Psalm 69:13

10.22 - Faint Not.
2 Corinthians 4:1

10.23 - Sowing.
Galatians 6:8

10.24 - The Sower.
Mark 4:3

10.25 - The Soil.
Luke 8:5-8

Index

October

10.26 - The Seed.
Luke 8:11

10.27 - All Or Nothing.
Philippians 4:13

10.28 - Choose The Fear.
Proverbs 1:29

10.29 - Thirsty.
Psalm 42:1-2

10.30 - Delight In Him.
Psalm 37:4

10.31 - The Results Of Delighting.
Isaiah 58:14

November

11.01 - Therefore...Give Thanks.
2 Samuel 22:50

11.02 - Thanks In Prayer & Praise.
Psalm 105:1

11.03 - A Thankful Voice.
Psalm 26:7

11.04 - In Every Thing.
1 Thessalonians 5:18

11.05 - Peaceful & Thankful.
Colossians 3:15

11.06 - Songs Of Thanks.
Colossians 3:16-17

11.07 - A Testimony Of Thanks.
Romans 1:8

11.08 - Sacrifice The Thanks.
Hebrews 13:15

11.09 - Rooted With Thanksgiving.
Colossians 2:7

11.10 - Thankful He Is In Control.
Daniel 2:23

11.11 - Thankful To Serve.
2 Timothy 1:3

11.12 - Thankful To Be Enabled.
1 Timothy 1:12

11.13 - Thankful That He Hears.
John 11:41

11.14 - Thankful To Remember.
1 Thessalonians 1:2-3

11.15 - Thank Him For Growth.
2 Thessalonians 1:3

11.16 - Thank Him For His Word.
Psalm 119:62

11.17 - Thankfully Effectual.
1 Thessalonians 2:13

11.18 - Thankful Despite Persecution.
Daniel 6:10

11.19 - Thankful Before The Miracle.
Matthew 15:36

11.20 - Thankful To Speak Of Him.
Luke 2:38

11.21 - Be Thankful Unto Him.
Psalm 100

11.22 - The Cause Of Thanksgiving.
2 Corinthians 9:11

11.23 - Thank Him For His Gift.
2 Corinthians 9:15

11.24 - Thank Him For His Goodness.
Psalm 107:1

11.25 - A Good Thing To Give Thanks.
Psalm 92:1-5

11.26 - The Trade For Thankfulness.
Philippians 4:6

11.27 - The Blessing Of Thanksgiving.
Psalm 34:1

11.28 - The Hope Of Thanksgiving.
Psalm 71:14

11.29 - Thanks Given For Others.
2 Corinthians 1:11

11.30 - Thankful For The Victory.
1 Corinthians 15:57

December

12.01 - The Word.
Psalm 119:1

12.02 - God With Us.
Isaiah 7:14

12.03 - For Unto Us.
Isaiah 9:6

12.04 - Herein Is Love.
1 John 4:10

12.05 - Highly Favoured.
Luke 1:28

12.06 - Favour Over Fear.
Luke 1:30

Index

December

12.07 - Faith Over Fear.
Luke 1:34

12.08 - From Barren To Blessed.
Luke 1:36

12.09 - Be It Unto Me.
Luke 1:38

12.10 - On This Wise.
Matthew 1:18

12.11 - Magnify Him.
Luke 1:46-47

12.12 - Raised To Be Bold.
Luke 1:57

12.13 - There Came Wise Men.
Matthew 2:1-2

12.14 - Days Were Accomplished.
Luke 2:4-6

12.15 - Let Him In.
Luke 2:7

12.16 - Good Tidings Of Great Joy.
Luke 2:8-10

12.17 - A Saviour.
Luke 2:11

12.18 - Wrapped With Love.
Luke 2:12

12.19 - Glory To God.
Luke 2:13-14

12.20 - Let Us Now Go.
Luke 2:15

12.21 - Made Known.
Luke 2:16-17

12.22 - They That Heard.
Luke 2:18

12.23 - Keep & Ponder.
Luke 2:19

12.24 - Glorify & Praise.
Luke 2:20

12.25 - His Name Was Called.
Luke 2:21

12.26 - Seeking Him.
Luke 2:49

12.27 - Purged To Be More Fruitful.
2 Corinthians 4:17-18

12.28 - Broken & Binded.
Psalm 147:3

12.29 - Prepared To Trust.
Isaiah 26:4

12.30 - Seeking Peace.
Philippians 4:7

12.31 - Delight In Peace.
Psalm 37:11

Holidays

There are themes throughout the year that center around specific holidays. **Each theme is meant to direct our focus toward how we can best delight in the Lord throughout each holiday season.** Since some holidays do not fall on the same date each year, listed below are the dates where these can be found.

Resurrection Sunday - April 12-17, 19-22

These 10 days are themed around the season that we celebrate the death, burial and resurrection of our Lord and Saviour, Jesus Christ.

Thanksgiving - November

The entire month of November has a theme of thankfulness woven throughout each page. My hope is that we can focus our hearts and minds toward a revival of thanksgiving that is shown in our day-to-day lives all throughout the year.

Christmas - December

The first 25 days of December are centered around the miraculous birth of Jesus Christ and the reason He came.

About Us

*"Delight thyself also in the LORD;
and he shall give thee the desires of thine heart."*
Psalm 37:4

From this verse comes the inspiration behind the name of this ministry. It is a reminder that if we delight ourselves in Him, He promises to give us desires according to His will for our lives.

In 2012, the desire for a design ministry began. The Lord has since opened door after door to allow that desire to become a reality..."*Commit thy way unto the LORD; trust also in him; and he shall bring it to pass.*" Psalm 37:5

Delight Thyself Design Ministries began as a media ministry at Teays Valley Baptist Church of Hurricane, WV. Shortly after that, the Lord began to direct us toward reaching people with the printed Word of the Gospel. A tract ministry was born, and has since continued to grow as the Lord leads. In 2014, we began shipping tracts to missionaries across the world with little to no material with which to reach their field. **Please pray with us** that the Lord will continue to provide resources to print the tracts the missionaries are requesting.

We ship tracts free of charge to anyone willing to distribute the printed Word of the Gospel of Jesus Christ. If you would like to receive a sample pack or box to distribute, please visit our website, delightthyself.com.

Gospel tracts customized with a church's contact information are a great way to spread the Gospel and allow others to contact your ministry. We design custom material for likeminded Independent Baptist Churches, which helps fund the printing and distribution of our stocked Gospel tracts which are sent for free all across the world.

We are so thankful for those whom the Lord has provided to support this ministry on a monthly basis or through one time donations. If it were not for these people, this ministry could not exist today. We claim Philippians 4:17 for this method of support, *"Not because I desire a gift: but I desire fruit that may abound to your account."*

If you would like to receive ministry updates, follow us on social media or send us your email address to receive our newsletters.

What Can One Tract Do?

One tract was sitting in the office of the home of a young man named, Hudson. When he found it, he read over it and the phrase "the finished work of Christ" began to work on his heart about his need for salvation. He then surrendered his life to Christ, and was burdened for the people of China. This man was who we now know as J. Hudson Taylor, the missionary who brought the Good News of the Gospel to China.

One tract was given by a friend to a man named Joe. Over the next several months, the Lord used that tract to put him under conviction, cause him to go to church and walk the aisle to trust Christ as His Saviour. When he got up, he saw his pregnant wife beside him. She had also came forward by faith to accept Christ. This is the testimony of the parents of the founder of this ministry. One tract led to their salvation, a Christian heritage, and the start of this ministry. Without God using a man to give that one tract, this ministry would not exist today.

One tract has now yielded nearly 3 million tracts to date being sent all across the world, and only heaven will reveal the fruit that remains. To God be the glory, for great things only He hath done.

Isaiah 55:11
"So shall my word be that goeth forth out of my mouth:
it shall not return unto me void,
but it shall accomplish that which I please,
and it shall prosper in the thing whereto I sent it."

**Will you allow God to use you
to spread the printed Word of the Gospel?**

Delight Thyself
DESIGN MINISTRIES

delightthyself.com

The Bible Way To Heaven.

*"Jesus saith unto him, I am the way, the truth, and the life;
no man cometh unto the Father, but by me."*
John 14:6

We Are All Sinners.
"For all have sinned, and come short of the glory of God."
Romans 3:23

We Were Sent A Saviour.
*"But God commendeth his love toward us, in that,
while we were yet sinners, Christ died for us."*
Romans 5:8

We Were Supplied A Gift.
*"For the wages of sin is death;
but the gift of God is eternal life through Jesus Christ our Lord."*
Romans 6:23

We Can Confess, Believe & Call.
*"That if thou shalt confess with thy mouth the Lord Jesus,
and shalt believe in thine heart that God
hath raised him from the dead, thou shalt be saved.
For whosoever shall call upon the name of the Lord shall be saved."*
Romans 10:9,13

It's that simple.

The Bible says… **Whosoever.**
Once you see yourself as a sinner, if you will simply *"call upon the name of the Lord"*, you can be saved from spending eternity in the Lake of Fire separated from God. You may say…"It's not for me." or "I'll never be good enough.", but God said… **Whosoever.**

God is not willing that any should perish.
That includes you.

If you have trusted Christ as your Saviour,
or would like more information, please contact us.

delightthyself.com

www.ingramcontent.com/pod-product-compliance
Lightning Source LLC
Chambersburg PA
CBHW070418010526
44118CB00014B/1805